C0-APN-084

GETTING YOUR WAY—THE NICE WAY

GETTING YOUR WAY—THE NICE WAY

*A Guide for Parents
and Grown-up Children*

CAROL C. FLAX, Ph.D.
and EARL UBELL

Copyright © 1980 by Carol C. Flax and Earl Ubell

All rights reserved. No part of this book may be reproduced, stored in a re-
trieval system, or transmitted in any form by an electronic, mechanical, photo-
copying, recording means or otherwise, without prior written permission of
the author.

Manufactured in the United States of America.

First Wyden Books edition: November 1980

First Wideview Books edition: May 1982

Wideview Books/A Division of PEI Books, Inc.

Library of Congress Cataloging in Publication Data

Flax, Carol C.
    Getting your way—the nice way.

    Previously published as: Mother/father/you.
    1. Aged parents—United States—Family relation-
ships. 2. Middle age—United States—Family
relationships. I. Ubell, Earl. II. Title.
HQ1064.U5F495   1982   646.7′8   81-70084
ISBN 0-87223-789-3   AACR2

To parents and adult children everywhere . . .
including our own.

CONTENTS

FOREWORD
by Dr. Thomas Gordon

That the quality of human relationships is principally determined by the specific language people use when they talk to each other is an idea so powerful that it deserves as much public recognition as we can give it. This book by Dr. Carol Flax and Earl Ubell will contribute to greater public awareness of this idea because it speaks to the needs and problems of so many adults. What adult doesn't want smoother and deeper relationships with his or her own mother and father?

My professional focus since the early sixties has been on helping parents learn how to improve their relationships with their children by learning certain skills of effective communication. In this work I've been given ample evidence that proves how widespread is the need of parents for better relationships with their children, at all ages and in all countries. My book *Parent Effectiveness Training (P.E.T.)* has been translated and published in fifteen foreign countries, and the brief course I designed in 1962, also called P.E.T., is being taught in most of the European countries, in the United States, Canada, Brazil, Mexico, Australia, New Zealand, Malaysia, Japan, and South Africa.

Parents everywhere, it seems, want help. And they get it when they learn to speak a new language with their children—a constructive language that replaces language that is destructive to children, a "therapeutic" kind of communication that replaces language that makes kids emotional cripples.

Now the authors of this book strike new ground by showing adult children how they can apply this new nurturing language, as the authors call it, to bring about better relationships with their parents. Here is a creative new application of an important idea. And I already have evidence that it will improve these often troublesome relationships, because graduates of the P.E.T. course sometimes reported using their new communication skills successfully outside the parent-child relationship—with their employees, their bosses, their associates, and their own parents. Some of them even suggested I could have named the P.E.T. course *People Effectiveness Training* because the skills work in all people-to-people relationships. There are *universal* problems in relationships between all kinds of people, so there are *universal* communications skills for dealing with these problems constructively. Take the skill of listening to someone who has a problem. Your twelve-year-old who feels she does not have any close friends needs someone to listen attentively and empathetically no more or less than your seventy-year-old mother who complains that you don't visit her often enough. At every age people experience loneliness, dissappointment, and pain. Dr. Flax and Mr. Ubell document this fact with numerous dialogues in which adult children try to deal with typical problems their older parents encounter in their lives. One of the strengths of this book is the inclusion of so many of these real-life conversations, some illustrating destructive and ineffective listening, some demonstrating nurturing listening. Readers who make an effort to learn and practice this empathic, non-judgmental kind of responsive listening will find for themselves just how potent it can be in removing the usual barriers that obstruct communication between older parents and their adult children.

For most children who have grown into adulthood it's never easy to make the shift from having been the needful and dependent child to taking on the role of a counselor to their needful and often dependent parents. But with the specific skills offered in this book, you can make this transition. You'll learn when to be silent (wordless listening), when to check on the accuracy of your listening (checking listening), and when to mirror back your parents' deeper feelings (nurturing listening). With these skills you'll feel comfortable becoming your parents' helper.

As the authors emphasize, however, what they offer is not the typical kind of help most people are all too ready to give—advice, preaching, teaching, answers, and solutions. Readers of this book will discover they'll need to bite their tongues and suppress their temptation to "take over the ownership" of their parents' problems. Dr. Flax and Mr. Ubell wisely point out the necessity of letting older parents search for and find their own answers and solutions.

But being a counselor for your parents is only one way to improve your relationship with them. After you learn the skills of helping your parents with their problems, you'll be ready to ask, " But what do I do when my parents cause *me* problems?" Or, "How can I get my parents to listen to *my* problems?"

Older parents inevitably say and do things that make their adult children feel angry, disappointed, or "unfaired against." The authors wisely don't neglect the fact that this troublesome relationship can't be a one-way street with the adult child always in the helper's seat. Older parents do things that irritate and interfere—they make unusual demands that are hard to meet, they embarrass their grown-up sons and daughters, they invade their privacy, they nag, they hassle, they dominate.

So how do you get them to listen to you? How do you make them more considerate of your legitimate needs? How do you protect your right to have a satisfying and rewarding life of your own without their control?

To handle these common situations, the authors offer a second set of communication skills to help you find the courage and honesty to assert yourself, to confront a parent whose behavior is unacceptable in some way, to send clear messages that Flax and Ubell label "call for help" and "cries of pain." Such messages can be destructive and harmful to a relationship because the language we use is often blaming, judgmental, critical, and shattering to our parents' self-esteem. To avoid such put-downs, the authors will show you how to assert and confront in "I-language"—messages that communicate clearly how the adult child feels, in contrast to "You-language" that always points the finger of blame at the parent.

It will require practice to learn these more constructive ways of asserting yourself and confronting your parent. But the rewards are worth it. You'll feel understood, because you'll be sending clearer and more honest messages. Your grievances will be out in the open, not smoldering inside. And you'll feel good about yourself, because your words will match your feelings—no playing games, no behind-the-back complaining. You'll also feel you're in charge of your life, not dominated by your parents.

The basic foundation on which these two-way communication skills rest is a specific philosophy about how relationships must be lived in order to be mutually satisfying and mutually nurturing. The principle: I'll listen to you when you have problems, but I expect you to listen to me when I have problems. I want our relationship to be a reciprocal one in which both of us are getting our needs met—nobody loses, both win.

Psychologists are beginning to discover evidence showing that whenever relationships get out of balance (are less fair to one than to the other) they will deteriorate. Relationships that endure, that deepen and have intimacy, are those in which both parties feel there is mutuality and reciprocity—what psychologists call "social equity" or "fair social exchange."

I prefer to describe them as "democratic relationships." Without them—in families, in schools, in offices and factories, in all our institutions—having a democratic *nation* will never be more than an illusion.

INTRODUCTION
Why and How and Who

In this book, we explore the mysterious, yet well-traveled region of the human psyche: the relationship between children and their parents. So much has been written on this subject that the idea of another book must give pause to anyone dipping into these pages. We have created this work because we believe we have something different to say, something of deep significance about that mysterious parent-child bond.

First, this is a book about and for adult children, while most writings concern young children. We look at the issue from the point of view of the adult child struggling to strengthen a relationship with a parent.

Second, we recognize that there have been recent efforts to examine the ways adult children respond to their parents. Some writers probe deeply into the underlying psychology of the ties between adult children and parents. Others try to advise adult children on their difficulties in escaping or managing a controlling parent.

Yet as we read these books, we find that the theories and case histories give the reader no tools with which to approach the parent. You can identify with the analysis, but you are left asking: "But what do I do?" Or the "advice" is laid out in convoluted psychological jargon that leaves you with the same question.

We hope we have provided a new and practical way to re-establish or to improve shattered or injured relationships. We have striven to put at your disposal the most up-to-date research in psychology. We have tried to avoid jargon so you will find little familiar psychological chatter. We have emphasized, instead, practicality.

Third, our approach is through communication. What we say and how we say it to our parents controls, more than anything else, the relationship between you and them.

In doing this, we have relied heavily on the works of many psychiatrists and psychologists. They include Sigmund Freud, Carl Rogers, B. F. Skinner, Thomas Gordon, and Albert Bandura. Their number is too great to list all by name, but we are greatly in their debt.

We want especially to mention Dr. Sharon Gadberry, of Adelphi University, who undertook to put the principles of nurturing communication to practical test. She also gave our manuscript a searching review. Her many cogent comments kept us on the right track. Lori Ubell also deserves credit as an editor for her sharp reading of our words as they came from the typewriter. Her clear eye was able to save us from many an egregious error.

Finally, our families. We thank them, each one, for putting up with absences and diversions. For Carol Flax, thanks to her husband David, and her children Anita, Laura, Maria, and Sam. For Earl Ubell, thanks to his wife Shirley, his children Lori and Michael, and grandson Ethan. We hope they are pleased with the result.

GETTING
YOUR WAY—THE
NICE WAY

/ 1 /

Our Toxic Language

"I'm forty years old and my mother still tells me to be careful crossing the street."

"My father knows I need the money for my business. He's got plenty and won't give me a dime, even though I beg him. He always was a stingy bastard."

"My father is seventy years old and it kills me to see him losing his mind. I really don't know what to do. I'd hate to put him in a nursing home."

"My mother-in-law is always telling me what to cook for her son, and when I do it, I didn't do it right. Someday I'm going to dump the spaghetti on her head."

"My father never loved me. Even now he seems to turn his back on me."

"My mother isn't capable of loving anyone."

These are cries of pain. The pain of being locked in emotional combat with a parent. But these are cries from adults

... adults who have living mothers or fathers. They are adult children. Half the American adult population has a father or a mother still alive. Many of these adult children suffer silently. Others, unable to cope with the battle, have cut themselves off from their parents: they never see them, never call them. For these adult children, their parents, though biologically alive, are psychologically dead.

It is one of the great tragedies of American life that far too many adults have "lost" their parents not through illness but through devastating psychocombat. The battles rage over money, health, housing, grandchildren, visits, telephone calls, sex, anything. Through interviews, special training programs, and a therapist's experience, we have collected a wealth of real conversations between adult children and their parents. We have edited them to hide identities and to bring out the important points. Some issues are trivial but ignite searing conflict. Others go to the core of the adult child's being, there to wreak profound psychological destruction. Yet all these battles, as we will show, are preventable or can at least be greatly eased—once you know the right strategies.

Ann is twenty-four years old, married to Richard, son of Arnold, who is forty-five. (In-laws are also parents.) Here is their dialogue as Ann reported it to us.

ARNOLD: You really look sexy in those jeans.

ANN: Oh.

ARNOLD: You have a very nice figure. I can see why my son is attracted to you. In fact, I am, too. Would you like to have lunch in my office today?

ANN: I have a date with Richard.

ARNOLD: I'm more man than he'll ever be. Let me show you.

ANN: I've got to rush off. Good-bye.

What is Ann to do if Arnold continues his advances? Can she stop him without damaging her marriage? How will

Richard feel if he finds out? If Arnold were just another man, Ann could rebuff him with little risk. But Arnold is her "parent." You could call Arnold's words poisonous—they attack Ann, seek to dominate her sexually, and demean her by mocking her husband.

Arnold speaks a toxic language. It is poisoning the relationship between himself and his children. Surprisingly, Arnold may not be aware of the venomous nature of his communication. Indeed, many of us do not realize that what we believe to be innocent remarks or questions are the ingredients of a toxic language.

Like Ann, you may be one of those adult children trapped in an emotional vise created by a dominating parent who speaks the toxic language. Or you may have an aging helpless parent. Or a parent who asks for help you cannot give. Or you need help that your parent won't give. Or you have lost the loving tie that binds you to your parent and you want to find the hand again.

Modern psychology has mapped a way toward a true and rewarding relationship with parents. Until recently only professionals possessed that skill. Now anybody can understand and apply this new knowledge of the human psyche. We will show you that road. It has worked for others. And it can work for you, even (as we'll show later) if Arnold is your father-in-law.

Through communication—spoken and unspoken—adult children can find their way back to their parents. To replace toxic speech we offer a nurturing speech that encourages mutually rewarding relationships. That's what this book is about: the strategies and tactics of how to nurture your parents and put your relationship on a new and happier footing. We believe—and many scientific studies have shown—that if you learn the skills of nurturing communication you can change the behavior and perhaps the thoughts of those around you. You can build trust; you can get help; you can give help; you can ward off hurt; you may find love.

We have seen men and women learn this new, nurturing language. We have seen that when they speak to people with their new language, the others in their lives act differently, gently, helpfully. We have seen them turn their new skills softly to their children, spouses, and parents. And in some measure, their new speech changed all their lives. We heard:

"It was as though I didn't ever know what to say; now I can talk."

"One day my son looked at me and said: 'Ma, you really listen!' "

"My mother and I were fighting all the time. Now we have those heart-to-heart talks that I used to read about."

Problem? Problem? Whose Problem?

Maybe you have no problem with your parents. They are supportive, helpful. They don't interfere. You like them and they like you. You visit them frequently and when you don't, you're writing to them or telephoning. You know that they are there for you. You are like Charles, forty, whose mother, Cecily, is sixty-five. Successful in business, Charles commutes to his fine house and growing family in the suburbs. Cecily prefers to live in the city in the same run-down neighborhood where she reared her family and where her friends still live.

Charles visits her at least once a week and does the shopping for her at the local supermarket.

CHARLES: I bring her gadgets, faddish things to keep her up to date. She's only sixty-five. She expects me to visit. I like to see her. I love her and want to see her. It's my doing, really, not hers. I've never missed. If I did, I don't think she would be upset. She's the only one who still calls me "Chucky," my boyhood nickname. You know, I like it; I like the whole scene. My wife knows and accepts it; she has no mother. She never comes along, though.

Or you are like Angela, thirty, unmarried, living with her mother in the family house.

ANGELA: Whatever my mother wants I take care of. It's better that way. She knows what to do and it makes everything easy. Yes, I do check in with her because I don't want to worry her. Dad left us enough money so that neither of us has to work. But we don't go out often, except to church on Sunday. I spend my time quietly writing letters and reading. She doesn't have many friends. Neither do I. We don't have many visitors. I guess I've accepted my fate. My older brother and sister live out of state. My dad died when I was in high school and I've been with mom ever since. It isn't too bad.

Or you are like Charlotte, twenty-seven, divorced with two young children living in Washington, D.C. Her father, Maxwell, fifty-seven, is a politician in their home state.

CHARLOTTE: My father is a physical and verbal bully. He's hit me with everything. Fists. Shoes. Books. And words. Especially words. He's tough, demanding, selfish. I did what he said but not very well. He wanted success for me. I failed and thwarted him. I didn't go to Radcliffe the way I was supposed to. Once—to get his attention—I stole pens from the five-and-dime. I got caught, and you know what he said? "Do you know what this could do to my career?" He still dominates me. I owe my divorce to him. He taught me how to avoid men. I avoided my husband. I didn't let him in my life or in my body.

Of the three—Charles, Angela, or Charlotte—who has problems with the parents? Some would say all three. Some none. It depends on your point of view. Charles may merely *say* he's happy and be oblivious to the guilt he feels if he doesn't visit. Angela, who seems dominated by her mother, may be taken at her word: "It isn't too bad." And Charlotte may be remembering a cruel father now a thousand miles away and unable to rule her any longer.

As we look from the outside, we cannot tell who has a problem with a parent. That evaluation rests with the adult child. And the motivation to change the situation therefore comes from the adult child, too, from you. However, you sometimes do experience unhappiness and cannot pinpoint the source. You may be afraid to indict your parental relationship: after all, parents and children are supposed to love one another. You may close your eyes to the damage that a parent inflicts on you. You may never have paused in your anguish to try to understand where your bad feelings come from.

If you feel like pausing to reflect on your relationship with your parent, here's a simple checklist that may assist in opening up the question for yourself.

Are you *unhappy* about any of the items below?

1. My parent always asks me too many questions. —Yes —No
2. My parent is always telling me what to do. —Yes —No
3. My parent demands too much money from me. —Yes —No
4. My parent interferes with the way I raise my children. —Yes —No
5. I cannot get my parent to take care of his (her) health. —Yes —No
6. My parent is foolishly spending his (her) money. —Yes —No
7. I really have nothing in common with my parent and I hardly see him (her). —Yes —No
8. My parent has to go into an old-age home and I cannot make him (her) go. —Yes —No

9. My parent constantly nags me to
visit or to telephone. —Yes —No
10. My parent frequently manipulates
me into situations I don't need or
like. —Yes —No
11. My parent wants to move in with
us and I hate the idea. —Yes —No
12. My parent is always criticizing
my women (men) friends and
what I do with them. —Yes —No

This is a very abbreviated list of parental behaviors that
cause unhappiness in adult children. Many stem from the
flow of toxic speech between parent and adult child and can
be "cured" by our nurturing language.

Where the Poison First Grows

In childhood. Of course. We all know that. We start life
dependent upon our parents for food, warmth, emotional
support. We remain dependent for many years. The relationship is one-sided, the parent holding most of the responsibility and power. It is an unequal relationship. Each parent
has his or her particular style of exercising that responsibility
and power. Each has a way of communicating with children:
judgmental or judgment free; mocking or sympathetic; directive or supportive. And that style carries over the years
into the adulthood of the child. If your parent was directive
when you were growing up, your parent will direct you now
that you are an adult. If your parent fired toxic words at
you—blame, mockery, judgment, put-downs—you will feel
the fire of the same words today.

But maybe it began before your childhood: with your parents' childhood. More and more research suggests that the
way your parents were treated as children is the way they

will treat you; and the way you, in turn, will probably treat your children. To break a poisonous chain, someone must change the style of communication. For many, the one-sided relationship that existed when you were young now needs to be changed into a mutual relationship, with mutual nurturing, help, support, respect.

Parents may want to unlearn their parental role of power and responsibility: of no longer taking personally—if they ever did—their adult child's mistakes. The dominated adult child who desires freedom needs to learn to handle parental disapproval no matter how expressed. Older parents continue to act toward their adult children as if they still had the responsibility of bringing them up even though the kids grew up decades ago.

Our parents act toward us as they were acted upon: The parental language of our parents mostly mimics that of their parents. And our parents also inherited the techniques of discipline, praise, judgment of their parents. So when your mother or your father talks to you, you may be hearing the voices of your grandparents.

Those voices can poison the relationship between you and your parents. You say things you don't mean. You hurt the other. Others say things the way they have learned to say them. They hurt you. It is verbal poison. And for many of us the toxic language has become a habit. To begin to change, we must first examine what it is we will be changing.

The Wounds of Words

The words that hurt vary from family to family. But in the last thirty-five years—beginning with the pioneering work of Dr. Carl Rogers—scientists have discovered the words and phrases that wound. Here are some examples:

1. "No daughter of mine should work as a waitress!"
2. "Why didn't you call me last week?"

3. "Nobody seems to want to take care of me."
4. "You're really thinking of marrying that girl?"

Even on paper, it is easy to see that the receiver of such statements has sustained a body blow.

Statement No. 1 says that the adult child's choice of work is trivial and the choice has disappointed the parent.

Statement No. 2 demands that the adult child call the parent at least once a week out of duty, not out of love.

Statement No. 3 is the beginning of a guilt trip: Why don't you take care of me? You owe it to me.

Statement No. 4 attacks the choice of mate, one of the most sensitive choices you can make in a lifetime.

Such words can inflict incalculable damage on the adult child, especially because most children have been taught that they should not answer back. But adult children do "answer back," and the result is combat:

PARENT: No daughter of mine should work as a waitress.
YOU-THE-CHILD: I can't find any other job.
PARENT: I told you to *study* in school!
YOU-THE-CHILD: Why are you always bringing that up?
PARENT: Because you wouldn't listen! If you had listened to me, you wouldn't have to work as a waitress.
YOU-THE-CHILD: And if you'd been so smart, you and daddy wouldn't have divorced.

The dialogues differ greatly. Some take longer to draw blood. Others continue over several days. The wounded adult child sometimes is silent after the final thrust. The parent withdraws even more. The strange thing about such fights is that they feed upon themselves. The fighters cannot seem to get out of them, and every effort to do so seems only to escalate the conflict. A toxic comment draws one in return—and another and another.

A fury grips the fighters. After a point, they cannot hear

the other or themselves. The venom flows unchecked until both are exhausted emotionally or until one gives up, the arsenal spent. The "winner" feels no triumph, only sadness, loss, and emptiness.

The Nurturing Language

In this book, we are going to show you a new language, a healing language. It grew from the modern knowledge of communication between human beings. More than that, the scientific evidence strongly suggests that this language is the only one that can sustain a loving, trusting relationship.

It is a language that shuts off combat.
It can be heard and understood by another person.
It inspires trust.
It is a language of negotiation.
It allows you to understand the other person.
It changes behavior.
It is a language of mutual regard, perhaps of love.

For these reasons we call it the *nurturing language* because it nurtures relationships . . . builds them. The word *nurture* conveys nourishment, support, caring, growth. The new language *is* a nurturing one.

Four Communication Principles

The new language stands on four central ideas. Because they are so important, we'll return to them again and again.

1. *People (parents) will tell you what they are thinking if they feel you are listening.*

PARENT: Harry Williams died last week and I didn't want to go to his funeral.
YOU-THE-CHILD: You couldn't face Mrs. Williams.

PARENT: That, and so many of my friends seem to be sick or dying. I just didn't want to meet any of them.

YOU-THE-CHILD: They're all getting on in years.

PARENT: So am I. Although I'm in pretty good shape. I still jog. And I go to work. I don't feel that old.

Here you are *searching*. By listening you gently explore the true feelings and thoughts of the parent. Searching through effective listening is the only way to learn what another is thinking. Direct questions do not work because, as we shall learn, questions make people feel unsafe. If they feel unsafe, they fear to reveal their inner thoughts. They are afraid that somehow the information will be turned against them (people often disparage those who have confided in them). There is no trust.

So parents often volunteer information in code at the outset, hoping that you will somehow guess the meaning or that you will take the clue and help them to explore that inner world safely. They are seeking trust. Searching builds trust; toxic language breeds distrust:

PARENT: Harry Williams died last week and I didn't want to go to his funeral.

YOU-THE-CHILD: What's the matter with you? Are you a baby? You've insulted Mrs. Williams.

The noxious quality of the adult child's reply can only turn off the parent to further revelations. There can be no meaningful dialogue. The bond between them weakens.

Effective listening often helps the other person think more clearly. If you listen and the other person knows you are listening, he or she can try out new thoughts safely without fear of being put down. And in this way, as psychotherapists have learned, a person often works out his own solutions to his problems.

Dr. Carl Rogers, one of the first to understand the benefits of a nurturing language, made it a central idea of his client-centered therapy. He believed implicitly in the power of individuals to heal themselves. But they need the support of a truly listening therapist.

The Foolishness of Mind Reading

Many people believe they know what another person is thinking, that they can often read minds. But very few people can perform mind reading no matter how well they think they know the other person. The futility of doing so has been demonstrated in many scientific studies. One study shows—surprisingly—that even trained psychologists or psychiatrists cannot read minds with any consistency. Nor can they predict their patients' behavior with any greater certainty than the patients' relatives can.

Yet we often base our actions on what we *believe* other people are thinking or will do. Sometimes we guess right; often we guess wrong. The sensitivity of human relationships prohibits too many wrong guesses.

"I know Mary won't mind if I don't invite her to the party."

"Dad really wants to go to a nursing home. He just won't admit it."

"I know just what mother is thinking: she thinks she can get money from me and from Jack."

If you were making such surmises and guessed wrong, you could deeply hurt Mary, dad, and mother. Instead we'll show you how to employ your searching skill to understand what your parent really thinks, feels, wants, and needs, and in that way build a better bond between the two of you.

2. *People will hear what you say only if they believe that you hear what they say.*

We call this *listening-to-speak*. Listen first; then speak.

If you do not believe a person is listening to you, you well may feel anger. If you are angry, you cannot hear what the other person says. We are often angry with our parents because we do not believe they hear us; and they are angry with us for the same reason. There is no listening; you cannot speak. No listening-to-speak.

PARENT: My friend Mary sees her daughter almost every day.
YOU-THE-CHILD: Don't expect me to come running every day.

The parent reached out indirectly by sending a thinly coded message to her adult child. The adult child heard and understood the parent's words. The response made that clear. But the adult child did not listen to the parent's inner world. The adult child did not allow the parent to reveal the inner need. Without listening to that plaintive call, however awkwardly put, the adult child cut off all further negotiation. The adult child spoke without listening. There was no listening-to-speak.

PARENT: Harry Williams died last week and I couldn't go to his funeral.
YOU-THE-CHILD: Come on, dad, you have plenty of years ahead of you.

The parent, again indirectly, expressed a common fear of older people: the fear of death. Psychologists now realize that while all of us fear death, as we grow older the defense against the fear weakens. Did the adult child listen? No, the adult child trivialized the father's fear. And the father learned he cannot confide in his adult child.

Unfortunately, many of us have not learned to listen, to let the other know that we want to hear more. That we want to hear about the other person's inner world. We hear the words but we do not listen. The distinction is important. To listen effectively the other person must know that we are listening.

And the most difficult thing to do is to listen to our parents because we have, many of us, lived our lives not listening to them. So they do not listen to us.

3. *People will hear a cry of pain or a call for help if the cry or call is genuine with feeling.*

We have given the name *genuine assertions* to such cries or calls. They assert our feelings or our needs.

The important part of this principle is the phrase "genuine with feeling." If we ask for something or utter a cry of pain but cover up our true feelings, the message we send the other is out of line with the words of the message. It doesn't ring true. Feelings—true feelings—lubricate communication. Without them, we cannot listen; we cannot speak.

PARENT: Jimmy failed math? I told you you don't know how to handle that boy! You're going to make a nothing out of him if you keep this up.

YOU-THE-CHILD: I'm doing the best I can. His father always interferes, so I can't make him do what I want.

Here the parent moved in with a club. The adult child, feeling some responsibility for the son's failure, defended herself weakly by attacking her husband. Yet the underlying feeling is that of a wounded child. The adult child needed succor, not accusation.

A parent often inflicts such pain on an adult child, and the adult child cannot say: "You hurt me." So the parent has a ticket to cause more pain. In time it becomes harder for the adult child to cry "Ouch!" A cry of pain in the form of a genuine assertion can end the parent's damaging behavior. Here is one such genuine assertion:

PARENT: Jimmy failed math? I told you you don't know how to handle that boy! You're going to make a nothing out of him if you keep this up.

You-the-Child: Mom, Jimmy's only failed math. I *am* terribly upset about it. But it hurts even more to be told that I'm mainly at fault and that I'm ruining my son's life.

We'll show why this communication will stop the attacks and how it helps open up a dialogue between parent and adult child.

Further, many of us have not learned to ask for help in ways that encourage others, particularly parents, to help us. We demand or beg instead of asserting our needs and allowing others to *choose* to help us.

You-the-Child: Mother, I need you to come over to baby-sit Loretta tomorrow evening.

Parent: I'm really too busy at home to baby-sit tomorrow. You'll have to find somebody else.

As in this dialogue, we too often prescribe how we want help. We give our potential helper no choice. Which leads to another important principle:

4. *A person will help you if there is a choice to help.*

Always give a choice to the other person. No choice, no help.

A person who is told what to do and how to do it loses self-esteem. It is as if you are saying: "I know you're too stupid to figure it out, so here's what to do." Under those conditions most anyone resists. Most people would rather figure things out for themselves; having done so, they are more willing to help.

Furthermore, if you say: "Do it this way," your suggestion may conflict with the other person's plans. Most people would reject your request because they cannot do what you want without giving up something they have planned. Without letting them figure things out for themselves, they never come up with an alternative.

You-the-Child: Mother, I have a PTA meeting tomorrow night and I cannot find a sitter for Loretta. It's really an important meeting because I'm going to be elected president.

Parent: Well, I'm pretty busy tomorrow night. My next-door neighbor has a teenager. I'll check and see if she'll sit.

In this dialogue, the adult child stated her need and left open the means by which that need is to be met. Given a choice, the parent agreed to help find a baby-sitter, since she cannot sit herself. And it could be that if she fails to find one she may discover she is not so busy after all.

We'll show you what there is in the above message that gives you the best chance of getting the help you need from your parent. Or how to offer help to a parent who needs it.

Parents can help: with baby-sitting, work, guidance (parents have had experience), affection, emotional support, and sometimes even with money.

Parents need help: with money, emotional support, affection, transportation, and guidance. (Parents are not omniscient when it comes to their own life decisions.)

We offer, then, four principles of communication. Four principles of a nurturing language, a language that does not poison relationships:

Searching, or listening
Listening-to-speak
Genuine assertions
Giving a choice

They look simple, perhaps deceptively simple. Yet all four have firm underpinnings in modern scientific psychology. They make communication effective between people. And when there is effective communication, there is relationship.

Building a Relationship

If you can learn the four principles and how to apply them—and almost anyone can—you will find that your parent's behavior toward you will change. And from that changed behavior you can build a new relationship on almost any level you desire. Later in this book we will discuss the nature of the relationship you want and how to achieve it.

Your parent doesn't talk to you? You can achieve a conversation free of hostility. It has been done by others with their parents.

Your parent ignores your needs? You can get help from a parent when you need it; perhaps not everything you want, but something.

Your parent won't take help from you or anyone else? He's sick and won't see a doctor? She lives in an apartment too big for her to take care of? He is too old to be left alone? You can help if you know how, and your parent will accept the help.

Your parent refuses to give or accept emotional support? Your mother seems unsympathetic to your divorce? Your father puts you down for the job you have? It's tough to do, but you can achieve a relationship that is mutually supportive. We'll show you how.

All too good to be true? Not if you learn the skills of relationship, of communication.

The Psychological Trap

"My father is too old to change!"

"My mother gets too much pleasure out of making me miserable!"

"My mother is too selfish to help anybody!"

"My father can't love anybody."

"My mother-in-law is a bitch and nothing will change her!"

"My father is paranoid!"

Each complaint is common. Only the last uses psychological jargon. But each is a psychological statement. Each statement tries to make a quick psychological analysis of the parent. And that's the trap.

First, it is almost impossible for nonprofessionals to make an accurate psychological diagnosis. Yet we try all the time. We don't call it diagnosis. We say we're sizing up a person. Or that we "know" him. Or we describe her character: "She's honest." "She's brave." "She wouldn't hurt a fly." "She'll kill to get what she wants." We know. Or do we?

Even with years of experience and psychological tests to help them, psychologists and psychiatrists have a difficult time diagnosing sick patients or characterizing normal people. The nonprofessional can hardly hope to do better.

Second, even if you are correct in your diagnosis, that doesn't mean that your parent will always behave in the same way. Mounting scientific evidence demonstrates that people change their behavior as they face different situations. Even if their behavior is habitual, a changed psychological environment will change the behavior.

Third, to act on the basis of the diagnosis you made means you have to know more about psychology than you now know. Much more. And it would take you years to learn it.

Suppose you decide that your mother is narcissistic. What is your response? Or neurotic? Now what do you do? Or paranoid? Whole books have been written on just one characteristic and how to treat it. Psychological patter makes good party talk, but for ordinary folk psychochatter is just impractical.

What we are suggesting will work for almost *any* diagnosis and with almost *any* personality.

It doesn't matter what is going on inside the other person. What *you* do, what *you* say, will govern the relationship just as powerfully as your parent's hang-ups. And with more skill on your part, you don't have to worry about the correct psychological word to describe your parent's behavior.

We are saying (and in some circles it is considered radical): If you deal effectively with the here-and-now, with the moment-to-moment flow of your relationship with your parent, you can strengthen the bonds that bind the two of you in loving regard. You do not need deep analysis. You do not have to understand what is going on in your parent's mind or heart on any deeper level than your parent chooses to reveal.

If you establish communication on a trusting basis you will find:

1. Older people will change their ways. Being old does not necessarily mean being rigid. (Older people are merely more wary. They need more reassurance than young people before they plunge ahead.)

2. People who get pleasure out of inflicting pain will lose the pleasure and will stop inflicting pain.

3. "Selfish" people can and will help others if properly approached.

4. "People who cannot love" will take some steps toward a loving relationship if they feel safe.

5. Paranoia—the fear that the world is ganging up on you —can be reduced (perhaps not ended) with trusting communication.

All these effects—and more—can come from the new language of trust and love: the nurturing language. It works.

/ 2 /

What's on Your Parents' Minds

"Can I let myself enter fully into the inner world of another person's feelings and personal meanings and see these as he or she does?"

The "I" of this question is Carl Rogers, the psychologist who pioneered in interpersonal communication.

For Dr. Rogers this question is central to the helping process in psychology. To be a good therapist, he says, a person needs the capacity to understand, to experience, to feel the other person's thoughts, needs, and feelings. More than verbal skill, a therapist needs empathy in this sense. As Dr. Rogers continued to study psychotherapy scientifically he realized that his question could be asked about any two people. If you can answer his question "Yes; I can enter into the other person's inner world," then you can achieve a helping, mutually supportive relationship. At least it can be a relationship in which hostility and combat fade to the mimimum.

It is extraordinarily difficult to enter into the interior world of another person. It is even more difficult to enter without threatening the other person and without judging his or her feelings and ideas. That interior world is carefully and closely guarded. Think about how vigilantly you protect your own inner world. Do you let others in on your most secret feelings and thoughts—even your wife, your husband, your lover? Don't you keep something hidden?

Direct questions ("How are you feeling? Why don't you cheer up?") achieve little because the answers come back covered over with meaningless facts or in some deep code. Consider the most banal of exchanges:

I: How are you?
You: Fine. And you?
I: Fine.

Clearly nothing has been learned, even though the question tries to get at something that lies in the interior world. We have degraded that question so that the only possible answer is trivial ("Fine"). The other person may be suffering incredible emotional pain.

Between parents and their adult children, the questions and answers are even more tortuously guarded. They have been twisted into weapons (you'll learn more about these later). Questions and answers cover up hurts, fears, needs. The range of hidden hurts, fears, and needs of parents is very great, frequently greater than those of their adult children.

Yet no matter how well you know your parents, any attempt to read what's on their minds is doomed to be wrong more than half the time. You can know their thoughts only if they *allow* you to enter their interior world. And they will not let you in if they feel threatened or judged. Of course, the same goes for you; you, too, keep that secret place barred against prying questions.

So there you have a dilemma: To foster a mutual and helpful relationship, you need to enter your parents' inner emotional domain. How can you penetrate their interior world if they feel threatened in any way? And how can they not feel threatened if they suspect that you are trying to breach the carefully erected walls to that world?

The dilemma strikes deeper. Between two people "help" may mean nothing more than being understanding, sensitive, sympathetic. Help can also include money, transportation, visits, etc. You cannot help your parents in these or any other ways unless they allow you (however slightly) into their world of feeling, and your parents cannot or won't help you unless you permit them somehow to step into your world. Each is afraid that the other will "use" the information to strike.

We will show you how to solve this puzzle with the nurturing language. In the process you will be able to deal with very real problems that face adult children and their parents. We now discuss some of those real-life difficulties from the point of view of the parent.

It is hard to guess the exact nature of the problem with which your parent may be struggling, but if you know the possibilities, you may find it easier to understand what your parent may be telling you. It is a beginning toward trying to explore the feelings of parents and the conditions that affect those feelings.

Loneliness

Before the 1930s, 80 percent of persons older than sixty-five lived in homes owned or rented by other people—children, grandchildren, others. Today 80 percent live in their own homes, either with a spouse or alone. The change came about because of Social Security, which provided enough money so that more older people could live on their own.

We can also attribute the change to the transformation of the United States from a rural country into a citified society with people living in apartments or small suburban houses rather than in large rural homes. In bygone days, the large homes or farmhouses could accommodate an extra grandparent. You didn't need an extra bathroom. But now there are too many older people—24 million of them, one out of ten Americans—to be housed in the old way.

So millions of older people—the parents—live alone. Studies show that many of them do not have an opportunity to speak more than a few words each day to another person. For some, weeks pass before they exchange any words at all! When a couple live together, the interchange between them may have become stereotyped. A chasm of silence sits between them. In short, your parents may be starkly alone, lonely.

How do you know if they are lonely? They may tell you if you ask them. More likely they won't tell you, but it could come out in other ways. They may phone you incessantly. They may not phone you at all. They may nag you to visit; they may reject your offer to visit. They may gain large amounts of weight; they may lose weight. They may complain of many disease symptoms, yet have no detectable disease; or they may be very ill and not complain at all. Each behavior marks a possibility of loneliness; but you can know only when you explore your parent's thoughts and feelings.

Again, direct questions are of no help:

You-the-Child: How are you feeling?
Parent: Better.
You-the-Child: Better? I didn't know you were sick. Are you not well?
Parent: Just a headache.
You-the-Child: Well, take some aspirin. That always works. Have you been to the doctor?
Parent: For a headache? Don't be foolish.

It is perfectly possible that the parent in this conversation has been to a doctor, had extensive x-rays, and been diagnosed to have a brain tumor. Yet the parent withheld the information from the adult child. Why? It's difficult to say simply from the exchange of a few words. The parent may fear that if the adult child suspects real illness, she would reject him even more. Or the parent may be so afraid of being sick that he denies the illness not only to himself but to anybody who asks him about it.

Or it may go something like this:

PARENT (on the phone): Sally? I'm terribly sick. I have such a pain in my stomach I can't stand it.

YOU-THE-CHILD: The same old pain?

PARENT: It's different. It's shifted over a little.

YOU-THE-CHILD: But, mom, you had x-rays only two months ago! The doctor couldn't find anything wrong. Just take some antacids. You'll be all right.

PARENT: If you could come over for a little while this evening, it would help me to stand the pain.

Clearly, the problem is lack of human contact, not illness. The lack of human contact can easily produce, in your parents, hypochondriasis—the belief that they are or will become ill, when there is no illness present. They complain about every little ache and pain—all to get your attention. On the other hand, millions of older parents get along very well without their adult children. Studies reveal that older people get more in the way of conversation, understanding, and help from their friends of the same age than they do from their adult children. The parents, being older, have more in common with their older friends than with their adult children.

Older people do help each other. They are unselfconscious about asking another older person for money, transportation, a visit, company on a trip to the store or to the South Seas.

So while many decry the retirement ghettos of Florida and California, those living arrangements provide, on a steady basis, many of the emotional and physical needs that adult children do not, cannot, or will not provide.

Nevertheless, whatever contact does exist between parent and adult child has great importance for both. Those contacts establish a link with the past and a sense of ongoing family, which in America is central for millions. Even you. And you can make those contacts pay off—even when the parent is not lonely.

Health

The human body, though wonderfully constructed to repair itself, does suffer from the years of abuse of living. Young people who feel an ache shrug it off in the knowledge that by tomorrow it will be gone. For those who are in their fifties and beyond, a pain signals something deeper, something far more threatening.

Older people, then, are more concerned with their health, more worried about bodily functions. You hear from them more talk about bowel movements, urinary tract problems, vision, hearing, aches in the joints, teeth, head, and chest. Many complaints reflect illness. And they need to be taken seriously.

Many symptoms go along with growing older. Joints hurt after exercise. Nearsightedness increases. Old infections come back again and again. Digestive pains abound. Because the pains can have more ominous meaning, older people dwell on them. For many, a symptom reminds them of the inevitable. It also reminds them of their dwindling capacities. And with the reduced ability to run, read, play, and engage in sex comes self-devaluation: "I'm no good anymore."

The question: "How are you?" directed at older persons cannot be answered casually. If pressed to answer, they often respond with some banal, meaningless words, because to give a real answer may mean cataloguing their aches and pains. And that never goes down well. However, many parents will reel off just such a catalogue without hesitation. It is their way of reaching out for contact and understanding, even though they know it often fails.

Many older people have a chronic illness. Of those over sixty-five close to half of the men and 40 percent of women live with some activity limitation. They suffer from disabling health problems: rheumatism, heart disease, kidney malfunction, high blood pressure, and on and on and on. The average person with a chronic illness may be taking six medications a day.

The reactions vary from stoicism ("I can't bother anybody about my troubles") to utter dependency and all the gradations in between. What your parent does depends on how your parent was reared to deal with illness and on how you-the-child react to that illness. You cannot change how your parent was brought up; you can only change your reactions.

You-the-Child: I see you're home today. You don't look sick, but you certainly are sick a great deal lately. Seems you are sick and at home more than you are at work.

Parent: Seems like you're here all the time checking up on me—whether I'm sick or not.

You-the-Child: You don't want me to come over and help you when you're sick. You make more work for mother.

Parent: You make me feel it's my fault I'm sick and that I wished this on myself.

You-the-Child: Well . . . maybe you did. You don't work as often as I know you could and you don't make much money either. If I didn't help out, where would you and mom be?

Parent: Just because we borrowed a thousand dollars last month—and I'm paying you interest—doesn't mean you own us!

That gets everybody nowhere. You want to find ways to get the parent to deal realistically with illness; to help the parent find proper medical help; to take medications; to provide care at home; to find rehabilitation; to decide on surgery. You-the-child can help, but, as you may have learned, direct offers of help are rarely taken, at least not gracefully.

Lest we paint too grim a picture of older people, this generation of aging parents is remarkably healthy compared with former generations. Looking at the numbers more cheerfully: Half the men and 60 percent of the women have *no* activity limitation. They show great zest for life: Tennis at sixty is common; marathoners in their sixties pop up every year; one out of five men is still working after sixty-five. Although fewer women work, a substantial proportion who did work continue to do so.

Although capabilities do decline with age, there is substantial physical strength, emotional stability, sexual prowess, and intellectual function well into the eighties. Louise Nevelson continues to sculpt in her eighties. Konrad Adenauer was the leader of his country at eighty-five. George Bernard Shaw turned out literary works at eighty, and Lillian Hellman is still a literary producer in her seventies.

And one marathoner—Noel Johnson—learned to run at seventy and ran in the New York City marathon at eighty, finishing the course in under six hours. The physical training had other benefits for Mr. Johnson. In an interview he said: "I was a dud at seventy; I'm a stud at eighty."

These are unusual men and women, to be sure. But they represent only the most visible segment of the healthy population of old people. While adult children of such people should be thankful for the continued health of their parent, the activity sometimes upsets them. They look askance at an eighty-year-old disco dancer. They think there is something wrong with a sixty-five-year-old man who dates and has sexual contact with thirty-five-year-old women. Or the reverse: their older mother dating younger men. For these aging parents, the capability exists and they take advantage of it. For them health is not an obvious issue. But it will become one with their advancing years. And that *is* an issue.

Money

The aged are the poorest class of people in our country. Men over sixty-five average eight thousand dollars a year from all sources, with half of them getting less than five thousand. Women are far worse off, averaging half of what the men get. While most men over sixty-five are married, most women are widows and living alone. Forced retirement cuts income in half for most Americans. Only one person in four has saved enough money on his or her own to enjoy a comfortable retirement.

Social Security has kept many from starving. New federal programs of supplemental cash bring them out of deep poverty if pensions and Social Security are not adequate. Medicare and Medicaid have prevented the impoverishment of the aged due to illness, but they do not provide everything.

So parents often need money from their adult children. Strangely, adult children who are well frequently cannot find a few dollars to raise their parents' standard of living. We are not speaking of saving parents from starvation; that is usually achieved through government programs. We are talking about money to go to the movies; to buy new clothes; to give a grandchild a gift; to take a vacation.

Often parents need help but cannot ask for it:

PARENT: Things are so expensive these days. I can hardly buy hamburger!

YOU-THE-CHILD: Yes, Harry and I feel it all the time. We're not going to get a new car this year because it's just too much.

PARENT: Yes. Social Security doesn't keep up with it.

YOU-THE-CHILD: And gasoline has gone to the sky.

Clearly the parent was sending a message about money. The signal was ignored. The conversation could have gone like this:

PARENT: Things are so expensive these days. I can hardly buy hamburger!

YOU-THE-CHILD: I know. It must be difficult to keep up.

PARENT: My Social Security payments have fallen way behind my bills.

YOU-THE-CHILD: You haven't got enough to live on.

PARENT: It's not that. It's just that I have no money to do anything outside of eating. I hardly ever go to the movies anymore.

This interchange brought out the true state of affairs. And now the parent is in a position to tell what he or she needs; you-the-child can choose how you want to help. How to achieve this result with some consistency is one aim of *Mother/Father/You.*

Sometimes the money problem sits with the adult child. The parents have the financial stability; the adult child needs help. Parents withhold such help for many reasons: They fear giving up their dwindling assets; they do not trust their adult children to be money wise; to give up money to the adult child is to give up control.

For some reason, even very wealthy people seem unwilling to part even with small amounts as they get older. The reason may vary from person to person. Merely to label a parent stingy solves little. The label does not get at the underlying motivation, and the label flung at a parent does not pry money loose. The statement: "Pa, don't be so stingy! Give a little!" stimulates little but anger.

Finally, there are parents who seem no longer able to manage their money.

Fifty-year-old James's mother, Jenny, eighty-one, was the beneficiary of her late husband's $100,000 insurance policy. Jenny put all the money in the savings bank at low interest. Between the interest income and her Social Security check she barely scrapes by. And inflation is tearing that income to tatters.

James has been trying to convince his mother to put the insurance money into United States Treasury certificates of deposit at high interest. That would give Jenny another five thousand a year.

But Jenny has been adamant. She has never heard of certificates of deposit. Having lived through the depression of the 1930s, she is fearful of anything but savings banks. And James simply cannot get her to change her mind. When he tries, she says, with some validity: "You treat me like a baby."

Fears

Fear of death. Fear of getting sick. Fear of being assaulted. Fear of falling. Fear of dying alone. Fear of being abandoned. Fear of losing money. Fear of losing love.

As parents get older their fears multiply. Their resiliency, emotional and physical, declines. They are less able to rationalize their fears.

Jane's mother, Yvonne, sixty-eight, and father, William, seventy-one, live in Indianapolis. Jane lives in Chicago. William is a retired army general. When William was on active duty, he and Yvonne were real go-getters. Wherever they were stationed, they occupied the center of social and army activities. Yvonne was an accomplished pianist.

Now he suffers from angina—heart pains. His wife is in pretty good health. They rarely leave their house because William feels his age and illness as bringing on imminent catastrophe. Their main amusement consists of watching television and drinking, too much, Jane thinks. Once avid travelers, they will not even visit their daughters in Chicago and San Diego. Contact comes via telephone about once a month and a visit from their daughters once a year.

The daughters ask: "Why don't you get out of the house? Take a trip. Why do you drink so much?" The questions aim at rousing their once active parents. To no avail. The answers come back: "We don't feel like it." "The trip is too much for my heart." "We hardly drink at all. Why, I used to be able to put away a quart of scotch. I don't do that anymore." And the parents retreat from their daughters, talking to them less and less. The retreat is due to fear: fear of a heart attack, fear of spending money, fear of their daughters' criticism. The alcohol damps down the fears, reduces the anxiety.

How does an adult child deal with a parent's spoken and unspoken fears? Certainly not by provoking more fear: fear of criticism, fear of being judged or abandoned or not living up to the adult child's expectations. Yet the adult child can easily provoke fear, often without realizing it. We will show you a language of calm that allows an approach to a fearful parent. And through that language, the adult child can give support and help for which the mute, scared mother and father cannot bring themselves to ask.

In-laws

The scene is a nightclub.

"Two women meet in the street to talk about their children's new marriages," says the comedian. "One says: 'My daughter married a wonderful man. He spares her nothing. She has credit cards to all the best shops. She doesn't have to get up until noon. And what's best, she has a maid to wait on her hand and foot.'

"The other woman," continues the jokester, "sighs sadly and says: 'And my son married a good-for-nothing. She spends spends spends on clothes. She sleeps like a lazy dog until noon and she doesn't do a thing around the house.'"

The mother-in-law joke has supported many a stand-up comic in a grand style. It works so well because it touches the core of the in-law difficulty. The parent always owes his or her primary allegiance to the adult child, who reciprocates with loyalty. The in-law can rarely win that loyalty. So the relationship always starts off asymmetrically: parent and adult child against spouse. In the conflict, the adult child is squeezed between parent and spouse.

Listen to this exchange between an older woman and her daughter-in-law, who shares household chores with her husband:

MOTHER-IN-LAW: Women are really stronger than men. Don't you think you should do the Saturday morning cleaning and let him rest and watch the ball game?

DAUGHTER-IN-LAW: I work hard, too, and I'm tired. We have decided to share the housework.

MOTHER-IN-LAW: I always did the work. My son never had to do my work nor did his father either.

DAUGHTER-IN-LAW: But you didn't work outside the house.

MOTHER-IN-LAW: No, I've always given my full attention to my family. It's a full-time job, you know.

Against such a superior combatant, the daughter-in-law hasn't got a chance, unless, again, she learns the language of negotiation. We are not forgetting that there are fathers-in-law with all the signs of the in-law syndrome. Fathers-in-law side just as readily as mothers-in-law with their children against the spouse.

Interference

"When are you going to have children?"

"This apartment is too small for you and Bill."

"You're too easy on your children! Let me show you how to discipline them."

"You're too strict with your children."

Many (if not most) parents consider it their right and duty to continue to "show" their adult children how to run their lives. To the adult children such acts or suggestions are gross interference. But it works the other way, too:

"Put your money into certificates of deposit, mother."

"That woman you're going out with is just after your money, dad."

"Go to the doctor. You don't seem well."

"This apartment is too big for you now that you're alone!"

Interference stems from a variety of motives. Much of it is habit. A parent cannot let go of her or his adult children's lives after a lifetime of wiping their noses. A parent is also motivated by the fear of loss, loss of the adult children. Only by seeming to be part of the continuing life of the adult child can the loss be averted. And finally, for many older parents the need to feel useful by running another life dominates their thoughts.

Recently, Brenda, twenty-six, moved into her own apartment. Elinor, her mother, comes to visit often.

BRENDA: I have the feeling I'm still living at home; you're always here!

ELINOR: I thought you'd be lonely and want my company.

BRENDA: Not all the time, every day. You don't seem to take the hint.

ELINOR: I cleaned for you and watered the plants.

BRENDA: I don't want to hurt you, but if you don't let me know before you let yourself in, I'm going to change the locks. I need to have a place of my own.

ELINOR: You were always trying to hide things from me. As a child, you were so secretive. You never told me anything. I knew we shouldn't have let you have this place.

BRENDA: What do you think I do here, screw every guy in town?

ELINOR: How dare you talk to me that way?

For the adult children who interfere in their parents' lives, motivation is also multiple. For one adult child, it is the fear that the parent in old age has become helpless, physically, emotionally, and intellectually. The roles have flipped;

the adult child has become parent to the parent. The scenes play out in reverse.

For other adult children, the parent-child flip has not taken place but they see it coming on the horizon. So they attempt to take measures that will "save" their aging parents from harm.

Many aging parents seek dependency on their adult children. One seventy-five-year-old father announced to his daughter that in a few years he would like to live with her and her husband. A California woman counsels her son not to take a job in Chicago, not because the job is ill-suited to her son, but because she will be deprived of the help he has given her.

MOTHER: You'd think you'd stay in San Diego.
SON: I can't pick and choose where to be located. I'll never get a job if I do.
MOTHER: Can't you just find a job in San Diego? Even if you did, you'd probably get your own apartment.
SON: That's right.
MOTHER: You'd think you'd stay home and help your parents for a few years.
SON: What if I got married right away?
MOTHER: That's different; you'd be starting a new life then.
SON: Are you saying that I can only move out if I get married because that's when I'd be starting a new life?
MOTHER: That's right.
SON: What if I never get married? Can I ever leave?
MOTHER: Of course, when you're older.
SON: What's the cut-off age? What is older? Twenty-eight? Thirty-five? Sixty-five?
MOTHER: I don't know! You sound like it's a prison. We don't ask much of you.

In any case, interference, whether by the parent or the adult child, creates tension. It usually does not achieve its stated goal: amelioration of the other's condition. And at worst, when successful, interference also succeeds in turning an adult into a dependent child.

Sex

Few issues create more tension between adult children and their parents than the sexual mores of the adult child or the sexual activity of the parent. There are generational differences of great magnitude today. In our parents' youth divorce was rare; now there are almost as many divorces as marriages. We Americans have gone in for serial monogamy; and that is difficult for our aging parents to understand or accept.

They see living arrangements between young and middle-aged couples that would have scandalized whole towns: men and women living together without being married; gay couples of both sexes, many with children, sharing homes openly; men and women espousing mates thirty years younger. All of this is reported openly not only among celebrities but among ordinary people as well. Yet your parents remember when, in the 1950s, Ingrid Bergman's movies were boycotted because she left her husband for another man.

Your parents may have had it dinned into them that there was something "dirty" about sex and that it was particularly dirty for old people. The phrase "dirty old man" is often appended to a man over fifty who retains a lusty sexual appetite and doesn't care who knows it. The pressures from your parents' peers work against their sexual interests. And adult children counsel their parents against sexual involvements. The advice often takes other forms:

YOU-THE-CHILD: Aunt Ida tells me you have a new girl-friend.
PARENT: Yes, a very nice woman.

YOU-THE-CHILD: Don't you think you should wait?
PARENT: Wait? For what?
YOU-THE-CHILD: Well, mom has only been dead eight months.
PARENT: I loved your mother, I need a friend.
YOU-THE-CHILD: You could wait.
PARENT: I've waited long enough.
YOU-THE-CHILD: You have no respect for mom.
PARENT: Don't tell me how to live my life!

In fact, most older men and women have considerable capacity for sex. The death of or divorce from a spouse dims that capacity often only temporarily. Family pressure against sex can have a catastrophic impact on the parents' lives. Yet many studies now show that continued sexual activity is important for their emotional as well as their physical well-being. Indeed, recent observations suggest that regular sexual intercourse diminishes arthritic pain.

The parent can exert a strong impact on the adult child's sexual life. The power of a parent to disapprove and to interfere, even with an adult child, can lead and has led to tragedy. Marriages have been disrupted, relationships broken up. And in the case of sexual activity outside the mainstream—for example, homosexuality—parental disapproval has been emotionally destructive to both parent and adult child.

Often, the parent lashes out at an adult child in a situation when the child needs comfort. The parent is caught between old feelings and needs and the adult child's "wayward" behavior. Meg, twenty-eight and unmarried, has been having an affair with a married man. Her parents know it and have cautioned her repeatedly. Her father, Andrew, has been particularly vehement.

MEG: Lyle and I have broken up.
ANDREW: Well, that's to be expected. And good riddance.

MEG: But you don't understand.

ANDREW: I understand only too well. He's had his fun. I hope you'll find someone with better sense.

MEG: But that's not it. I think we'd still be together.

ANDREW: And he'd leave his wife? Fat chance! Look, he's forty years old and he was a little restless.

MEG (crying now): That's not it! That's not it.

ANDREW: Then what is it? He's gone. Good.

MEG: I'm going to have his baby.

ANDREW: Damn! So now the dumb slut wants to bring the bastard home.

Handling this sensitive dimension of human activity requires delicate and understanding communication, not combat.

Other Problems

How do you get an aging parent into a nursing home when the parent doesn't want to go? What do you do with a senile parent? A seventy-year-old woman has a forty-year-old boyfriend; is he after her money? A mother doesn't eat properly. A father won't let his adult children visit. A mother demands daily visits.

Everybody knows that in relations between parents and adult children problems abound that may fester for years, poisoning the love that many want. Parents and adult children are trapped, as we've said, by their language—toxic dialogue that does not allow the solution to these problems.

Our language of mutual support, the nurturing language, gives you a clear road to the solutions. It doesn't matter what the problem is; careful application of the new way of communication can achieve a mutuality. It may take longer than you first expected, but in time you will find a way to help your parents or get them to help you, as much as they can.

/ 3 /

A New Skill: Searching

Now you are ready to learn the new language. The first skill
—the basic one—is listening, because through listening we
nurture the other person's feelings. Listening nurtures by
giving validity to those feelings: "If he's listening, then what I
feel is true and important." If we do not listen, we trivialize
the other's feelings: "He's not listening. He doesn't care. My
feelings don't count."

The new language lets you search into your parents' interior world of feelings. It is a world they have kept hidden, but
it governs their relationship to you. If you can put yourselves
into that world, you can build a relationship with your
parents. You can in turn make your needs and pains known to
them.

In Chapter 1, we spoke of the four principles of communication. We gave one of them a shorthand name: searching. In effect, the principle states that:

People (parents) will tell you what they are thinking if *they feel* you are listening.

Many people believe they are listening to another person because they have heard and can repeat back every word spoken to them. They try sometimes to prove they were listening by such a repetition: "I was listening. You just said: 'I'm not feeling well.'" But hearing the words is only part of listening. You have to do more than parrot another's words to prove you are listening. Remember, the other person has to believe you are truly listening. Let's see why.

Think of this situation: You want to tell your parent something that is troubling you but you are afraid to open yourself up:

PARENT: You look worried.

YOU-THE-CHILD: It's nothing.

PARENT: I can tell by that look on your face that something's wrong.

YOU-THE-CHILD: Well, I had trouble at work. My boss said my work was sloppy.

PARENT: I always told you that you were a slob. You just wouldn't listen to me!

No wonder you're afraid. If a parent strikes at you verbally when you are looking for understanding, the chances are that next time you will try to hide what you wanted to say. The conversation might go like this:

PARENT: You look worried.

YOU-THE-CHILD: It's nothing.

PARENT: I can tell by the look on your face that something's wrong.

YOU-THE-CHILD: I told you nothing's wrong! Please stop nagging me!

PARENT: I know you're hiding something.

YOU-THE-CHILD: Oh, please!

And so on.

Of course, it works the other way, too. Parents are afraid to confide in the adult child if they may be judged, evaluated, or made to look silly. Yet people do need to confide, to elicit understanding and sympathy. Each of us keeps trying to introduce hidden material, hoping that we will not be punished for revealing it.

The Opening Signal

We try by sending out a tentative signal. A little message of no apparent importance. A worried look. A sigh. A remark out of the blue ("People are really terrible"). Or a non-sequitur response to a question:

PARENT: Can you come over for dinner tonight?
YOU-THE-CHILD: I got a letter from my alumni association.

The signal says to the other person: "I have something on my mind. Is it safe to proceed?" We call this an *opening* or an *opening signal*. It is intended to open communication. Safely! So the person who opens up does so in code, or with minimum commitment. You can't get hurt that way.

Unfortunately, in American society we have mostly lost the language for saying: "I hear you. Tell me what's troubling you." So we block the other from proceeding with safety. The closer the relationship—parent-to-child, husband-to-wife—the harder it is to allow the other to talk about his or her deep concerns. We fear the revelations.

We feel responsibility. We want to control, to judge, to change, to correct.

All this shuts off communication from our parent's deep emotional recesses. And it is the emotions that govern our parent's behavior.

In the new language, you communicate to your parent:
"I've heard your signal. Proceed with safety."
"I'm listening to what you say. I won't judge you."

"I hear that you're troubled. I'm ready to help."

You could speak those words, but if they were the only sentences in your new language you would soon sound awkward and strange. Listening consists first in picking up the tentative signal. Then you acknowledge to your parent that you have heard it. ("I heard what you said. Go on.") In return, your parent will reveal more of what that signal means. And you acknowledge that. So you proceed by listening and acknowledging. And as you do, you will see the miracle: Your parent will begin to tell you things about herself or himself that have been kept hidden for decades. You will begin to understand your parent's fears and needs. And in turn and in time, your parent will listen to you. Listening takes in the other's words and feelings. Listening does not advise. Listening does not judge. And when the other believes you have listened, he or she will be ready to hear what you have to say.

Three Kinds of Listening

You will find that true listening is a complex skill. It comes in three varieties.

1. Wordless Listening

With *wordless listening* you show the other person by the look on your face, the set of your body, and the tone of your voice that you want to hear more about what the other has to say. With wordless listening you can pick up on the opening signal.

PARENT: I cleaned the whole house today.
YOU-THE-CHILD: Mmmm . . . [Or any other sound that suggests that the parent should continue.]

The other sounds might be: "Uh-huh," "Yes," "Really," "Well," "Oh," or "Ahhhh." They are best uttered flatly, not as questions. If you say: "Really?" that may be heard as if you were doubting that your parent had the energy or the will to clean the house.

Or if you accompany the word with a tone of surprise when you say: "Well!"—it is as if you were saying: "Well! It's about time you cleaned up the pigsty." And that, of course, shuts off communication with a click.

The only idea to be communicated to your parent is: "I hear you. Please tell me more if you want to." Surprisingly, it is not easy to avoid a judgment even at this simple level. It takes practice. Later we'll show you how to practice this skill. It is only with practice that you can achieve the highest level of communication. For now, you might try just uttering out loud one of the words as if it were in response to an opening signal.

2. *Checking Listening*

After you have acknowledged the opening signal with wordless listening, your parent will probably want to continue. Because your parent may not want to tell you the whole story right away, he or she may issue a second statement in code. The coded message hides the true meaning of what is on your parent's mind.

Essentially, you want to say to your parent: "I've heard your statement. Is this what you mean?"

You are checking out *your* understanding of the coded message. We emphasize that it is *your* understanding that is being checked, not your parent's ability to communicate. The onus is on you. That's why we call this second variety *checking listening*. It is intended to check out the new message.

PARENT: I cleaned the whole house today.
YOU-THE-CHILD: Mmmm . . .
PARENT: I was running up and down the stairs twenty times.
YOU-THE-CHILD: You worked very hard cleaning the house.

Reflection: Your statement is a simple interpretation of what your parent has said. Carl Rogers called this *reflection:* You reflect back to the other person his or her ideas as you heard them. Reflection says to the other person: "I heard what you said. This is what I understood you to mean." You are trying to enter the interior world of your parent to see that world as your parent sees it.

In a study Dr. Rogers did many years ago, he found that simple reflection encouraged his clients to speak and to seek for solutions to their problems on their own. If the therapist gave advice or gave a *psychological* interpretation, or talked about himself or his reasons for his actions, the client usually stopped talking.

Reflection encourages your parent to continue because it is safe. When you are checking the meaning of a message you are trying to interpret its meaning on the simplest level. The implied question is: "Is this what you mean?" Not: "This is what you really mean?" You are not trying to make a psychological interpretation. You may be wrong in what you believe your parent has said, but that doesn't matter.

Suppose the exchange went as follows:

PARENT: I cleaned the whole house today.
YOU-THE-CHILD: Mmmm . . .
PARENT: I was running up and down the stairs twenty times.
YOU-THE-CHILD: You worked very hard cleaning the house.
PARENT: No, it wasn't very hard. I found it easy.

The second reflection inaccurately stated your parent's meaning. The point is that your parent continued the conversation and knows that you are really listening. You are not repeating the words; you are trying to understand them, and that encourages more revelation.

Sometimes you can check out the meaning of a communication simply by repeating the last words of the speaker. You could have said, in the example above:

"You ran up and down the stairs twenty times."

Such a statement still encourages the speaker because it says: "This is what I heard you say."

Checking listening, then, has two forms: the *simple repeat* and the *simple interpretation*. The simple interpretation usually produces better results, but you can fall back on the simple repeat if you do not know what to say. If your parent hears the simple repeat too often, your parent may say: "Why are you repeating everything I say?"

You can ignore the question or you can make a simple interpretation:

"You're bothered when I repeat what you say"; or

"You feel I'm repeating what you say."

It is hard to deny that you are repeating when you are doing so. It is best to encourage your parent to express his or her feelings about your attempts to understand what is being said.

Some Variations: To avoid the problem of your parent's becoming annoyed with checking listening because it sounds as though you are endlessly repeating his or her words, you vary the form of the response. Here are some variations:

"*You're saying* that you ran up and down the stairs a lot."

"*I understand* that you worked hard cleaning the house."

"*I hear you saying* that you cleaned the whole house today."

"*I don't understand*: you cleaned the whole house."

"*Let me see* . . . you cleaned the whole house and you ran up and down the stairs."

"*It sounds as if* . . ."

"*You mean that* . . ."

The italicized words provide the variation. The skill is to change them frequently in a natural setting so that your language doesn't sound contrived or stilted. Again, it takes practice. Later in this book we will describe role-playing, which will show you how to practice *the nurturing language* by assuming different roles with your family and friends.

Caution: Reflection in question form may be damaging; for example:

"Are you saying that you ran up and down the stairs twenty times?"

In question form, the statement can be misinterpreted as a criticism. It can be heard as: "Why did you run up and down the stairs?"

In this case the parent can think: "She doesn't like the idea that I ran up and down the stairs." As we will show in the next chapter, questions can corrupt innocent meaning and put the other person on the defensive. Many, many people are particularly sensitive to questions. So when you are checking listening, a statement in a declarative voice avoids misunderstanding.

As with wordless listening, checking listening must be accompanied by a tone of voice that strongly suggests that you want to hear what the other is saying. Your facial expression and, if possible, the set of your body also expresses interest. For example, if you stand with your arms folded, you are signaling disbelief and guardedness. It is also easy, in an unguarded moment, to turn a simple sentence into mockery by a change of emphasis.

"So . . . you ran up and down the stairs twenty times!"

Checking listening is your single most useful tool because it is simple and requires little thought or creative effort. You don't have to be clever. You don't have to make a complex psychological analysis. On these two grounds, the nurturing language stands above all other schemes for "handling" people. It doesn't require you to be tricky or insightful, only interested, sincere, and motivated. You can bring checking listening into play rapidly under almost all circumstances. You will rely on it frequently—perhaps ten times or more in an encounter with your parent.

Here are some parental signals and how you might respond to them:

PARENT: I can't come to visit you next Tuesday.
YOU-THE-CHILD: You have something you're doing Tuesday.

PARENT: Your face looks flushed and not well at all.
YOU-THE-CHILD: You think I'm ill.

PARENT: I have this stock that dropped ten points. What would you do with it now?
YOU-THE-CHILD: You don't know whether to sell the stock.

PARENT: Why are you dating Alice? She's been everybody's girlfriend.
YOU-THE-CHILD: I don't understand. You think Alice is not a nice woman.

PARENT: I really think that you and your brother should chip in and help us out with about forty dollars a week. Then we'd be comfortable.
YOU-THE-CHILD: You're saying that you and mom need forty dollars a week to make ends meet.

Each time the first—almost reflexive—response is to listen. You want to know the full meaning of your parent's statement before you speak. If you speak without listening, you may not get to your parent's true thoughts. The first signal may camouflage something more important, more urgent, more painful:

PARENT: I can't come to visit you next Tuesday.
YOU-THE-CHILD: You have something you're doing Tuesday.
PARENT: I'm busy.
YOU-THE-CHILD: Hmmm.
PARENT: Well, I might as well tell you. I have a doctor's appointment to check some bleeding I've been having.

A direct question to this parent would have brought an evasion. Only because she felt safe was she able to confide her medical problem to the adult child.

3. *Nurturing Listening*

Nurturing suggests support, nursing, caring, and acceptance. The third kind of listening will help you to support and to express caring for your parent. Almost always, a communication of support and caring evokes a desire to continue speaking, a desire to bring up more hidden thoughts and feelings.

Nurturing listening is the most powerful skill you will have in reaching out to your parents. It is powerful because it deals with feelings. And feelings—much more than reason—guide behavior.

An example of nurturing listening:

PARENT: I cleaned the whole house today. [opening signal]

YOU-THE-CHILD: Mmmm . . . [wordless listening]

PARENT: I was running up and down the stairs twenty times. [continues talking]

YOU-THE-CHILD: You worked very hard cleaning the house. [checking listening]

PARENT: I hardly sat down. My knees wobbled at the end. [produces more hidden material]

YOU-THE-CHILD: Cleaning that apartment must be an awfully big job. You must be just knocked out! [nurturing listening]

PARENT: I didn't want to say anything, but I did get some pains in my chest. [comes up with the most hidden fact]

The parent was not a complainer and would have kept her chest pains secret from her daughter if the daughter had run the exchange as follows:

MOTHER: I cleaned the whole house today.	[opening signal]
DAUGHTER: What? You know you you're not supposed to overexert yourself!	[criticism]
MOTHER: It was nothing. I just took a warm bath and I was as good as new.	[hiding the facts]

Nurturing listening requires careful attention, not cleverness. First, you look for the emotional content of your parent's message. Then you reflect it back sympathetically. The reflection tells your parent that the confidences will be lovingly handled. That allows your parent to open up to you. And both of you will quickly get to the core of what may be standing between you. And it allows your parent then to hear what you say.

Steve is fifty and his father, Frank, is seventy-nine. Frank's wife, Mary, died three months ago after half a century of marriage. The loss has devastated Frank. He wanders about his house (he now lives alone), stopping from time to time to weep. Nobody in the family knows the extent of his grief. Everybody keeps telling him that time will heal his wound, that he has his own life to live, that he should get up and do things, take a trip or a vacation . . . all designed to "cheer up pop." In public he does keep a stiff upper lip. He rarely leaves the house, giving some lame excuse. The family wants him to get out and to be the once-bouncy man that he was. Steve visits him alone one evening.

STEVE: How're you doing, pop?	[question]
FRANK: Just fine. Just fine.	[cover-up]
STEVE: You're doing fine.	[checking listening]
FRANK: As well as can be expected with your mom gone.	[opening signal]

STEVE: You really still feel mom's go-   [nurturing listening]
ing terribly.

FRANK: Truthfully I didn't think it   [opening up]
was going to be this bad.

STEVE: After fifty years you must miss   [nurturing listening]
not having mom to talk to.

FRANK (his eyes growing watery):   [bringing up hidden
Steve, almost every hour of every   material]
day! Everybody seems to want me
to forget her, but I want to remember!

STEVE: You want to do something to   [checking listening]
help you remember.

FRANK: I know it sounds foolish but   [the hidden need]
I want to visit the places where
Mary and I had a good time and I'd
like to take Harriet [his oldest
granddaughter] with me.

At no time did Steve ever give his own opinion of what his
father should do. He never gave advice. He never tried to
cheer his father up. All he did was listen in the new way. That
allowed Frank to open up without fear of being put down for
wanting to do something that the family might think was
foolish.

People do want to be understood. Most of all they want
their feelings to be understood. One way to signal your parent
that his or her feelings are understood is to identify those
feelings just as Steve did when he identified Frank's longing:
"After fifty years you must miss not having mom to talk to."

Your parent may be feeling anger or satisfaction, disap-
pointment or gratification, sadness or happiness, depression
or elation, fear or security, anxiety or calmness, or any of a
score of different emotions. When you reflect back the particular emotion your parent may be feeling, you are saying:
"I understand."

Unless you listen very carefully, you may not hear your parent's emotions. And if you do not hear, you cannot feel. That's what your parent (and all of us) want: that someone be able to understand—to feel—their feelings.

Here are some emotional expressions from parents and some possible nurturing responses:

PARENT: I wanted so much to be able to visit with little Jeff.

YOU-THE-CHILD: You're *disappointed* that you can't see your grandson this week.

PARENT: The Social Security increase came through. We'll have some extra money now.

YOU-THE-CHILD: You feel some *relief* from money pressures with the Social Security raise.

PARENT: Whenever I talk to Ellie she treats me like a child. I'm a grandmother and I've lived a good deal longer than she has!

YOU-THE-CHILD: You're *angry* that Ellie doesn't treat you as an equal.

PARENT: I have this pain in my chest whenever I take a walk. I wonder if it's the angina coming back.

YOU-THE-CHILD: You're *afraid* you may be having your old heart trouble again.

PARENT: Now that Thanksgiving is over and everybody has gone home I can take a load off my feet and go back to my normal life.

YOU-THE-CHILD: You're *enjoying* the calm after the storm of all those people here.

After nurturing listening, your parent will be willing to go deeper into his or her feelings. Example: a mother is visiting her daughter on a Sunday afternoon.

MOTHER: It gets dark early these days. [opening signal]

DAUGHTER: Yes. [wordless listening]

MOTHER: You never know who you'll run into. [opening up hidden material]

DAUGHTER: You're *afraid* something will happen. [nurturing: identifies mother's fear]

MOTHER: Yes. Mrs. Henry was mugged last month walking along the street. [reveals nature of fear]

DAUGHTER: So you're afraid that if you go home after dark something like that will happen to you. [checking listening]

MOTHER: Yes, that's why I want to go home early. [reveals need to go home early]

The mother was not only afraid of going home on dark streets, she also was fearful of telling her daughter that she had to leave early. By nurturing listening the daughter allowed her mother to express her true feelings. The daughter, of course, has some choices now: She can offer to see her mother home; suggest her mother stay the night; or she can simply agree with her mother's need to be home early.

Another example: A son has borrowed money from his father and is late with a payment.

FATHER: The mail must be slow this week. [opening signal]

SON: You were expecting something. [checking: The son had no idea what the father wanted]

FATHER: You know damn well what I was expecting. [closer to what is going on in the father]

SON: You were expecting a payment and you're angry that it's late. [nurturing: identifying the father's need and anger and reflecting it]

FATHER: At least you could have [the true need: ac-
called me to tell me that it was knowledgment
going to be late. from the son]

The son's reflecting the father's emotion allowed the father calmly to state his need. The revelation of the father's true needs opened up many possibilities for the son. He could agree to call his father in the future when his payment was going to be late; he could explore further his father's feelings about being called. The son tuned in to the father's feelings and gave the relationship some options.

Don't Try to Be Freud

We made the point in Chapter 1 that you don't have to be a psychologist to apply the nurturing language. In professional psychological analysis, we examine the other person's behavior and words and then form some idea of that person's inner world and personality. From that, then, the "psychologist" moves to alter the other person's behavior. It takes years to learn. And even then, therapists do not interpret perfectly.

All of us do some psychologizing. We say: "Bill is so rigid" or "Lucy is too emotional." We base those judgments on home-grown analysis of their behavior and words. We act on the basis of those characterizations. If Bill is rigid, we put our proposals to him in the strongest terms to overcome his rigidity. If Sally is too emotional, we avoid giving her tasks that will stir up her emotions.

We sometimes go further: We guess a person's next move based on our analysis of his motivations. We say: "I know Jim so well, I almost know what his next words are going to be."

That may be fine for poker where we back up our hunch with a bet. But trying to "use psychology" may backfire. Between people a wrong guess poisons the relationship. Scientific studies show that even the most empathetic of us guess wrong at least half the time. Here's what can happen:

Jane, twenty-seven, works as a high school teacher; her father, Edward, forty-eight, owns a furniture store. Jane wants to go back to school to get a doctorate in history. She needs her father's help. She has sized him up over the years as being stingy and hard-driving. So she "knows" he will turn her down.

JANE: Dad, I'm planning to take a leave from school and go back to the university to get my doctorate. I have some money saved but I need more from you. I know you don't like to give me money, but I do need it and you owe it to me as your daughter. You should give me the money.

EDWARD: What's this? You're telling me what I should do? I'm not one of your pals whom you can order around. If you want to go back to school that's your business. I paid for college and that was almost too much. You should be married by now. If you get a doctorate you'll be smarter than most of the men and then you'll never get married!

Did Jane guess her father's motivations correctly? She'll never know. She never gave him a chance to express his true feelings about her plans. She challenged him on just the grounds about which he is probably most sensitive: his apparent stinginess and his duty as a parent. And, of course, he defended himself with all the weapons a parent can muster.

As we go along, we will show how the nurturing language expresses your needs so that your parent can respond to them. We'll help Jane ask her father for help. But the first step is to search into your parent's interior world and not to assume what is going on inside that unexplored region. Only by listening in this new way will you learn what your parent really wants, thinks, and feels. You want to open up your parent's interior world, not to psychologize but to prepare your parent to open up to your wants, thoughts, and feelings.

A Look Back

Listening is the most important tool in an interpersonal relationship. If you show your parent that you are truly listening to what he or she has to say, your parent will open up his or her interior world to you. We call this searching. Only by searching can you prepare the way for an exchange in the nurturing language. Searching is a prelude to allowing your parent to listen to you.

Wordless listening encourages your parent to continue talking after an opening signal. With wordless listening you utter simple sounds or words: "Hmmm," "Ahhh," "Really," "Well," "Yes," "Oh," or "Uh-huh." Your tone of voice and facial expression says: "I want to hear more."

Checking listening reflects back to your parent the ideas he or she has expressed. It encourages your parent to open up hidden material safely. Again, your voice and expression show sincerity and interest.

One form of checking listening is the simple repeat: You repeat to your parent, almost unchanged, the words just uttered. You can vary the word order or put a phrase in front of the repeat to introduce variety. The phrases include: "You are saying . . ." "You mean . . ." etc.

Another form of checking listening is the simple interpretation. You make a guess at the meaning of your parent's statement. It is more powerful than the simple repeat and is more likely to encourage your parent to bring out hidden needs, thoughts, and feelings.

Nurturing listening reflects back to your parent the emotional content of his or her speech. It puts into different words the emotional status of your parent. It expresses caring and sympathy for your parent's point of view. While it is more difficult to do, it is more effective in encouraging your parent to bring forth the hidden needs, thoughts, and feelings. With nurturing listening, you will find it critical to match the tone of your voice and expression sincerely to the emotions your parent vocalizes.

Things to avoid: questions, criticism, judgment, advice. Avoid also psychologically analyzing your parent . . . you probably will be wrong and it will lead you to say or do something that will make your parent clam up.

/ 4 /

Recognizing the Weapons
Fired at You

With the old toxic language of parent–adult child relations, both sides tend to mount powerful verbal, material, and sometimes physical weapons. They are part of the attack and counterattack that mark the unloving exchanges from which so many suffer.

It is not unknown for adult children and their parents to resort to blows when the going gets deeply personal and frustrating for one or both. Frequently, such fights occur in families who have long histories of physical abuse of children. It is not a problem easily solved even with the nurturing language. However, mastery of the language by the adult child can reduce the chances of physical violence.

Of course, most adult children and their parents forgo physical violence. Material weapons more often come into the struggle. The parent or the adult child can withhold money from the other.

"If you marry that woman, don't expect a cent from me."

"Go ahead. Open a business. But you're on your own."

The giving of money can also be a weapon because the giver often demands control with the gift.

"If I give you a hundred dollars a month I should have some say over how you spend it."

"If I give you money for food, you shouldn't spend it on clothes or going out."

Clearly, the most common weapons are verbal assaults in many forms. Even material weapons (withholding money, placing an elder in a nursing home, exclusion from a family occasion, etc.) are verbal at the start. Verbal weapons can be trivial; or they can wound so deeply as to cause despair and sometimes suicide. When they are used against us, most of the time we recognize them for what they are. But sometimes they are so subtle they escape our attention. We realize only dimly that we've been had.

In this chapter we will reveal the weapons for what they are so that you can recognize them. If you know what they are, you can avoid or counter them. In subsequent chapters, we show how to avoid and to counter weapons by speaking the nurturing language.

Judgment

Almost all parental weapons aim at control; the same control parents exerted on their adult children when they were growing up. Some weapons are meant to inflict pain. Parents often want to achieve both goals. The basic weapon is judgment: to declare something is right or wrong, not up to standard—the parent's standard. The parent may judge the adult child's behavior, taste, speech, dress, belongings, children—the list exceeds imagination:

"We never went to work without a tie."

"Your wife ought to let you sleep late on Saturday."

"Your children need more discipline."

"You'll never get a man if you keep going around with those girlfriends of yours."

"Just because you're so hungry for sex is no reason to let that woman lead you around by the nose."

"That is just the wrong thing to do."

These clearly attacking statements aim at controlling the adult child's behavior. They express *negative* judgments with the goal of changing the adult child's behavior to one acceptable by the parent's standard. They leave no room for the adult child's choice of behavior, and when there is no choice there is a slim chance of help or listening.

What most people miss is that *positive* judgments also subtly attempt control. They say to the adult child: "You have measured up to *my* standards. Keep up the good work."

Some examples:

"I like it when you wear a tie. It makes you look so neat."

"Alice is very good to let you out of household chores."

"Tommy was so well behaved at dinner. You've done such a good job with him."

"I think Penny is such a nice girl. You're smart to have picked her for a girlfriend."

"I like to see you independent from women who chase you."

"Oh. You did that so well."

The trouble with these compliments is that they carry a hidden message: "I know what's good for you and I will tell you when you are doing well. If I withhold praise, you'll know you are doing something wrong."

As we examine other weapons, we will see that they also frequently come in two forms: positive and negative. The negative obviously demeans; the positive also disparages but it is unrecognized. Praise, however, generates the same kind of effect on exchange of views: The receiver of the positive judgment declines to reveal more of his inner world.

All of us have been taught to be wary of flattery. We so easily see others succumb to it but may be oblivious to the fact that we are the target of flattery. One interesting thing about flattery is that it works to make you feel beholden to the flatterer even when you know you are being flattered to get something.

Here's an interesting little experiment: Say to someone you know: "I'm going to flatter you and I don't really mean it. I just want you to tell me how you feel when I do it." Then say something especially nice about that person. You will be amazed to learn that the flattered one liked what you said even though you announced that you didn't mean it. But the next thoughts following praise are red lights to emotional traffic.

Why is this so? Judgment of any kind tends to arouse psychological defenses, our way of protecting our dignity, independence or self-esteem. We think:

"What did he mean by that?"
"Does she really mean it?"
"What does pop want?"
"How does she know that's any good?"
"He's just saying that to get on my good side."

And when we think such thoughts we are not going to expose more of our inner world to more praise or blame. The poet Emily Dickinson understood the two faces of judgment when she wrote:

> Blame is just as dear as Praise
> and Praise as mere as Blame.

Of course, we have been talking as if only the parent fires the guns of judgment. The adult child also has learned to aim blame and praise (probably from a blaming or praising parent). If the parent criticizes the adult child's money management, you can bet that the return salvo will criticize something about the parent.

How can you avoid judgment and at the same time offer a compliment? Were we not always taught to compliment good work? To reward something nice somebody has done for us with words of praise? This is tricky. In principle, you cannot compliment without judging. After all you are applying a standard of good and bad when you call something good.

We will go into this in more detail when we show you how to counter weapons like judgment. For now, the important thing to remember is to judge the behavior, not the person. Or better, judge the product of the behavior and not the behavior. Again, listen to the difference between a compliment in the old toxic language and the same compliment rephrased in the nurturing language:

"Tommy was so well behaved at dinner. *You've* done such a good job with him."

Compare that with this:

"Tommy was so nice at dinner. I really enjoyed sitting with him."

The new language version eliminated the word "you" and changed "well behaved" to "nice." The first change removed the praise from the person. The second avoided the implication that at other times Tommy may not be well behaved.

Toxic version judging the person:

"I think Penny is such a nice girl. You're smart to have picked her for a girlfriend."

Nurturing language version praising the product:

"I think Penny is such a nice girl. I know she must make a very good friend."

Again the "you" is eliminated. It is the fact of Penny's niceness that is praised.

Toxic:

"I like it when you wear a tie. It makes you look so neat."

Nurturing:

"That's a good-looking tie . . . so colorful and neat."

The nurturing language versions allow praise without shutting off parent-child exchange. If a new language version cannot be found for a compliment, then it is better not to utter it. The same thing can be said of negative judgments—

criticisms. If you criticize the product or the behavior, not the person, you can avoid cutting off conversation.

Praise and blame—judgments—are difficult to handle. As you will see, the nurturing language can be used to make your ideas known without stirring the hostility of your parent. The language will help you to put up a defense against judgment that discourages your parent from using blame or praise and that encourages loving give and take.

Questions, Questions, Questions

When your parent cross-examines you with a barrage of questions, he or she has fired a most insidious weapon. It is not at all obvious that the question-as-weapon is so powerful a control tool. But as you read the following conversation try to hear it in your mind's ear:

PARENT: How are you?
YOU-THE-CHILD: Not bad. And you?
PARENT: Fine. Fine. How is Emily?
YOU-THE-CHILD: She's okay.
PARENT: And your job? What's happening at work?
YOU-THE-CHILD: Everything's all right.
PARENT: Where are you going on vacation this year?
YOU-THE-CHILD: I don't know.
PARENT: And how's Emily?
YOU-THE-CHILD: I told you. Emily's fine.
PARENT: I just wanted to know how she was. Are you going out tonight?
YOU-THE-CHILD: Probably.
PARENT: Where are you going?
YOU-THE-CHILD: I don't know.
Etc.

Such conversations drone on and on in many families. They represent the parent's attempt to find an opening to enter into the life of the adult child. To block the parent's judgment of the adult child's actions, the adult child responds with the tiniest amount of information possible without lying. In that way the adult child attempts to discourage questioning and denies the implication that the parent has a right to know such things. Yet monosyllabic answers seem often to increase the parent's insistence on wanting to know. Monosyllabic answers signal a rejection, and the parent will probably redouble the effort to be accepted by asking more questions.

The question as a parental tool harks back to the adult child's early life. Parents believe they then had the right to ask anything of the child and the child had an obligation to answer and to answer truthfully. If the parent treated the answers as items to control the child's behavior, then over the years, the maturing child learned evasive answers. A famous book had a title that summed it up: *"Where Did You Go?" "Out." "What Did You Do?" "Nothing."*

Questions are weapons because they place the onus on the answerer. Actually, the burden of the question belongs to the questioner. Like this:

"Did you see my keys?" instead of "I misplaced my keys. I need help finding them."

"Are you going out tonight?" instead of "I'd like some company tonight."

"Are you free next Thursday?" instead of "I'm planning to have the family over to dinner Thursday."

"How much did you pay for the new car?" instead of "My car is breaking down and I'm afraid I need a new one."

Questions that begin with "Why did you . . ." or just with "Why" are judgmental questions:

"Why did you write to Sheldon that I'm not well?"

"Why are you combing your hair that way?"

"Why are you going to the beach?"

"Why do you let Johnny run loose like that?"

Because they judge implicitly the person to whom they are directed, "Why" questions most effectively cut off responses that have any meaning except at the surface. In the hands of a desperate parent, "Why" questions often have an edge of hysteria that can easily be detected. The answers mean little except as a pause for the next question. The questions tumble out one after another in relentless succession. The target of the questions feels helpless, unable to do anything except answer, and often in a way that provokes more questions. The target feels like a hostile witness being queried by Perry Mason.

Sometimes the questions are unrelated. They zigzag across the field and provide a difficult moving target:

PARENT: Where did you park the car?
YOU-THE-CHILD: Behind the house.
PARENT: Where's Stanley?
YOU-THE CHILD: He's coming later.
PARENT: How's your upstairs neighbor? The one with cancer.
YOU-THE-CHILD: She seems to be getting along well.
PARENT: How did you like *Star Wars*?
YOU-THE-CHILD: I thought it was very exciting. How did you like it?
PARENT: Okay. When are you going on vacation?
YOU-THE-CHILD: We haven't decided yet.

Zigzag questions are often the parent's urgent call for connection. But the questioner does not know how to follow up the answer with a connecting response. In effect, neither does the adult child. The responses indicate a desperation of trying to get out from under the questions. Such a pattern suggests that the parent is an addict to questions; the parent cannot stop asking without feeling a deep loss. The questions and having someone to question become more important— more rewarding—than the answers.

The zigzag questioner often skims the surface, never daring to confront the responses at any deeper level because that may be dangerous; the questioner may have to reveal part of himself.

Some zigzag questioners shoot into very personal areas without regard for the consequences:

PARENT: How are you and Mildred getting along?
YOU-THE-CHILD: Not bad.
PARENT: And Mildred's leg? Is it healing?
YOU-THE-CHILD: It seems to be getting better.
PARENT: Are you happier in your job?
YOU-THE-CHILD: Oh, yes. Things are fine.
PARENT: Did you talk to your father? [The parents are divorced.]
YOU-THE-CHILD: Just last week.

Though these questions provide many, many opening signals, the replies fail to open up the conversation to any deeper level. As we will show, this type of zigzag questioner can be more easily engaged in a meaningful exchange than the questioner who stays on the surface. We'll return to these examples and show what to do to divert questions and to bring the parent into discussions of the hidden thoughts, feelings, and needs.

Just now, here is another principle of our new language:
Never ask a question; never answer one.
What? Never? Well, hardly ever.

Many questions are mere requests for information: "Which bus do I take to get to Elm Street?" "What time is it?" "What's the address of the phone company?" And these can be answered most of the time without difficulty. But when you're dealing with an addict questioner, even such simple requests may have to be addressed with care.

A question is best treated as an opening signal for the respondent to go into listening, not answering. It is the language of listening that will help the adult child fend off the addict questioner.

Should and Ought

The two most demeaning words in the old toxic language are "should" and "ought." They have cousins: "must," "have to," "is essential that," "need" and "duty." They are almost always preceded by the pronoun "you." The adult child hears:

"You should change jobs."
"You ought to look for another apartment."
"You must call your brother."
"You have to control your children."
"You need a new overcoat."
"It's your duty (obligation) to contribute to my income."

Like blame and praise, "should" and "ought" express a parental standard of behavior or obligation but in a more direct way. If you listen carefully to conversations—your own and those between others—you will hear the two words and their variants extremely frequently. They show that people want others to do things their way. They convey that the "should-sayer" knows better or best. They come under various guises—demands, suggestions, advice.

However they are used, they get the hearer's back up; they imply a lack of confidence in the hearer's ability to do, to think, or to feel. They attack the hearer's independence or sense of freedom.

Think of what the daughter must be feeling in this conversation:

MOTHER: How much do you make a week?
DAUGHTER: I make one hundred twenty-five dollars.
MOTHER: Is that all? With your education, you should be making a lot more. Ask for a raise!

Not only has the mother attacked her daughter's competence; she has set a standard that she expects her daughter to attain. As bitter icing on the bitter cake, the mother provided advice: "Ask for a raise." Advice always contains a "should," hidden or overt. Because "should" attacks independence, so does advice. And advice, once accepted, creates dependency in the taker. As with questions, then:

Never take advice; never give it.

To some, this little nurturing language proverb smacks of advice itself. We offer it not as advice but as a psychological law. Let us add: Never take advice; never give it—*if you wish to avoid falling into the trap of dependency.* We'll explore this maxim in detail as we discuss the giving and taking of help.

Why Direct Orders Don't Work

Fifty years ago, parents easily directed their children. Parents had almost total authority over children. The children obeyed. Parents obeyed their authorities, too: bosses, clergy, politicians, police—all commanding powerful retaliatory weapons to exact obedience. Bosses could fire you; the clergy could damn or excommunicate you; politicians could affect your job or living space; and the police your freedom.

Most of those weapons have weakened considerably. Unions protect workers against arbitrary discharge (even where unions do not exist employers have softened discharge procedures). The power of the clergy has waned and their communicants do not see their eternal fates so much controlled by the clergy. And so, too, the domination of politicians and police has declined.

We have become more democratic, more sensitive to the rights of individuals, less willing to allow others to hold sway over our lives. Although many decry these changes as a loss of discipline, the net effect, we believe, has been good. We are all freer now.

Children participated in these changes. While they take parental direction—the "shoulds" and "oughts"—at young ages, they resist more and more as they grow older. While an eight-year-old will obey an order to be on time for dinner, a sixteen-year-old will frequently disobey it, and a twenty-year-old ignore it. Direct parental control grows weaker according to the age of the child, the kind of directive given, and the family environment. But parents do not easily give up trying to control their children.

More and more parents are learning ways of allowing children to decide about and to acquire behavior that succeeds in modern society. Much of the psychological background for those new ways comes from Dr. Carl Rogers. Dr. Thomas Gordon, a former colleague of Dr. Rogers's, has prepared a brilliant manual for parents that incorporates most of those ideas. The book is called *P.E.T.: Parent Effectiveness Training* (Wyden). It has been enormously successful in showing parents how to deal with their children as human beings. Scientific experiments demonstrate that parents can learn the new skills and to apply them. Many of Dr. Gordon's ideas, coming as they do from Dr. Rogers and his successors, overlap with ours because of their similar ancestry.

Belittling

Belittlement is a form of judgment; belittlement makes little of the other person's feelings, thoughts, and behavior. When you belittle a person's feelings, ideas, or behavior, you guarantee that that person will defend himself by withdrawing from the conversation, i.e., by not listening, or by striking back.

Parents belittle adult children by:

Outright criticism:

"You never were very good at picking your friends."

Joking:

"If you dress like that you can get a job in a circus."

Mocking:

"Look who's going into business!"

Teasing:

"It looks as though you've been sleeping in your suit."

Exaggerating:

"If you go around without socks you'll catch pneumonia."

Trivializing:

"Come on! You'll get over it! There are lots of other men. Laugh a little."

All belittling has the same implications: "Your feelings are not valid. Your ideas are stupid. Your behavior is unacceptable. Your needs are sham. You are no good."

Mocking, teasing, and joking are extremely common weapons. They are almost always offered with a sense of goodwill. In some quarters the put-down joke has been refined to a high art form. It is seen as good-humored joshing. In some families, teasing is the preferred communication. It's all in good fun. But teases hurt. And they stop real exchanges.

Trivialization is the most insidious of the armory. It is always offered to make the hearer feel good, to cheer him up in the face of adversity.

"Losing a job isn't anything to be worried about. There are others."

"Look, grandma's death affects me as much as anybody. But you don't see me going around moping!"

"A broken pitcher is not a major catastrophe."

These and similar statements declare the hearer's true feelings to be invalid, which is unfeeling and, indeed, impossible.

A person who has lost a job is suffering from rejection. He or she needs acceptance, not to be told that the loss is trivial.

An adult child who is grieving over the death of a grandmother needs comfort and sympathy rather than to be told that the grief is inappropriate.

If you have broken a favorite pitcher, you are full of self-blame. It is a valid feeling that needs gentle understanding so that you can put the accident into perspective. If your parent says that the pitcher was meaningless, it makes you feel as though your feelings are meaningless. And that probably makes the self-blame more intense.

To deal with a parent's belittlement of your behavior, ideas, or feelings requires first that you recognize what has happened. If you do identify the weapon correctly you will be able to counteract it with the nurturing language and without resorting to counterbombardment.

Defensiveness As a Weapon

We often say another person is defensive. What we really mean is that he or she is explaining actions and thoughts too much. There is always an excuse or a reason or an explanation, and these often go beyond what is needed in the situation. For example:

PARENT: I wanted to visit you last Sunday but my friend Henry came by and we got to talking and pretty soon it was too late.

YOU-THE-CHILD: We all missed you.

PARENT: I couldn't help it. You know Henry, he just talks and talks. And I couldn't be rude, could I? I really wanted to come to your house. You know how much I like to be there. But Henry wouldn't budge.

YOU-THE-CHILD: That's okay.

PARENT: And then I had to give him something to eat, and that took time. You understand, don't you?

YOU-THE-CHILD: Sure.

Clearly the parent had no interest in exploring the child's feelings about the parent's not having visited, but was only interested in justifying the missed visit. So defensiveness—overexplanation—is a weapon that announces: "I'm not interested in your feelings, needs, or thoughts in this situation. I want you to listen only to me and my thoughts."

Defensiveness, then, subtly undermines the other person. After all, the parent seems to be explaining a behavior that affects the child negatively. The parent expects the child to accept the explanation and thereby smooth over any hurt feelings. But what defensiveness does is wipe out any possibility of the child's getting his feelings out safely to the parent.

Sometimes defensiveness is a frontal attack:

PARENT: You really should keep an eye on Warren. He fell off his tricycle and skinned his knee. If he rides his bike, a good mother would be outside with him.

YOU-THE-CHILD: I'm a very good mother! I hate it when you imply that I don't know what I'm doing.

PARENT: I didn't mean to say you were a bad mother. You should know by now that I have great confidence in you. You take me too literally. You do that all the time. I was talking about "good mothering." And that could be anybody, not you particularly.

YOU-THE-CHILD: But you just said that a "good mother would be outside with him."

PARENT: Come on now! My words don't have to be taken letter by letter. Would I say anything bad about you? I've told you that I have confidence in you. What more do you want?

This parent tries to get out of having said something bad about her adult child by "explaining" what she *really* means. She makes the weapon more potent by putting the burden on the adult child for understanding her "true" meaning: "You take me too literally," etc. Such defensiveness takes refuge in the parent's concept that the adult child should be able to read the parent's mind. Sometimes this is stated as:

"You know me too well to believe that I would say anything bad about you [or your spouse or your child or your whatever]."

"You ought to realize that when I say thus-and-such I really mean that-and-such."

"Everybody understands what I mean except you."

"No thinking person would interpret what I said the way you have."

Parents (and other persons, of course) delicately inject the defensive weapon when they find themselves trapped by their own behavior. The clue is explanation. They have not been asked to explain themselves and then they do. Usually they defend themselves against criticism or implied criticism. They more urgently want to keep criticism at a distance than they want to learn from the criticism.

Implied criticism occurs when the adult child defends against a parental attack. In the example above, the adult child counterattacked by saying that she hated her mother's telling her that she was not a good mother. The parent's counterattack was defensiveness, ripe with explanation and shifting the burden to the adult child.

With the nurturing language, defensiveness can be countered without counterattacking. Essentially, we avoid arousing the parent's defenses so that he or she can concentrate on your message.

Manipulation

Parents who are long used to controlling their young children by direct order often shift to subtle manipulations to control their adult children. A manipulation in this sense employs underhanded, unfair, and scheming methods to get one's own advantage. (In this sense, we say parenthetically, the nurturing language is not a manipulation. It depends on open-handed, fair, and nonscheming language to set the stage for negotiation. Neither side gains an undue advantage over the other.)

One favorite method of manipulation is for the parent to have a hidden agenda. The parent cajoles the adult child into agreeing to one item on the agenda and then ties that agreement to a concealed demand:

PARENT: Could you pick me up and give me a ride to the wedding?

YOU-THE-CHILD: Sure!

PARENT: Then it shouldn't be any trouble for you to pick up Aunt Sarah, too.

Or there is the parent who invites her daughter over for a Sunday afternoon. The daughter arrives to find the parent up on a ladder painting the dining room. There is nothing for the daughter to do except pitch in.

Some manipulations are inspired. We heard of one well-to-do father who sent his newly wed son a complete bedroom set because he thought his son needed more than a foldout couch. Trouble was, the son and his bride lived in a one-room studio!

Some parents wait to strike until a third party is present. They make a demand that is hard to refuse when another person is there whose judgment you fear or do not want to invoke. "After all," you're supposed to think, "how can I seem to be so unfeeling to my own mother by refusing her request in front of her friend?"

A favorite manipulation is to provoke guilt, the guilt of having crossed some moral standard or obligation.

PARENT: Where are you going on vacation?

YOU-THE-CHILD: We're planning to go to the shore.

PARENT: Have you taken a house?

YOU-THE-CHILD: Yes, but it's awfully small.

PARENT: How many rooms?

YOU-THE-CHILD: Only two bedrooms, just right for Mary and me in one and the other for the kids.

PARENT: I don't think I'll go anywhere this summer. Probably stay home.

YOU-THE-CHILD: I wish we could put you up, but there's no room.

PARENT: Not even in the living room?

You-the-Child: Not really. The kids will be in the way.
Parent: I don't mind if you don't.

And so on. To counter manipulations you had best open up the hidden agenda with the nurturing language. To counter manipulations you also need to recognize that parental standards of behavior need not apply to your current life. You have your own needs and standards of behavior. If they cross those of your parent, a common solution to competing wants can be negotiated through the nurturing language.

Although many weapons we have discussed come in two forms—positive and negative—manipulation, like questioning, comes in only one form. The opposite of manipulation is fair play or acceptance; both contribute to the negotiated solution through nurturing.

Superiority

Parents usually start out being smarter and stronger than their children.

Our social scheme has therefore given parents the right— some even say the duty—to prescribe the proper behavior for their young children. Parents tell young children what to eat, wear, say, think. Parents erect standards of right and wrong. They approve or disapprove of their children's friends, jobs, games, hairstyles.

With superiority comes power, power over the other. Parents exercise this power, often without realizing it. They can prevent or command behavior by their young children, determining where the young children go to school, who their friends are, what time they go to bed, where they go on vacation. And so on.

But children, sometimes to the parents' surprise, get smarter and more competent as they grow up. Step by step they begin to establish their own rules of behavior and thought. With parents who refuse to give up their superior position, there is likely to be more conflict as the children grow up, particularly in our society with its loosening of authoritative reins.

Nevertheless, many parents continue to assert their sense of superiority—being smarter, more experienced, richer—when their children become adults. They keep their power to command behavior. And they impose their superiority as a weapon:

PARENT: How much money do you have saved up?

YOU-THE-CHILD: About three thousand dollars.

PARENT: What are you going to do with it?

YOU-THE-CHILD: My friend, Al, is a stockbroker. I thought I'd let him invest it for me.

PARENT: Listen, I've been in business for forty years. I've made a lot of money, as you know. And the stock market is no place to make money. I know. I can't let you do it.

YOU-THE-CHILD: Al has a degree in business from Harvard. And his company has really put him up high fast. He seems to have done pretty well.

PARENT: Yeah. With other people's money. I never graduated from high school and I know about business more than a kid from college. For you the stock market is a place to lose money.

YOU-THE-CHILD: I still want to give it a try.

Although the advice may be sound, the adult child cannot easily listen to the parent when the parent is showing his superiority. The dogmatic approach of the parent arouses the adult child's defenses. He explains himself to no avail. The parent overrides the explanation with his obvious business success.

"I know better . . ."

"Everybody knows that . . ."

"Look. This is the way it is . . ."

"Now, here is how things work . . ."
"I've lived long enough to know . . ."
"If you're smart [as I], you'll . . ."
"That's wrong. Just plain wrong . . ."
"If you do this, what'll happen . . ."
The list of the know-it-all's weapons is quite long. You may add more if you wish. The point is that superiority suggests an unequal power relationship: one person dominating another. And that, by arousing the defenses of the person subjected to power, can shut off communication.

Certainty

Along with superiority, parents often express certainty. They leave no room for exploration, for understanding, or for experimentation. Like superiority, certainty shuts off communication because it, too, brings up the adult child's defenses.

"Here's how it works."

"If you take three pills a day, you'll get rid of your headache."

"The stock market has been on a long upswing. We expect the market will come down now. All indicators point that way."

"Aunt Mary is just senile. She has all the symptoms."

"Henry always was a fool about women and always will be."

The same material can be offered with some hesitancy that would invite participation:

"Here's how I *think* it works, though I'm not altogether sure."

"The indicators seem to suggest that the market may be coming down after a long upswing. But we've been fooled before."

"Aunt Mary's symptoms do worry me. I hope it isn't senility."

"Henry seems to be having trouble with women again. I wonder what goes on there."

In the same spirit, all the information we offer in this book bears the same caveat. We are reasonably sure that the nurturing language does promote relationships. It usually does, though not with everyone and not at all times.

Weapons Point Both Ways

We have mentioned almost casually that adult children also aim weapons against their parents. But it doesn't happen casually. It is in the nature of unhappy relationships that weapons are rolled out from both sides. And adult children make the relationship worse by resorting to the same weapons as their parents. Sometimes they do so to counterattack. Sometimes it is in anger over past pain inflicted by the parent. Sometimes the adult child has learned from the parent how to use certain weapons and uses them just as freely as a matter of long-accustomed habit. Sometimes the roles have flipped—the parent because of illness, loss of money, or status—becomes the child of the adult child.

Now here's a very important rule of the nurturing language.

If you want to be heard, lay down your weapons.

While many people get their jollies from firing verbal abuse, no relationship can be built in the middle of such battles. All sense of listening or wanting to listen disappears. And if you fire weapons at your parent, at worst you will get a blast back and at least your parent will find ways to shut you out.

Now that you know what the old toxic language contains, you have a good idea of what to avoid. So while listening is first, laying down the weapons is second. If you are a weapons user, you may be surprised at the change in your parent when he or she no longer hears them from you.

Now look at the weapons from the point of view of the

parent as the receiver. Try to check out how many you have
sent out today toward your parent and others.

Judgment. This weapon includes both praise and blame. It
declares that the other person's behavior is or is not up to the
speaker's standard. It shuts off communication because it
clearly attempts control. And few people like to be controlled
by another.

Imagine how a sixty-year-old man would feel if told by
his son: "You simply don't understand business today."

Or the son praising: "Gee, mom, you did a good job taking
those pills for a whole week."

Questions. These are the most insidious of weapons. A
question seems like an innocent request for information,
but it, too, aims at control by demanding an answer on the
questioner's terms. A question shifts the burden from the
speaker to the respondent. Rule: Never ask or answer a question.

Just think of a seventy-year-old woman in a nursing home
being bombarded with questions about her health, her
money, her home, her daily activities as if she were a teenager just returned from camp.

Should and Ought. They express the speaker's standard of
behavior but also carry the weight of social approval for that
standard. Few people like to be told what they "should" do.
So they do not listen.

Picture a forty-year-old daughter telling her sixty-five-year-
old mother that the mother should not drive the automobile
anymore.

Defensiveness. By explaining yourself, you shift blame to
the other person. Defensiveness proclaims that your judgment
takes precedence and calls on the other person to know
what's on your mind.

"Dad, I have to take care of my family first. Believe me,
if I had the money, I'd certainly help you out. But I just
can't right now. You understand that, don't you?"

Belittling. This is an indirect way of setting a standard. If you belittle a behavior or a feeling or idea, you are saying that those do not measure up to standard—your standard. Belittling invalidates the other's behavior, feelings, or ideas.

"You're always complaining about your aches and pains. I never hear it from anybody else. You're behaving like a child."

Manipulation. By using unfair, underhanded, or scheming methods, the manipulator gains advantage over another. Manipulation operates with hidden agendas, guilt promotion, lying, or secret moves. Manipulation rules out negotiation. It leaves the manipulated person afraid to deal with the manipulator. Trust evaporates. No relationship can be built on manipulation.

A brother to a sister: "If we tell dad that he can try out the nursing home we'll be able to get him there. And once he gets there he simply won't leave. It will be too hard for him."

Superiority. One person gets into a superior power position with respect to the other. When the relationship is unequal listening or negotiating is difficult. Another stopper is certainty. If the speaker sounds dogmatic, certain, and all-knowing, communication ends. And with it any chance of relationship.

"Mom, you must not be climbing those stairs every day. It's just too much for you at your age. Everybody knows you can hurt yourself that way."

"Investments today have to be handled by professionals."

Each weapon, then, can hurt your parent as much as it can hurt you. But more than hurt, weapons shut off discourse, and without discourse there can be no relationship worth the name.

/ 5 /

The Weapons Are Coming; the Weapons Are Coming

Many adult children shrink in abject terror when parents fire their shower of verbal weapons. A parent, easily slipping into the old role of controlling authority, mounts a barrage of questions that the adult child, like the young child, cannot deflect or stop. "Who?" "What?" "Where?" "How?" "When?" and, especially, "Why?" relentlessly bombard many an adult child.

Or parental judgments fly at the adult child with the parent sowing "shoulds" and "oughts" as if they were mines in enemy territory. Guilt stings remorselessly. The agony comes out as a stifled cry. Or—often—in real tears.

Or the parent belittles the adult child, mocking or trivializing the ideas, needs, and feelings of the bewildered offspring. The parent smugly gathers the robe of moral or intellectual certainty about himself or herself, sitting like a Supreme Court justice hearing an appeal from a death sentence. Who can struggle against such emotional authority?

Such were the weapons we described in the last chapter. What can an adult child do to deflect parental attacks? Counterattack? That's often recommended by friends and even professional counselors. It does work. Sometimes. Usually, the parent, with long experience in attack tactics, knows how to parry and thrust better than the adult child. And the adult child loses. And so does the parent because the adult child is hurt and resentful, feels small and like a loser. Communication worsens.

Parents operate from a stronger power base than do adult children, of whatever age. Parents have on their side society's admonition to adult children to "respect" parents: "You can't talk to your mother that way!" Mother may be an incredible monster. Likewise father. But that doesn't matter: Honor thy parents!

In any case, attack and counterattack usually lead to an escalation of the battle. The epithets become more vicious. Passions rise to a peak from which neither combatant can descend. Such fights end in emotional exhaustion; the relationship, such as it was, torn once again into shreds.

Parents often cannot help themselves. They have been at it too long. They have felt the rewards of controlling their children and they do not want to (and often cannot) give up those rewards. To relinquish their weapons, they need to *feel* that the old ways do not work, that there is no thrill in punishing you. They cannot be convinced by argument. They need to be emotionally weaned from expecting your habitual responses to their habitual ploys. You can do it; many, many others have. It does take patience and practice.

How then does an adult child deal with parental weapons effectively and without crippling side effects? Silence sometimes helps. The parent often gets an emotional lift—a reward—from evoking an agonized response from the adult child. (Indeed, some parents are addicted to the rewards of weaponry.) Silence—a nonresponse to a weapon—does not reward. The weapon may not be used soon again. But silence may also be followed by an imperious demand:

"When I ask a question, I want an answer!"

"If I give advice, I'd like the courtesy of knowing that I've been heard."

"Answer me!"

Using the New Language Against Weapons

The real power to slow, deflect, or stop a parental assault lies with the nurturing language. It does not stimulate a counterattack. It does not fire the heat of battle. It cools angry passion. Blessed peace can be yours. You can begin to build a loving bond between your parent and you.

You start with listening, a basic part, but only part of the nurturing language; it also includes the genuine assertion by which you make clear *your* needs or *your* pains. And also listening-to-speak to open up the other person to hear what you have said, to hear your genuine assertion. To wean your parents completely from weaponry, you usually need listening plus genuine assertions plus listening-to-speak. But listening alone can often turn the tide.

With the three styles of listening—wordless, checking, and nurturing—you have enough power to slow the torrent of weapons. You can turn off the questions, the judgments, the "shoulds" and "oughts," the belittlement, the mockery, and even, in part, the overweening parental authority. ("I'm your father, dammit. Listen to me.")

We ask you to try to turn aside weapons with listening alone at first because you may get quick relief from some of the more burdensome of parental abuses. You can then build on the foundation of listening the rest of your nurturing language. You will not succeed in turning aside each weapon each time. But we think that with the power of listening you will deflect many attacks. And that will motivate you to learn the rest of our language to build a connection of decent feeling between you and your parent.

Judging the Judgments

Strangely enough, the best way to ward off judgmental attacks by parents (or by anybody else, for that matter) is to invite them to judge more, to explain what they mean, and, finally, to judge their own judgments. For example:

PARENT: Your hair is a mess.	[opening signal—criticism/judgment]
YOU-THE-CHILD: You think my hair is messy.	[checking/reflection]
PARENT: Yes. You had it cut too short.	[more information—less nasty]
YOU-THE-CHILD: You liked it when it was longer.	[checking/interpretation]
PARENT: Yes. I prefer long hair to short hair.	[attack deflected—criticism general, not personal]

With this child's searching (the invitation to judge the judgment) the parent revealed a general dislike of short hair. Out of habit, the parent had used the general dislike to mount a personal attack on the adult child. As the parent is made to feel safe in exploring the true meaning of his or her judgment, the need to attack diminishes. As the hidden agenda comes into the open, the original "reason" for attacking no longer seems valid to the parent. Notice that the adult child always did checking listening without a question. If the adult child had responded with "My hair is a mess?" the parent could interpret the question as a challenge to the judgment: a counterattack and the battle would be on.

That example was simple: Usually arguments about dress have minor emotional overtones, although we know about plenty of screaming fights over parental criticism of nails, ties, shirts, dress, etc.

Let's go to a more difficult arena where emotions run deep.

PARENT: Susan is not good for you. If you marry her, you'll regret it. [opening signal/ criticism]

YOU-THE-CHILD: Susan is terrific! We get along very well. [defensiveness/ challenging judgment]

PARENT: You say that now. But after you're married, you'll find out what she's really like. [more judgment/ deeper attack]

YOU-THE-CHILD: Look, I know what I'm doing. I'm twenty-eight years old and I have a right to make up my own mind to do what I want without any advice from you. [more defensiveness]

[threat to cut off communication]

PARENT: Yeah. You never were any good at deciding anything. You couldn't tie your shoelaces unless dad or I showed you how. Look what happened to you and Martha. You bought her a ring and the next thing you know she's off with somebody else. Same thing is going to happen again. [belittlement/ mockery]

YOU-THE-CHILD: Susan is different. Why are you always putting me down? Why isn't anything I do any good to you?
You're not a mother—at least not mine. [defensive/on the ropes]

[counterattack]

As you can see, the parent can mount powerful weapons. None of the defensive counterweapons work. They merely intensify the attack. Finally, the adult child is driven to petty name-calling. Like any powerful weapon, name-calling can end the attack, but it can also smash the relationship.

Now let's see what the nurturing language can do to the same dialogue:

PARENT: Susan is not good for you. If you marry her, you'll regret it. [opening signal/ criticism]

YOU-THE-CHILD: I'll be sorry if I marry her. [checking/reflection]

PARENT: She's too flighty and she doesn't seem serious. [more specific criticism]

YOU-THE-CHILD: You think she doesn't really care for me. [checking/interpretation]

PARENT: I think she likes you well enough. [backing down]

But I keep thinking about what Martha did to you [taking the ring and then taking off]. I don't want to see you hurt again. [expressing fear]

YOU-THE-CHILD: It worries you that Susan will hurt me the way Martha did. [nurturing/ reflecting parent's fears]

PARENT: I am not sure she will. She is so young—only twenty. It's hard for me to see her married so young. Of course, I was married at nineteen. But times were different then. [hidden material]

We know such a dialogue does sound a little too pat because we've edited if for length. Usually there are a lot of fits and starts. There are mistakes. At early stages, few people speak the nurturing language perfectly. So a dialogue of this kind may take fifteen or twenty minutes as the adult child backtracks over errors or deals with fresh attacks that seem to arise from nowhere. We saw the slow accumulation of skill in reports of actual exchanges between parents and adult children who have been trained in the nurturing language by Dr. Sharon Gadberry and her students at Adelphi University on Long Island. And we have trained adults with similar results. Despite the halting pace of early learning, it has amazed us how well the new language works.

The pattern is always the same. The parent attacks. The adult child listens. The parent becomes more specific in judgment. The adult child listens some more. The parent reveals some hidden emotion or thought. The adult child shifts into nurturing listening. The parent reveals hidden fears, thoughts. The attack subsides.

The Other Side of Judgment

Blame or criticism is clearly judgment. And both are clearly weapons. Praise, you will recall from Chapter 4, is also judgment. Praise says: "I approve of what you do because you live up to my standards." There can be underlying motives: envy, fear, manipulation. The nurturing language can reveal the hidden thoughts behind praise:

PARENT: I do like your new living room furniture. You do have such good taste. [opening signal/ praise]

YOU-THE-CHILD: You like my taste. [checking/reflection]

PARENT: Well, it does look expensive. Velvet comes high, I know that. It must have cost you a lot. [specific]

YOU-THE-CHILD: You think I spent too much. [checking/interpretation]

PARENT: It looks like it. [hidden agenda]

Some might say: Why not leave well enough alone? Why not accept praise with a gracious "thank you" and let the hidden agenda remain hidden? First, hidden feelings have a way of cropping up in other contexts. Second, it is better to understand your parent's true feelings about you and what you do than to allow a sham to be played. A relationship founded on play-acting can be fragile at best.

In the situation above, the parent revealed her hidden concern for the adult child's having spent too much. There may be other hidden items. The parent may be in financial need and be angry that her adult child found money to buy overly expensive couches but could not find money to help her.

Praise also implies a threat to withhold praise if the standards of the parent are not met in the future.

PARENT: I'm so pleased that you were promoted at work. I always knew you were clever and hardworking. Wonderful! [opening signal/ praise]

YOU-THE-CHILD: You're pleased. [checking/reflection]

PARENT: Oh, yes! I like my children to succeed. If you work hard you can always make it. [more specific]

YOU-THE-CHILD: Hard work gets the promotion. [checking/reflection]

PARENT: And the cash. [more specific]

Now the adult child clearly understands the parent's standards. The praise was rooted in the parent's desire to have his adult child make money. If the adult child agrees with the standard, all well and good. If not, the adult child has won an understanding of the parent's position and can better deal with it.

Block That Question!

Ask me no more questions;
I'll tell you no more lies.

So goes a bit of child's doggerel. It expresses folk wisdom
about the power of questions to provoke falsehoods. Although
shading the truth is a ready way to deal with questions used
as weapons, falsehoods, while sometimes winning the day,
lose in the end. The parent clearly sees through some falsehoods. Or we enmesh ourselves in a tangle of falsity from
which we cannot escape.

We turn to lies (or more often evasions) in dealing with
the torrent of questions because, as we pointed out in Chapter
4, questions place the burden of the give-and-take on the
respondent. We try to stop the endless flow of questions by
giving partial answers or false answers, hoping to satisfy. But
we fail, because the questioner seeks ever more answers.
Answers are the question addict's "fix."

Questions also drive—uninvited—directly to the respondent's closely guarded interior world. Questions also provide
parents with powerful tools for manipulation.

Our guiding principle to the problem of questions:
Do not answer questions; do not ask them.

It sounds simple. In practice, it is difficult to carry out. In
our society, a question demands an answer. Not to answer
seems at least rude and, at most, hostile. So we take the easy
way: We answer. And the answer usually drags in another
question and we are in the vicious cycle of question and
answer, question and answer.

In the nurturing language, we distinguish between *answers*
and *responses*. An answer is a reply to a question that truly
seeks information. Most questions from parents are not
information-seeking. So you do not answer. A response is a
reaction to a stimulus—a provocation. Treat parental ques-

tions as stimuli, as weapons or potential calls for help or cries of pain or opening signals or manipulations. You respond with the nurturing language. You do not answer.

You *answer* questions when you are assured that they are true requests for information. So answer simple questions like:

"How do you get to Montvale?"

"Where is the salt?"

"How high is Mount Everest?"

Be more cautious and *respond* to questions like:

"What are you doing Thursday night?"

"How much money do you have?"

"Have you heard from your brother?"

"Why did you let Andy ride his bike after dark?"

These questions easily lead into attacks or demands. And as such they are better handled by the nurturing language. You reveal the hidden agendas to open the way to negotiation. You remove the question-as-weapon.

The following dialogue opens with a question made famous by Sophie Portnoy, the Jewish mother in Philip Roth's novel *Portnoy's Complaint*. It is a question noted widely among Jewish mothers. But it is also a question employed on such a grand scale in all communities that you would have to say that all mothers (and fathers) are, in respect to the question, Jewish mothers.

PARENT: When am I going to see you? [Mrs. Portnoy's question]

YOU-THE-CHILD: I don't know. I am so busy with work these days I hardly have time to do anything outside of work. [defensiveness/ evasion/half-truth]

PARENT: It seems to me you could find time for your parents. We always seem to have enough time for you. [open attack]

Portnoy's response to Sophie was: "You're seeing me now!" He delivered his answer as his mother was driving off in a taxi, so she had little chance to follow up. However, no *answer* ever satisfies the Sophie in our mothers and fathers. There are *responses* that do satisfy.

PARENT: When am I going to see you?   [opening signal]
YOU-THE-CHILD: You're anxious to see   [nurturing listen-
    me again soon.   ing/interpreting
                                                    feelings]

PARENT: You know I like to spend time   [more information]
    with Bruce [the grandchild].
YOU-THE-CHILD: You feel you don't see   [checking/interpre-
    him enough.   tation]
PARENT: I would see him every day if   [expresses feeling]
    I could.
YOU-THE-CHILD: You would see him   [nurturing listening]
    every day but you know you can't.
PARENT: Oh, I know that. I wish there   [wants to negotiate]
    were some way we all could get to-
    gether more often.

This exchange from a real-life situation shows two aspects of the nurturing language. One: Nurturing listening deflects the initial power play of the question. Two: It opens up the parent's interior world and the hidden agenda. Now, negotiations can begin.

It is very difficult not to *answer* questions. Our impulse—drilled into us over the years—is to answer. That's why questions are such powerful manipulators. So the first thing to do when a question comes your way is to stop and to shout silently (in your head):

"STOP! That's a question. Don't answer!"

That will give you enough time to formulate a *response*. Sometimes the pause will be enough to deflect the question. It is the equivalent of silence. Wordless listening also gives you time to gather your wits, especially if the queries rattle on one after another.

PARENT: Where are you going on vacation?	[opening signal]
YOU-THE-CHILD: Hmmmm.	[pause/wordless listening]
PARENT: You're not going to the shore again, are you?	[new question/more information]
YOU-THE-CHILD: You're worried that we're going to the shore.	[nurturing listening]
PARENT: Last year it rained when I was there. And the house was too small with all the kids.	[hidden fear]

Questions often have more than one meaning. "Why did you buy that car?" may mean "Why did you buy that particular car [Chevy, Ford, etc.]?" Or it may mean "Why did you buy any car at all?" A possible response to clarify the meaning can be: "I don't understand that question."

Here's how that works with more intimate questions:

PARENT: Why do you let Luther [the adult child's husband] treat you so badly?	[opening signal]
YOU-THE-CHILD: I don't understand the question.	[checking listening/ clarification]
PARENT: Why do you let him keep you in that terrible house? He can afford a better place.	[more information]
YOU-THE-CHILD: You don't like the house.	[checking/reflection]
PARENT: You know I don't. Why do you have to ask?	[dogmatic/shifting the burden]
YOU-THE-CHILD: Hmmm.	[pause/wordless listening]
PARENT: You must love him an awful lot to put up with it.	[concession]

Questions sometimes come at you so fast that it is difficult to bring up a response even if you do pause. You may, therefore, find it useful to have some stock responses well in hand. They will be for you what steps are for a dancer: well practiced, smooth, almost reflexive. You can bring them out rapidly. If you have a variety at your command, your responses will sound real (as they should be) and natural.

Your parent will believe that you are truly listening. And, of course, you are. Any attempt to fake listening will, in time, be discovered and expose your attempt to change your language as a manipulation. That is an issue with which we will deal in detail. At the moment, as we mentioned before, a manipulation is taking unfair advantage through unfair means. If you fake listening, that is unfair and a manipulation.

With that warning in mind, here are some responses that may help you get out of a question trap and into the listening groove:

"I don't understand that question."
"I don't understand the *reason* for the question."
(This response will help when the parent asks a sequence of unrelated questions that seem to come from nowhere.)
"You have a reason for asking."
"You (are) (sound) concerned about . . ."
"You (are) (sound) worried about . . ."
"You (are) (sound) eager to . . ."
"You (are) (sound) disappointed that . . ."
"You (are) (sound) angry about . . ."
"You want to know about . . ."
"You want to . . ."
"You feel that . . ."
Here are some frequent questions and some responses:

"When are you going to Chicago?"
"You have a reason for asking."

"Why is Andrew's face so pale?"
"You are worried about Andrew."

"Why did you tell dad that the doctor put me on a diet?"
"You sound angry that I told dad about the doctor."

"How are you and Patrick getting along these days?"
"You want to know how our marriage is doing."

"Why don't you make the broccoli with cheese the way Steven [her son] likes it?"
"You feel Steve doesn't like the way I make broccoli."

"Why should I pay all my Social Security to the nursing home?"
"I don't understand the question."

When you are dealing with a zigzag questioner, you may have to field many responses to stop the flow. Pauses are powerful in slowing down the torrent. The zigzag questioner gets his or her reward from asking the questions. Your answer is a cue to ask the next question. By pausing or using wordless listening, you do not cue the next question.

Some question experts have a habit of repeating the question:

"Why should I pay all my Social Security to the nursing home?"
"I don't understand the question."
"Why should I pay all my Social Security to the nursing home?"
"I repeat, mom, I don't understand the question."
"I mean, it's unfair. It doesn't leave me any money for myself."

A repetition of the response prefixed with "I repeat . . ." usually brings forth some material that is hidden by the question.

Sometimes, particularly impatient or domineering personalities may fling an imperious demand in your face:

"Come on. Answer the question."

"When I ask a question, I expect an answer."

"What are you trying to do? Pull psychology on me?"

There are several possible responses to such all-out attacks.
They all come to one thing: more nurturing language.

"You're angry that I'm not answering your questions as
fast as you would like."

"You need fast answers to your questions."

"You feel I am not answering your questions."

"You feel that I am trying to put something over on you."

"My answer doesn't sound right to you."

You may also find it helpful to repeat the previous response
just as in dealing with a repeat question. The repetition conveys the idea that you really meant your last response. And
you did. Sometimes the other person simply doesn't believe
you.

You have another way to deal with such gross attacks. You
can show your own feelings by issuing a cry of pain at being
subjected to such relentless interrogation. That skill—emit-
ting genuine assertions—will be dealt with later. You will
probably need genuine assertions along with the listening
skill to deal effectively and sensitively with the question barrage.

Turning "Should" and "Ought" into "Maybe"

"Should" and "ought" and their cousins are parents' favorite
words for imposing their standards on their children, young
and adult. They have brought out these word weapons so
often and for so long that they have become almost reflexive.
The parent brings out the "you should" whenever the adult
child mentions something about his or her plans. The parent,
of course, knows better. He or she always has known better.
That is the message.

Adult children handle the imposition in different ways. Some discuss none of their plans or activities with their parents. They keep the conversation abstract—about the weather, the latest news, foreign affairs. In short, they shut their parents out of the relationship because of a need to avoid the "shoulds" and "oughts." The method "works" in avoiding parental meddling but it reduces the relationship to the thinness of tissue paper.

To many adult children, the failure to discuss the important activities and plans in life with one's parents represents a true loss. Yet they give it up rather than face the imposition of parental standards. Others feel they have done something wrong—in psychological terms, they feel guilty—when they ignore parents' often well-meant advice. But again: The burden of the "shoulds" is just too great to bear.

With the nurturing language, you can turn the "should" into "maybe," into an idea that can be examined dispassionately. You can fully understand your parents' standards, compare them to your own, and then choose on your own what to do.

At the same time, your parent will not be upset about your not exactly following his or her "advice." You can have the benefit of your parents' experience; parents do know some things we do not. They have lived longer. They may even have learned by their mistakes and successes.

Dealing with "should" and "ought" is similar to dealing with questions. Listening comes first. Understanding what your parent means leads to your being able to be cool in the face of parental superiority. You can bring out the same stock phrases because "You should" is identical to "Why don't you . . .?"

A young woman scolded her five-year-old son and three-year-old daughter for playing in the street.

MOTHER-IN-LAW: You shouldn't pun-   ["should"]
   ish and scold the children.

You-the-Child: They know they're   [defensiveness/
not supposed to play in the street.   explaining]

Mother-in-law: But they're so small.   [second "should"]
You should explain to them that it's
wrong.

You-the-Child: Sometimes I feel that   [more explanation]
immediate action is necessary for
understanding. And this is one of
those times.

Mother-in-law: Well, I have to say   [dogmatic]
that I don't agree.

You-the-Child: You've made your   [cutting off]
point.

Mother-in-law: You really should   [third "should"]
read some psychology books.

You-the-Child: Bullshit!   [crash]

Such dialogues are common between mothers-in-law and their adult child's spouse. Fathers-in-law are not immune from the conflict either. The underlying psychological conflict can be interpreted in many ways. The mother-in-law is jealous. The father-in-law feels frozen out. The spouse feels caught between the parent and the adult child. In general, however, in-laws act like parents. The spouse—loath to accept his or her own parents in their role—usually doesn't accept the in-law for the same reasons.

Our experience with the nurturing language tells us that the above dialogue can be redirected as follows:

Mother-in-law: You shouldn't pun-   ["should"]
ish and scold the children.

You-the-Child: I shouldn't punish   [checking/reflec-
and scold the children.   tion]

Mother-in-law: You could explain to   [weaker "should"]
them that it's wrong.

You-the-Child: You feel explanation is more effective than scolding in this situation.   [checking/interpretation]

Mother-in-law: I admit they were doing something dangerous. But scolding only scares them.   [defensive/backing down]

You-the-Child: It sounds as though you're saying there's a choice between stepping in to prevent danger and teaching them something.   [checking/interpretation]

Mother-in-law: It's not easy to be a mother. I know.   [sympathetic]

The nurturing language prevents the conflict. The mother-in-law has a chance to state her full case without feeling that she has to overkill to make her point. The daughter-in-law, in turn, has a chance to hear her mother-in-law out. She may disagree and probably could state so later (we'll show you how listening-to-speak helps her to do it). The net result is that one "should" has been weakened and the other has disappeared. Weapon deflected!

Defusing Defensiveness

Listening also helps blunt belittlement, superiority, and defensiveness. Of the three, the last is the most treacherous.

We say a person is defensive when he or she explains his or her actions or motivations or what "I really meant." Such a person feels attacked or feels he or she has done "something wrong" and is impelled to explain away the attack or the error. The defensive person makes no effort to understand what the other has really said. He or she is too busy making excuses. That such explanations are defensive and really attacks is hard for many people to grasp.

People who are defensive say, in effect: "If I explain what I really meant to do, I should be excused for doing it even if it hurt you or turned out not too well."

They are saying that there are times when their actions are "accidental" or "unmeaning" or "misinterpreted." Under such conditions, they feel they do not have responsibility for the injury they do and that explanation will heal the wounds.

We all know, however, that when the wound is inflicted no amount of explanation changes the fact that the pain was felt. We are reminded of an old cartoon by James Thurber that depicts a fencing match. The fencers wear masks and padding. However, one of the fencers has sliced off the other's head and says: "Touché!"

Another variant of the joke has one of the fencers saying: "Oops!"

The joke lies in our realization that nothing can put back the head lost in play or accidentally. And it goes deeper: The wound may heal, but the pain was real.

Defensiveness becomes a weapon when the wielder shifts the burden for his actions to the injured party. The weaponeer expects the other person to know what "I really meant." In the last chapter on recognizing weapons we listed some of the pet phrases of the defensive player. We list them again with some responses that weaken their power to hurt.

"Come on! How could you think I meant that?"
"You meant something else when you said George treats me badly."

"You know me too well to believe I meant that."
"You're saying I know you meant something else."

"No thinking person would interpret what I said the way you do."
"I don't understand what you meant to say."

"Everybody understands what I mean except you."
"You feel I purposely misunderstand you."

At first these responses bring forth more explanation. But as the parent explains more and more and realizes that you are truly listening, the defensiveness becomes transparent. The defensiveness wanes. It is when you do not listen that the parent redoubles his or her effort to make amends; to make himself or herself understood; or ultimately to shift the burden to you.

Remember the following dialogue from the preceding chapter?

PARENT: You really should keep an eye on Warren! He fell off his tricycle and skinned his knee. If he rides his bike, a good mother would be outside with him.

YOU-THE-CHILD: I'm a very good mother. I hate it when you imply that I don't know what I'm doing.

PARENT: I didn't mean to say you were a bad mother. You should know by now that I have great confidence in you. You take me too literally. You do that all the time. I was talking about "good mothering." And that could be anybody, not you particularly.

YOU-THE-CHILD: But you just said that a "good mother would be outside with him."

PARENT: Come on now! My words don't have to be taken letter by letter. Would I say anything bad about you? I've told you that I have confidence in you. What more do you want?

Now that you have some experience with the listening skill, you can plot out what the daughter can do to avoid her mother's defensive attack.

PARENT: You really should keep an eye on Warren! He fell off his tricycle and skinned his knee. If he rides his bike, a good mother would be outside with him.

YOU-THE-CHILD: You're saying I'm not a good mother because Warren fell off his bike.

PARENT: No, no. I didn't mean to say you were a bad mother. I only meant that Warren should be watched. You take me too literally.

You-the-Child: You're concerned about Warren and his bike.

Parent: Yes. I wish he would ride it when adults were around.

Some might say that the adult child was letting the parent "get away with it." The parent insulted the adult child and the adult child just "took it." Well, it depends what the adult child wants. If the adult child wants to get her jollies from striking back hard, then we recommend the original dialogue. But if the adult child wishes to build a relationship and reduce the number of times the parent resorts to the defensive weapon, the nurturing language is needed.

Dealing with Other Weapons

In general, if you listen very carefully to your parent, you will detect the weapons, the manipulations, the hidden agenda. If each statement is first treated as an opening signal and followed with one of the three forms of listening, then you will be able to distinguish a manipulation from a sincere effort at reaching out. If you listen, your parent will drop his or her habits in using attack as a means of getting your attention.

As we dealt with judgment, questions, "should," we can also deal with belittlement, mockery, manipulation. Listen. Listen. Listen. You will hear.

Let's listen in on a nurturing language conversation in which the parent makes demands on the adult child in the presence of a third party:

Parent: Jack, you're going to drive   [manipulation]
Mrs. Jackson home later, aren't you?

You-the-Child: You want me to take   [checking listening]
Mrs. Jackson home.

Mrs. Jackson: Oh, it's all right. I was   [information]
really planning to take the bus.

YOU-THE-CHILD: You were going to take the bus.	[checking listening]
PARENT: But it's such a long trip. Mrs. Jackson really can't take it.	[more manipulation]
YOU-THE-CHILD: You're worried that Mrs. Jackson is too ill to take the bus.	[nurturing listening]
MRS. JACKSON: Oh, no, not at all. I don't mind really. Really, Kathy, don't make him drive all the way there and back.	[information]
PARENT: Well, all right if you say so.	[concession]

In such cases you nurture both parties. You have not refused to drive Mrs. Jackson. You could still choose to do so, but the choice is now yours.

Sometimes, the adult child is caught between two parents, each trying to manipulate the other with the adult child as the agent.

MOTHER (to father): You're too fat! Stop eating that.

FATHER: Look who's talking! [stage whisper to daughter] She thinks she's so thin—look at her!

MOTHER: Your mother was fat. She was taller than your father. You were skinny before I married you.

FATHER: Skinny! [to daughter] You saw pictures of me before we were married. What do you think?

DAUGHTER: You want me to be a referee in this argument.

FATHER: I'm just asking if you thought I was skinny before I got married.

DAUGHTER: I repeat—you want me to be a referee in this argument.

MOTHER: Leave her alone. I'm tired of this anyway.

Listening placed the daughter in the position of being outside the argument. As the father tried to pull her in and the listening made that apparent, the mother understood what was happening and intervened to prevent it. The daughter could also have said that she was fearful that she might be drawn into the fight and that both of them would be angry with her. That would have told her parents her feelings and in a sense asked them for help to keep her out of the fracas. That statement of feelings is called a genuine assertion, and we'll shortly show you how to make one.

Hearing Your Own Language

We cannot leave this chapter without admitting that we have laid a pretty heavy burden on parents. We have shown them in their all too common roles of aggressors, manipulators, and attackers. We have done so because this book is addressed to adult children and deals with their problems. Yet our purpose is to build a relationship between parent and adult child.

It may be that over the years the adult child has developed particular styles for attacking with words. It is not unknown for adult children to turn the tables on their parents and to treat their parents as children. They then trot out the weapons they learned at the mothers' and fathers' knees. This is the point we made at the end of the last chapter.

When the nurturing language is brought into play the idea of "getting back" at your parents fades. You are "giving up" all your weapons. You are giving up judgment, praise, blame, questions, belittlement—the whole kit and caboodle. You are doing so to gain a parent.

/ 6 /

Play It Again. And Again

You are in an argument with your mother (or father). All the weapons are drawn. You've been through it a hundred times. Your heart is beating quickly. Your face is flushed. You feel like running away. You've promised yourself each time that you are not going to let this happen again. But here it is all over again. And you feel helpless.

Now we suggest a new way of speaking to your parents, and you say: "My God, I can hardly keep from throttling her [him]. How in the world am I going to remember all the new ways of talking? How am I going to make it sound natural? Besides mom [dad] is too quick for me. I'll never be able to get out the right words in time."

Many people have asked us these questions. They express doubt about the ability to learn the nurturing language. If we were face to face with you we would—using our language—explore what your doubts are all about. Perhaps then you could answer these questions for yourself.

But since this is not a face-to-face session, now we offer you a method to make learning the new speech easier and natural. It will help you when the crunch comes, when your chest hurts, when you cannot utter a word.

The method is called role-playing. With this powerful tool psychologists build their client's confidence, social skills, and emotional strength. In the same way you strengthen your confidence, skill, and emotional strength in the nurturing language. You play the role of adult child speaking the new language. You play the role with another person playing your parent. You remain cool while you handle weapons, build your language.

Role-playing can be enormously helpful in acquiring the new language. It is tough to learn any language—French, Spanish, Urdu, whatever—that differs from the one you have been speaking all your life. The nurturing language does differ from the way most people talk. For many of us, it might just as well be Urdu.

Most of us—the authors included—have been reared in a society in which control and attack have for a long time been part of the way we deal with each other. Much of the content of modern fiction, movies, television, and plays centers on control and attack and the spoken dialogue closely follows the rules of the toxic language. The most "interesting" plays are those in which the characters most deftly deploy their weapons. So the toxic language is much with us.

Each of us dresses in a speech personality shaped by our social environment—our parents, friends, teachers, bosses, literature, movies, etc. We have much invested in the way we speak. It is so much a part of our personality that to change our speech feels to us as if we were assuming a new and rather ill-fitting persona. Yet, although we wear them like old comfortable shoes, our old patterns of talking often serve us ill. They tear up relationships by tearing up feelings. We are not, after all, characters in well-made plays.

We judge and are judged. We throw questions. We answer

them. We offer advice—the "shoulds" and "oughts"—and we tease and mock and manipulate. And, in turn, we are teased, mocked, and manipulated. All, as if they were natural, born in us. No wonder that an attempt to listen, to reflect the other's words and feelings, seems awkward and ill-fitting.

Role-playing provides the practice to wear your new words comfortably and naturally. You bring the nurturing phrases to your tongue under conditions that are safe. After all, you are "only playing." There is no punishment for error. Since your partner is also playing, he or she will take no offense if you say something "wrong."

During role-playing, you may feel many of the same feelings as if your parent were there. That's good. It means that when your mother or father is present, you'll have the emotional strength to counter the real weapons.

Setting Up the Game

Role-playing is a game. It's not the real thing. But it is a serious game because it can train you to get at the core of your feelings for your parents. Any role-playing helps. If you can't set it up formally, you can simply ask someone to "please play my mother." The game will still pay off in understanding and practice. You can get more out of it by taking some preliminary steps.

Picking the Right Person

Ideally, your role-playing partner knows your mother or father very well. Your partner could be a spouse, a brother or sister, your adult child, or even a friend. Unless you are quite sophisticated in the nurturing language, it's not a good idea to play with a parent. Such "games" can turn into attack and counterattack and do damage to your parent-player or to you.

If you cannot find anyone who knows your parent, you can

brief your partner about the ways in which your mother or father usually deals with you. You can say, for instance: "She's always asking me a lot of questions." Or: "I can't seem to do anything right when she's around. At least that's what she tells me." Or: "My father has to go into a nursing home and he won't go. I think he's afraid we'll never visit him." A few clues usually give your partner enough to simulate your parent's behavior. Even if the play is not exact, it doesn't matter. Any response gives you something to chew on.

If you can find a partner already expert in some form of the nurturing language, so much the better. The game will move onto serious ground quickly and give you practice on some of the more difficult passages of give-and-take.

Picking the Right Place and Time

You can role-play anywhere, anytime. At dinner, in an auto, on a train, in bed, on a beach. Except: within earshot of your parent. To your parent—if he or she catches on—your "game" will seem like a plot. The level of distrust will rise and make it harder for you to enter your parent's inner world in safety.

Making the Rules

Rule No. 1: Once you figure out who is going to play whom, stick to the role until the game is over.

You can switch roles later but play the game in the same role until the end. Reversing roles may be important. You may want to play your parent to get some feeling about your parent's feelings. For example, suppose your mother is in a nursing home and she has been complaining about the food, the bed, the nurses. If you play your mother, you will begin to appreciate some of the problems she actually faces. You will be better able to help her. You may even find some way to alleviate some of her real troubles.

Rule No. 2: Keep the game on a very specific problem.

Some specific problems:
Stopping the flow of questions
Getting your father to the doctor
Getting your mother to stop criticizing your wife
Telling your father you can't take him on vacation
Asking your mother-in-law for money

Some general problems:
Getting your mother to be affectionate
Asking your father-in-law to stop meddling in your husband's business
Keeping your father from being depressed
Trying to make your mother happy

If problems are general, they usually are composed of a host of more specific difficulties. If you deal with the series of specifics, the general problem will be eased. If you tackle the general problem you will find few solutions.

If your father-in-law has been meddling in your husband's business, examine the meddling. Has he been showing up at the office unannounced and giving orders to your husband's employees? That's a specific. And that can be dealt with more easily than a general assault on meddling.

Rule No. 3: Have a specific goal in mind. How do you want the game to end?

"I want to be able to get my mother to stop bringing my son so many toys."

"I want to get my father-in-law to keep his hands off me."

"I want to negotiate how much money I give my father each week."

"I need to have my mother stop teasing me about my clothes."

You may not be able to achieve the goal in the game or in real life. In the game, your partner may not be able to understand how to conclude the game because he or she does not have anything emotional at stake. In real life you will have to negotiate. Your negotiation can fail. You may settle on a compromise. Or you may get what you want. You can be ready for all three possibilities. By role-playing you give yourself the best chance of reaching your target.

Rule No. 4: Play as realistically as possible.

The closer you get to reality, the smoother your nurturing vocabulary. And you *are* trying for naturalness. After a while, your responses to your parents (in fact, to everyone) will be so effortless that nobody will be able to tell that you have changed your speech.

Instead you will find that your parent will be less hostile, less inclined to use weapons. Other people will find you more interesting, more sympathetic. They will be more willing to listen to you and to help you. They will not know why except that they feel safe and comfortable in your presence.

Besides achieving smoother speech, realistic play enables you to get deeper into your feelings about your parents. If you are having problems with your parents, it is likely that your relationship skims along at the surface because you and they want things to be safe. Through realistic play, you may gain new insight into their lives.

Because speech is a habit—and a powerful one—realistic play enables you to change habits. As you speak the words out loud under conditions that simulate reality, your habit of speech will change. You will gain confidence in yourself.

Some Dividends from Role-playing

Most of all, role-playing makes the nurturing language part of your personality. It enables you to speak to your parents (and others) in a supportive way. You also collect some by-products from role-playing.

As we said, you solve specific problems that sit between your parents and you. As you role-play, your mind considers many options. You play out the options as you play the game. You have time to think. You do not have to blurt out the first idea that comes to mind.

When confronted with the real problem in real life, you

can respond to your parent with any of several options you have considered. Role-playing prepares you for any new trick. Having gone over several ideas, your mind is ready for a new one.

Take the problem faced by the young daughter-in-law, Ann, whose father-in-law, Arnold, makes sexual advances. Ann decides to confront Arnold with her unhappiness over his behavior. We'll show you how to do that in a later chapter on handling pain inflicted by a parent. The man could respond to her assertion in one of several ways. In real life, any of them could catch her unawares. In role-playing she could consider the following possibilities:

1. Arnold recoils, backs down. He is all apologies.

2. He takes her confrontation as encouragement. He redoubles his effort.

3. He says he was misunderstood and feels insulted.

4. He says she is being flirtatious with him and he is going to tell her husband.

5. He threatens to break her neck if she breathes a word about it.

As we pointed out, trying to read the man's mind is likely to lead to a wrong guess. In this case, a misreading could lead to disaster. But if these possibilities are role-played in advance, Ann will have had practice in handling them if they come up. Essentially, her fundamental tool will be listening.

But suppose Arnold comes up with a totally unexpected behavior? He breaks down and weeps with remorse. Having had the practice in dealing with the other responses, the young woman now has the insight to deal with the new one.

Here's another by-product of role-playing: You often decide to do nothing.

Suppose your mother lives in a distant city. You want her to come to visit you this Christmas instead of your going there. You role-play with your spouse. And during the game the incontrovertible fact stands out that your mother is really too ill to travel; that by encouraging her to move you would be putting her in danger. So you agree between yourselves to visit her.

Which brings up another dividend. If the person with whom you are role-playing is involved in your parental problem—that is, a spouse or your child or sibling—the role-playing tells your game partner what's going on. Your game partner, even if not interested in the nurturing language, may find it possible to help you.

Your mother has been asking you for more money for support. You are finding it hard to give her more because inflation has knocked out the pins from your income. You want to tell your mother that you can't increase the stipend, at least not now. So you ask your spouse to role-play your mother. As she does so she begins to see more of your mother's point of view; begins to feel what it's like to be an older person on a restricted income. By the end of the game, your wife may be saying to you: "Maybe we could cut back on some things and find a few more bucks for mom."

Recording the Game

Oh wad some power the giftie gie us
To see oursels as others see us!

—Robert Burns

Psychologists are making constructive use of a powerful psychological tool for helping us to see ourselves as others see us: the videotape recorder. At Michigan State University at East Lansing, Dr. Norman Kagan makes videotapes of doctors, interns, and nurses treating or interviewing patients. He then plays the tape back so patient and therapist can watch themselves on TV.

As they review the tape together, patient and therapist begin to see things they missed when they were in the heat of the treatment session. Both also feel again the same emotions they experienced during the session. One doctor—an expert in psychosomatic disease—completely overlooked the fact that his patient became ill with asthma whenever her mentally ill brother came home. In reviewing the tape, this became instantly clear to both doctor and patient. They could then work on the problem of home visits by the brother.

Dr. Kagan has also videotaped marital counseling sessions. As they review the tape, the couple draw closer together as they see themselves striking each other with verbal weapons, hiding their feelings and their thoughts.

Videotape recording of role-playing sessions has a similar effect. You see what you did wrong. You examine the feelings you had during the game. And you begin to see what you can do to improve your reactions and to understand what is going on inside you. (Of course, not everyone has TV cameras and videotape recorders, although the number who do is rising greatly.)

Dr. Kagan made a second discovery. He found that a simple sound recording gives you almost everything that a videotape will. And for learning the nurturing language, a sound recording is perfect. All you need is an inexpensive cassette recorder. You can get some of them now for less than twenty-five dollars. We have tried it. It revealed to us many of the difficulties in making our new speech natural.

If you are at home, you can easily record your role-playing game. Then listen to it with your game partner or alone. You will detect the most remarkable things.

Suppose you promised yourself that you would not answer a single question. If you try to remember whether you answered any questions you probably will not remember. Listening to the tape, you will hear yourself answering several questions.

Similarly, you will find yourself using weapons, falling into your "parent's" traps, getting upset, losing your cool. It's like watching a tape of yourself playing tennis or some other game; or like listening to a tape recording of yourself singing, talking, or playing an instrument. You can catch the defects that you prefer to overlook.

Finally, role-playing is fun. You can enjoy yourself because it is, after all, a high-level psychological game. You may be amused by your own foibles and errors as the game reveals them. You may be struck by sudden unexpected revelations about yourself or your parent:

"I never realized that living in our old house was so important for father."

"Yes, I do tease mother all the time! I can't seem to help it. But I realize I do hurt her without meaning to."

"You've caught dad's habit of saying, 'Eh?' to get approval for what he has just said."

We believe that role-playing is so important that we are tempted to make this sweeping statement: If you knew nothing about the nurturing language, role-playing might be just enough to give you the means to rebuild your torn relationship with your parents or to solve many of the problems you have with them.

/ 7 /

Genuine Assertions:
Calls for Help

How many times have we desperately wanted something from a mother, a father, a spouse, an adult child—yet we cannot ask because our emotions clog our throats? Or how many times have people close to us wounded us by their words and actions and we cannot open our mouths and scream in pain? Or if we do scream, it's because we have long passed the point of endurance?

Our parents intimidate us most. For most of our lives—or at least during the formative years of our lives—they held the absolute power to grant or to deny. They could hurt us with impunity. If we protested, they could threaten us with withdrawal of approval, support, and, worst, of love. Often they did. And still do.

In Chapter 3 we introduced Jane, twenty-seven, who teaches high school; her father, Edward, forty-eight, owns a furniture store. Jane wants to study for a doctorate in history. She turns to her father for help.

JANE: Dad, I'm planning to take a leave from school and

go back to the university to get my doctorate. I have some money saved but I need more from you. I know you don't like to give me money, but I do need it and you owe it to me as your daughter. You should give me the money.

EDWARD: What's this? You're telling me what I should do? I'm not one of your pals whom you can order around. If you want to go back to school that's your business. I paid for college and that was almost too much. You should be married by now. If you get a doctorate you'll be smarter than most of the men and then you'll never get married!

Jane could not have consciously designed a call for help more likely to turn off her father. She attacked him on three grounds: his dislike of sharing money, the neglect of his duty as a parent, and finally she launched a gratuitous "should" at him. It was almost as though Jane did not really want her father's assistance. More likely, her expectations having been rebuffed in the past, she leaped to protect herself against rejection by attacking first. Edward's counterattack is worth studying for its accurate aim at his daughter's heart.

To see how Jane could have increased her chances of getting some money, let's return to one of the first principles of the nurturing language:

A person will help you if there is a choice to help.

Jane gave her father no choice. She ordered him to give her the money. Not only that, she gave him no choice in the *manner* in which he was to help her. She asked for money specifically. Given a choice, her father might have found other ways to help rather than with money: for example, a place to live, a car, helping her to find scholarship money, etc.

Why do most people balk when they are directed to do something? Remember: These days each of us enjoys independence unheard of fifty years ago. Our bosses, parents, police, priests, and others in "authority" no longer have the dominion they once did over our minds, bodies, and spirits. "Who are you to tell me what to do?" is often the spoken or unspoken reaction to a direct order. Jane's father blasted her with it immediately.

Parents, especially, balk at directives—actual or implied—from their adult children. They're accustomed to giving, not taking, orders. An order is to them a form of lese parent, a sign of disrespect.

There is a deeper reason why an absence of choice promotes balkiness. Each of us harbors a creative impulse. We like to do things in our own way. We like to invent solutions to our problems. To be told to do something or how to do it cuts against our sense of individuality, against our creativity. It's as if we are being told that we are not smart enough, skilled enough, or kind enough to do the right thing on our own. Our integrity is maligned.

Adult children suffer most from this denigration at the hands of their parents. "Do it this way!" "Don't do that!" "Here, let me show you!" "You call that neat?" "Come home early!" "Write your grandmother!" And on and on. It's a wonder that we get out of childhood with our psyches in as good condition as they usually are. And no wonder that most people bear some emotional scars inflicted by parental directiveness.

Many parents suffered the same abuse at the hands of their parents, which makes them just as sensitive to commands as anybody else. In issuing a call for help, an adult child like Jane might keep in mind the principle of choice. She could have approached her father like this:

JANE: I'm thinking about giving up teaching for a while and working for my doctorate in history.

And that's all. It is an opening signal to discuss the topic of her school plans. It provides her father with the widest choice in discussing the problem. He is free to talk about it. Nothing has been asked of him.

The Secrets of the Genuine Assertion

If we are to follow Jane's example, we give our intended helper the widest choice while clearly stating our own needs. We call that statement a genuine assertion. We are asserting our needs. We are emotionally genuine—real—in the way we assert them. There is true feeling behind our statement. We do not fake it. We do not play-act.

The genuine assertion is one of the core ideas of the nurturing language:

People will hear a cry of pain or a call for help if the cry or call is genuine with feeling.

As we use the terms *call for help* and *cry of pain* we mean something special. Each has several well-defined ingredients; the most important is the genuineness of feeling accompanying the call or cry.

Many studies show that we respond more to other people's feelings than to their words. We judge others by the tone of the emotions they express. "He's a sourpuss." "She's such a sweet woman." "He doesn't have a mean bone in his body." "She's always smiling; it's good to be around her."

But the words are very important, too. People do hear what we say. A communication problem arises when messages can be interpreted in more than one way. We tend to be ambiguous when we fear the other person's reaction to what we say. In the above example, Jane first says she needs the money. In the next breath, she says her father doesn't like to give money. That gives her father two ideas to deal with; he picks the one that hurts. And he defends himself with an attack. People who are attacked are not free to deal with your needs, your problems.

A genuine assertion contains no attack on the intended helper. If your statement of need conveys an attack, your parent will focus on the attack, not on your need.

A statement containing an attack is aggressive, not assertive. And there lies the difference between being aggressive and being assertive. The dictionary tells us that *assert* means to state something positively, with assurance or with force. *To aggress* means to attack. People who take "assertiveness training," which is designed to help people state their needs positively, often err by emphasizing a forceful statement that borders on an attack. Forceful, aggressive statements reduce the possibility of obtaining help.

To lessen the tendency to include an attack in your assertion we offer Rule No. 1 in creating an effective genuine assertion:

A genuine assertion does not contain the pronoun "you" or "your."

Although you can mount an attack on another person without the pronoun "you," it is hard to do.

"You should" is a much more powerful attack than "one should."

"Why don't you . . . ?" cuts deeper than "Why not . . . ?"

"Your hair is a mess" judges the person directly. "I don't like messy hair" judges the hair and only by implication judges the owner of the hair. However, either way, it's a judgment, one weaker than the other.

"You never understand what I say" is defensiveness targeted on the other. "I can't seem to make myself understood" takes the heat off the other.

"You" always can be taken as an accusation. And if we are accused we defend ourselves. We are more involved with the defense than with the other's call for help. Our "creativity" is taken up with defense. And, besides, we do not like to help those who attack us. If we do help, we do so only grudgingly.

The Implied "You"

Clearly, when Jane opens the subject of her going back to school, her father may very well be on alert for some demand. He has had some past experience and he could give in to a little mind reading. He easily could read a "you" in Jane's assertion. That cannot be helped. However, Jane can more easily deal with the implied "you" than if an actual pronoun were there.

JANE: I'm thinking about giving up teaching for a while and working on my doctorate in history.   [opening signal]

EDWARD: So what do you want from me?   [reading the "you"]

JANE: You think I want something from you.   [checking listening]

EDWARD: You wouldn't be telling me this if you didn't.   [mind reading]

JANE: You're saying that's the only reason I'm discussing my plans.   [checking listening]

EDWARD: Oh, you probably want my approval.   [more mind reading]

JANE: You don't approve of my getting my degree.   [checking listening]

EDWARD: You probably have enough education.   [hidden material]

By patient checking listening Jane finally brought out one of the items on her father's hidden agenda (too much education). He attacked her with it in the first dialogue we reported. But this time he brings it out under conditions that do not add up to an attack. And Jane can handle it.

You can arrive at several deductions from Jane's and Edward's conversation. First, she neatly *responds* to (rather than *answers*) his question. She could have defended herself by saying "Nothing. Nothing at all." That would not have been true and would have brought other questions from Edward.

Second, Jane addressed her father with the pronoun "you" in her checking listening, not in her opening signal. In checking listening, "you" is not heard as an attack (unless you intone the sentences as questions). Rather Edward hears a real attempt by Jane to understand what he is saying. So "you" is okay in all forms of listening; it is kept out of genuine assertions.

Third, Jane did not return to her assertion. Her first goal was fully to understand her father's position on her wanting to get her degree. Until she explores his ideas she will find it futile to go further. Edward will not be listening. We'll get into that more when we discuss listening-to-speak, the art of making sure that your parent is psychologically tuned to your words.

All Assertions Have Three Parts

We have seen how ambiguity in an assertion encourages an attack. So Part 1 of a genuine assertion says:

State your single need or problem clearly without too many details.

"I need money to go to school."

"I cannot leave Jimmy [her son] alone while I go shopping."

"I'd like to have the whole family come to my house for Thanksgiving."

"We cannot take anybody else on our trip to the mountains this year."

"I'm buying a boat."

"My problem is that I have to get downtown and I have no way of getting there."

Stated simply, your need or problem cannot be easily misinterpreted, though sometimes your parent will misinterpret even when you have been careful. That happens because people do try to read your mind. They also hear what is on their agenda, not yours. Consciously or unconsciously, they are selective listeners.

When your need or problem is given as *your* need or *your* problem, you have not put the burden on your parent. You

are encouraging your parent to see your problem as your—
not your parent's—problem. To avoid confusion on this
point we suggest the pronouns "I" or "we." If you examine
our examples, you will see that we have cast the statements
that way.

In his book *Parent Effectiveness Training,* Dr. Thomas
Gordon calls such a statement the I-Message, because it is
focused on the "I" rather than on the "you." It also answers
the question: "What is the problem and who has it?" It
leaves the hearer free to help or not to help and to choose
the manner of helping.

Traditional request for help:

YOU-THE-CHILD: Mom, I have to go [call for help/
shopping. Would you baby-sit   no choice]
Jimmy for me, please?
PARENT: I have so much work to do at [refusal/attack]
home. Besides, you've spoiled him
so much I can't control him.

The nurturing language:

YOU-THE-CHILD: Mom, I have to go [call for help/
shopping I can't take Jimmy with   choice]
me. He's got a cold.
PARENT: If he's sick, you should stay ["should"/response
home.   to two ideas]
YOU-THE-CHILD: I should stay home. [reflection listen-
                                     ing]
PARENT: I hope he's not too sick. [expresses fears]
YOU-THE-CHILD: You're worried about [nurturing listen-
him.   ing]
PARENT: Yes. Five-year-olds pick up
so many things.
YOU-THE-CHILD: Well, it's only a [giving facts]
runny nose and he has no fever.
PARENT: That's good.

YOU-THE-CHILD: I really do have to go shopping.	[repeats message/ one idea]
PARENT: I have so much work at home.	[expressing concern]
YOU-THE-CHILD: You have a lot of work.	[checking listening]
PARENT: If you brought him to my house I could watch him for a few hours.	[creative solution]

At first, Jimmy's mother made an error. She presented her mother with two ideas: the need to take care of Jimmy while she went shopping and that Jimmy had a cold. Grandmother pounces on the problem of the sick child. So Jimmy's mother had to take the long way round before she could get back to her own problem.

Couldn't Jimmy's mother simply have given grandma the facts after the "should"-attack and short-cut the whole conversation? Possibly. The chances are that until grandma has a chance to examine her own feelings about the child's possible illness, she is not in a position to listen to "facts." Her head is not clear to deal in a creative way with her daughter's problem.

The Reason Why

The second part of a genuine assertion contains the *reason why* you need what you need or what will happen if you don't get your problem solved. By providing this information, you eliminate another source of ambiguity. "If I don't get this, that will happen." You avoid opening up a whole line of questioning about your motives or the legitimacy of your need. If you said to your father: "I need five dollars," the chances are that he will not ask why you need it. Most likely he would respond differently if you asked for a thousand dollars.

Part 2 of a genuine assertion says:
Always give the reason why you need what you need.
Let's see how both parts of a genuine assertion work together.

You-the-Child: I can't seem to keep up with my housework what with the children and my going back to school.	[problem/reason why]
Parent: I think you have to drop something.	[suggestion/advice]
You-the-Child: You think I'm doing too much.	[checking listening]
Parent: Yes, I told you not to take on school. What did you need that for?	[superiority]
You-the-Child: You don't believe school will do me any good.	[checking listening]
Parent: It's always good to go to school. When the kids grow up you'll be able to get a better job.	[backing down]
You-the-Child: Yes. Mmmm.	[wordless listening]
Parent: I don't know how you do it all.	[sympathetic now]
You-the-Child: I'm falling behind in my housework. I could get it done if the children weren't in my hair when I'm cleaning.	[repeats call for help]
Parent: Maybe I could come over and play with them while you clean.	[creative solution]

Notice that the second genuine assertion contained a more specific reason for not getting the housework done. That led the parent to suggest taking care of the children while the cleaning was done. In the original dialogue on which this nurturing language version was based, the adult child had asked the mother to help her clean. There was no choice and a refusal followed coupled with an attack.

Once More with Feeling

The third part of a genuine assertion—the part that makes it sound real, genuine—is the feeling, the emotion. Without feelings, your call for help sounds weak, and perhaps insincere. Without feelings, the nurturing language becomes an empty technique. Unless you express your feelings to your parent, he or she will somehow "catch on" to the moves you make as a technique. Your parent may not be able to discern exactly what you are doing, but your words will not carry weight.

Your parent may say: "Why are you talking so funny?" Or: "You're not really listening to me."

Remember, people do attend to your feelings and they respond to them as much as they do to your words, if not more so. If you try to sound cool, your parent will interpret your request as not being important. If it isn't important, then perhaps it's not worth asking.

Many people have difficulty in expressing their true feelings by tone of voice or facial expression. They have been taught not to wear their feelings on the outside. The result is a deficit in their ability to communicate effectively; they are not as believable as they could be. Others express themselves at fever pitch no matter what the issue: The failure to find toilet paper is delivered with the same intensity as the announcement of a marriage. Such people are as hard to read as those who mute their emotions.

Your relations with your parent may have reached the point where you take refuge in hiding your feelings. You fear that you will be manipulated because you have revealed something that matters to you. In the past, your parent has pounced on your revelations. So you keep your emotions hidden and perhaps ask for help in a way that indicates that refusal doesn't matter to you. You are trying to avoid being hurt by the refusal. But that, paradoxically, invites a turn-down. If it seems not to matter whether you get what you want, you parent will take you at face value.

One way to bring your true feelings to bear on your assertion is to label the assertion with the words that stand for the feeling. Some examples:

"I *desperately* need the money to pay off the mortgage this month."

"I need a car to take Beth to the ball game. If I don't get a car, we can't go and we'll both be *disappointed.*"

"I promised the Turners I would invite them to the country. I *don't like* to go back on my promises."

"If I don't find some way to get caught up on my house-work, I'll go *crazy.*"

"It would make me *happy* if I could find a way to get the family together once a year."

Part 3 of a genuine assertion is:
Put some feeling into it.

The Structure of a Genuine Assertion

To repeat: A genuine assertion has three parts. All three are needed to avoid ambiguity, to avoid attack, and to make the assertion genuine.

Part 1 consists of a simple statement of your need or problem without excessive details. The briefer the better.

Part 2 is the reason why. You are saying "I need this because." Or: "If I don't get this, that will happen."

Part 3 is the feeling. You color your assertion with your true feelings about what you want. If you have trouble expressing the feeling, try a word label.

It doesn't matter in which order you put the parts as long as they are all there.

"I desperately need somebody to baby-sit Jimmy so I can go shopping for food for the week."

"If I can't get somebody to take care of Jimmy I won't be able to do my weekly food shopping. That is going to leave me in a desperate situation."

"I must desperately do my food shopping for the week and I can't do it unless I get somebody to baby-sit Jimmy."

If you leave out any part, you will be dealing with your parent's response to the missing part. That's not necessarily bad. You may want to introduce one part of your assertion at a time in order to get your parent's feelings about each part before making a complete genuine assertion. In the end, however, the call for help as given by a genuine assertion has the best chance of success when it is complete.

No matter how little you feel your parent cares about helping you, a genuine assertion is most likely to touch your parent at his or her most human point. People do like to help each other. The genuine assertion, because it is free of aggression, makes it possible for your parent to help.

To make certain that the genuine assertion is free of attack, we leave out the pronoun "you." We stick to the pronoun "I" and "we." We cast our assertions as positive statements. We avoid questions. To prevent the mistaken impression that we are asking a question, we avoid allowing our voices to rise at the end of the assertion.

A genuine assertion is not magic (just close to it). The history of your relationship may be such that your parent finds it hard to believe your call for help. Or your parent may not hear you without a good deal of your supportive listening (see Chapter 9, "Listen First; Then Speak"). It may take time to rebuild your relationship so that your parent feels safe from attack from you and you feel safe with your parent. And finally, because we allow choice and creative solutions, we are prepared to negotiate our needs, to end up with something, not quite what we wanted, but something.

Now what about the cries of pain that we muffle when our parents hurt us? See the next chapter.

/ 8 /

Genuine Assertions:
Cries of Pain

Remember Ann and her father-in-law, Arnold, from Chapter 1?

ARNOLD: You really look sexy in those jeans.

ANN: Oh.

ARNOLD: You have a very nice figure. I can see why my son is attracted to you. In fact, I am, too. Would you like to have lunch in my office today?

ANN: I have a date with Richard [her husband].

ARNOLD: I'm more of a man than he'll ever be. Let me show you.

ANN: I've got to rush off. Good-bye.

Ann has had several such encounters with Arnold. She knows she cannot deal gracefully with them, especially because Richard works in Arnold's business. She is panicky that Arnold will make a physical play that she won't be able to handle at all. She is on the verge of collapse. Her solution: Avoid Arnold. She hasn't yet confided her problems to Richard. But Richard has reported to her the following conversation:

ARNOLD: How are you and Ann getting along?
RICHARD: Fine.
ARNOLD: You know, I mean, how is it coming along? You don't have any children. I know that many couples don't these days. But I was wondering, do you know if you can? I mean, well, you never were one with the girls and I often wonder how you got such a good-looker like Ann? She must have married you for *my* money.
RICHARD: (silence . . . he is wiped out)

Ann has been suggesting that Richard "stand up" to his father, but as she well knows, Arnold is a superior weapons handler, capable of inflicting even more severe punishment.

Perhaps you have thought of the following possible solutions:

"If I were Ann, I'd smack him and tell Richard what his father was up to."

"Arnold is such a boor. I'd ignore it and tease him out of it. Richard is such a momma's boy he'll never stand up to his father."

"I'd tell my husband to quit his job and get away from his father and that if he didn't I'd leave."

"Arnold sounds like a real man. I think, given Richard, I would find it hard to fend off his father."

Much depends on what Ann and Richard really want from Arnold. Does Richard really need the job or can he go out on his own? Does he want a loving relationship with his father? How about Ann? Can she support Richard in his confrontations with his father? Does she want Arnold to be a significant person in her life?

The Cry of Pain

In this case, the nurturing language provides the means of exploring these questions while at the same time taking the edge off Arnold's aggressiveness. The central tool is the *cry of pain.* It is a statement that says: "I have been hurt and I am in pain."

For many reasons, we find it difficult to say to another person that his or her behavior has resulted in injury to us.

*We may be loath to admit that somebody got the better of us.

*We may fear that a cry of pain will spur additional attacks.

*We do not want to reveal what hurts us so that our attacker will not fire the same weapons at us again.

*We believe that if we blame another for our hurt the tormentor will find other, more powerful, means of punishing us.

When our parents hurt us we avoid crying out for all these reasons plus the additional fear that our parents will withdraw their love. As young children we lived with the ever-present possibility that our parents might go away and leave us. Parents, often unattuned to children's need for security, do leave their children (to go to the movies, to go shopping, etc.). Unless parents take care, they may create fear in their children about their parents' ultimate return.

And, of course, it is not unknown for a parent to say: "If you do that I won't love you anymore." If not explicitly, parents often communicate that feeling implicitly. They say it by the way they punish their children's transgressions, by the rigidity of their control, by the "shoulds," the questions, and all the rest. They fail to treat their children as thinking, feeling human beings capable of negotiating a problem.

As we grow older, many of us still harbor the wounds and

fears of loss of love and abandonment. And parents quietly threaten withdrawal as a way of extorting from their adult children money, attention, submission, whatever. So we stifle our cries of pain. We do so until we are so choked up with them that we explode, emotionally. The results frequently rupture the relationship for days, months, and sometimes years.

Then, too, we cannot bring ourselves to be angry with a parent who may, in retaliation, withhold love. We cannot be angry with that person against whom society forbids us to be angry. We hold the anger in. By now, psychologists and psychiatrists have good evidence that held-in anger turns against the holder: We begin to blame ourselves for the parent's misdeeds; and that, in susceptible persons, creates depression.

Imagine Ann or Richard exploding in the face of Arnold's provocation. Who can predict Arnold's response? In his rage, Arnold could tear apart his son's marriage, something that he seems bent on doing anyway. Is that a valid risk for either Ann or Richard to take, especially if they care for each other? To do nothing also increases the chance that Arnold will do something quite foolhardy.

We suggest that Ann or Richard issue a cry of pain. It has all the ingredients of a call for help. It states simply and briefly the nature of the hurt. It tells the reason why the parent's actions and words hurt. It has valid emotional content. It does not attack or blame. It omits the pronoun "you." It is a genuine assertion. Instead of asserting a need or a problem, it asserts an injury. The injury can be physical or emotional.

It may seem strange that the cry of pain does not blame the tormentor. We think (old language) that a person who hurts us should be scolded for doing so. "You shouldn't hurt me!" we cry in our former language. But recall that you want to enlist your parent's help. The help consists of his or her not repeating or continuing the punishing behavior. If your cry is aggressive, not assertive, your parent will deal with the attack and not turn attention to the pain you are feeling. If you attack, your parent may feel pain, and he or she will be more concerned with his or her own pain than with yours.

Some Cries of Pain

Ann and Richard face an extraordinarily difficult problem with Arnold. His behavior is of long standing, which means that it may have become a habit, and habits resist change. Great skill is needed to penetrate barriers erected by habit. So before we get to Ann and Richard, let's look at some simpler examples.

SON: I took Marilyn to the Irish dance.	[opening signal]
MOTHER: You took Marilyn to a dance? When did you learn to dance? You couldn't even skip when you were a kid. You have no coordination.	[mockery]
SON: You don't think I can learn.	[checking listening]
MOTHER: You have no coordination.	[repeats, weaker]
SON: For years, I've been told that I'm a klutz. I'm tired of it. It upsets me a lot. It makes me feel worthless.	[genuine assertion] [cry of pain]
MOTHER: I didn't mean to hurt your feelings. You shouldn't be so sensitive.	[defensive/shifting the blame]
SON: You think I'm too sensitive.	[checking listening]
MOTHER: I didn't think you were so easily hurt.	[admits having gone too far]
SON: I don't like to hear again and again how clumsy I am.	[repeats genuine assertion]
MOTHER: Okay.	[agreement]

As in this example, a cry of pain is always preceded by listening. Although frontally attacked by his mother, the son first listened. As expected, the checking listening weakened the mother's attack.

Listening has another important effect. If you want someone to hear what you have to say, that person has to be sure that you will listen to what he or she says. Only after listening did the son deliver his cry of pain. Only then was it heard. The nurturing language requires that listening precede a genuine assertion. It is the listening-to-speak idea that we will develop for you later.

The cry itself was complete:

The simple statement: "For years, I've been told that I'm a klutz."

The reason why it hurts: "It makes me feel worthless."

The emotion: "I'm tired of it. It upsets me a lot."

And certainly no "you" to be heard.

We know the mother heard the cry because she became defensive. She also heard the implicit "you." Then, more listening to blunt the second attack. Finally, a repeat of the original genuine assertion to get mother's agreement.

Lets look at another dialogue, first in its original form, then as redone in the nurturing language.

FATHER: I heard that Jill [the grand-daughter] did well in school this report card. [opening signal]

DAUGHTER: Yes, she earned all A's.

FATHER: You never did very well in school. You were lucky they let you graduate. [attack: put-down]

DAUGHTER: I didn't do too badly. [defensive]

FATHER: Really you weren't smart in school at all. Jill must get her intelligence from me. I can remember my father telling all his buddies that I was his smartest child. [intensifies attack]

DAUGHTER: I can remember my father   [counterattack]
telling his buddies that I was his
dumbest, good-for-nothing child.
FATHER: Well, I wasn't far wrong.   [counterattack]

The daughter's final counterattack is an incomplete cry of pain. It doesn't give the reason why the father's statement hurts. It is contaminated by "my father," the equivalent of "you." It is far too aggressive to be left standing without a response by the father.

Let's look at the dialogue in the nurturing language.

FATHER: I heard that Jill [the grand-   [opening signal]
daughter] did well in school this
report card.
DAUGHTER: Yes, she earned all A's.
FATHER: You never did very well in   [attack: put-down]
school. You were lucky they let you
graduate.
DAUGHTER: You don't think I did well   [reflection/check-
in school.   ing]
FATHER: You certainly didn't come   [weakened attack]
out on top.
DAUGHTER: You were disappointed   [nurturing listening
that that I wasn't a prize student.   reflecting his
feelings]

FATHER: It would have been nice.   [his real feelings]
DAUGHTER: It makes me very unhappy   [genuine assertion]
to be told that I didn't do well in
school, especially when there is
nothing I can do about it now.
FATHER: I was just exaggerating. You   [backing down]
did better than most kids.

Again the same sequence: listening, genuine assertion. And, at the last, the complete cry of pain:
Simple statement: "told that I didn't do well in school."

Reason why: "when there is nothing I can do about it now."

Emotion: "I am very unhappy."

No "you."

If the daughter had said:

"It makes me very unhappy when *you* tell me that I didn't do well in school, especially when there is nothing I can do about it now," the "you" could have triggered another attack, most likely a defensive statement aiming to shift the blame to the daughter:

"I'm just talking about old times. It has nothing to do with now."

If the daughter had left out the reason why:

"It makes me very unhappy when I'm told that I didn't do well in school," the father can find an opening:

"Well, you took the tests; I didn't."

Completeness is essential if the genuine assertion is to have maximum effect.

Here is a telephone "conversation" between Arlene, sixty, and her daughter, Sally, forty. It is a particularly difficult situation because of the special weapon—silence—with which Arlene punishes her daughter.

SALLY: I realize I hurt you when I forgot to tell Shamus to pick you up.   [opening/apology]

ARLENE: (Silence)   [withdrawal of relationship—i.e., love]

SALLY: That was two days ago and you haven't spoken to me since.   [pleading]

ARLENE: (Silence)

SALLY: Why the silent treatment?   [question attack]

ARLENE: (Silence)

SALLY: We can't discuss our problems if only one of us talks.   [logic]

ARLENE: (Silence)

SALLY: I'm getting angry because you aren't answering me.   [aggressive, not assertive]

ARLENE: (Silence)

SALLY: I don't understand how you can be so angry over an honest oversight.   [defensive/shifting blame]

ARLENE: (Silence)

SALLY: For God's sakes, mom, talk to me! I'm miserable when you treat me this way!   [directive/incomplete assertion]

ARLENE: (Silence)

SALLY: If you don't talk to me now I'll make sure everyone in the family forgets to pick you up forever!   [open threat]

ARLENE: (Silence)

SALLY: Can't you see how miserable I am and how sorry I am because you weren't picked up?   [defensive/muddled assertion]

ARLENE: (Silence)

SALLY: Why do you treat me as if I don't exist?   [question attack]

ARLENE: I felt like I didn't exist when I wasn't picked up and was forgotten.   [perfect genuine assertion]

The roles are reversed. Although Arlene's silences are punishment (withdrawal of self), Sally hurls weapon after weapon in a vain attempt to break her mother's silence. When Arlene finally speaks, she delivers a perfect cry of pain. We have only Sally's report of what went on, but it's a good bet that Arlene's cry of pain was accompanied by a discordant emotion, i.e., rather than express hurt Arlene used the assertion to attack in a different mode.

Except for Sally's opening statement nothing in her responses suggests that she is remotely interested in what her mother may be feeling. She is interested in her own pain and in having her mother forgive her even when she expresses her pain in an attacking way. Clearly, the nurturing language would handle the situation differently.

SALLY: I realize I hurt you when I forgot to tell Shamus to pick you up.	[opening/apology]
ARLENE: (Silence)	[withdrawal of relationship—i.e., love]
SALLY: That was two days ago and you haven't spoken to me since.	[pleading]
ARLENE: (Silence)	
SALLY: You must be terribly hurt to be so quiet on the telephone.	[nurturing listening]
ARLENE: (Silence)	
SALLY: It really does hurt to feel left out and forgotten. You must be furious with all of us. I can understand why you don't want to talk.	[nurturing listening]

(By this time, most people would have said something. But Arlene is determined now to punish Sally. It would be worth one more round of nurturing listening. However, Sally decides to issue a cry of pain of her own.)

SALLY: I cannot stand this silent treatment! It makes me feel like an unloved child!	[genuine assertion]
ARLENE: Now maybe you know what it is to be forgotten! It made *me* feel unloved.	[hidden material]
SALLY: You felt that none of us loved you because we forgot to send Shamus to pick you up.	[nurturing listening]
ARLENE: Somebody should have remembered.	[more of the same]

SALLY: Hmmm.   [wordless listening]
ARLENE: Next time I'll have to make   [solution]
  sure nobody forgets an old mother.

Sally's cry of pain in this dialogue came after Sally attempted to understand the exact reason for her mother's silence. At the point that it became painful for Sally, she let her mother know. Her mother could very well have continued the silence. To break the silence, Sally would have needed more nurturing listening. Then she would repeat the genuine assertion with greater intensity of feeling: angrier, more unhappy, more disappointed.

Dealing with Arnold's Sexual Aggression

"Arnold will never change."
"He's deaf to all human approaches."
"He'll catch on and turn it against them."
"He's vicious and not worth dealing with. Besides, he's dangerous. They should get out fast."
All possibly true. Let's look at each item because each represents an important and prevailing view of human psychology. The first is heard everywhere: "People never change." It expresses the idea that people tend to behave in the same way under all circumstances. "Arnold is aggressive" means that Arnold always attacks. "Richard is submissive" means that Richard will always give in. "Ann is sweet" means that Ann will always take into account another person's feelings. We tend to label a person from a sampling of behavior in our presence.

Modern scientific investigation has shown that people do tend to behave in the same way under a variety of circumstances. In that finding psychology tends to confirm common sense, i.e., that we can to some extent "label" a person psychologically. But this is, as we have said, a very tricky business. It takes great skill, which most of us do not have.

A more important and useful discovery tells us that if circumstances change, behavior may change. If Ann can arrange the proper circumstances she can curb Arnold's aggression, encourage Richard to be less submissive.

To take the obvious example: A criminal living free engages in crime. In prison, his ability to commit crimes is severely limited. Prison changes circumstances. The criminal may continue to think criminal thoughts, but criminal behavior cannot easily follow.

A more everyday example: A worker who tends to procrastinate will produce more work if his boss monitors his activity. The close monitoring is a new factor that governs the worker's behavior.

A child who fails to do homework will do a lot more if teacher, parent, and child negotiate an agreement on homework. The agreement is a changed circumstance.

The nurturing language changes the interpersonal circumstances. And as those circumstances change, the individuals in the relationship change their behavior. If you change behavior—your language and your actions—your parent will probably change his or her behavior. This may take longer with some parents than others, but changes will occur.

So with Arnold. If Ann and Richard consistently employ their new language with Arnold, Arnold's behavior will change. And it will change in a direction that is less aggressive and more helpful. It has happened in many cases.

In a special program at Adelphi University, Long Island, Dr. Sharon Gadberry and her associates trained adult children in the nurturing language. The trainees could learn the language and to handle their parents' aggressive behavior. They also showed that the parent's behavior did change as the adult child's language changed. Here's an example involving Gloria, thirty-two, and her mother-in-law, Billie, fifty-eight.

BILLIE: How long is this project you're working on going to last? When will it end? [question]

GLORIA: You're asking me again when my project is ending. [checking listening]

BILLIE: Yes. I want to know when it ends. [repeats]

GLORIA: It's really annoying to be asked the same question over and over. I keep answering and it seems as though I can't make myself heard. [genuine assertion/ cry of pain]

BILLIE: I just want to know how long you'll be going back and forth like this. [defensive]

GLORIA: You don't remember when my project ends. [checking listening]

BILLIE: Next August. [remembers]

GLORIA: Good. That's right. I'd like not to be asked anymore.

The next time Gloria saw Billie, Billie did not ask the question. In the past, Billie had asked the same question each time. But now she seemed to be more cautious in going after Gloria with trivial questions designed to provoke and control Gloria. So behaviors do change under changed circumstances.

Now for the second item: "He's deaf to all human approaches." Can Arnold hear his children? With consistent listening and genuine assertions, the message will get through. Ann and Richard may have to express more and more of their hidden anger toward Arnold to penetrate his wall against his children's feelings. A genuine assertion permits the safe expression of anger; safe because to the hearer the anger you show will be directed against the behavior or the situation rather than against the hearer.

Suppose Richard had made the following cry of pain:

RICHARD: It makes me very unhappy to hear that Ann married me for money because that makes me feel I'm worthless.

Arnold could vary it for another attack:

ARNOLD: You're damned right. You're worthless!

After a period of listening, Richard could return to his genuine assertion with greater emotional content:

RICHARD: It's the most terrible agony for me to hear that I am worthless and that my wife married me for money! I simply cannot stand such language! It hurts as deeply as anything that anybody might say.

Arnold could still persist within the current dialogue to berate his son, even though Richard clings to the nurturing language. After all, in Arnold we are dealing with a longtime weapons handler. But it is our experience that in subsequent encounters people like Arnold modify their language; they do not persist in the face of being told again and again that they are causing injury.

Can Arnold "catch on" to the nurturing language and turn it against his children? He could say: "What's the matter? You using some psychology on me?" Plausible. He is clever. He may even have read this book. But the nurturing language can handle that by reflective listening:

"You feel I'm using some psychology on you."

"You think I'm taking advantage of you in some way."

"You have some problem with the way I talk."

"You don't like the way I talk."

(If your parent has read this book, so much the better. It will be easier for you to make clear what you are trying to do. You may be able to say: "Mom, I'm glad we now have the same language. I hope I can make myself understood. I hope I can understand you and your feelings.")

Such responses help Arnold examine what it is that he doesn't like about what Richard and Ann are doing. He may find out that he misses Richard's total submissiveness and Ann's embarrassment. And it could reveal to the couple how their speech may fall short of the full nurturing language. An example:

ARNOLD: What's the matter? You using psychology on me? [opening signal/attacking question]

RICHARD: You have some problem with the way I talk. [checking listening]

ARNOLD: Yes. It sounds strange. What's up? [information/question]

RICHARD: You don't like what I am saying. [nurturing listening]

ARNOLD: You never talked this way before. [information/no attack]

RICHARD: I'm trying very hard to understand what I'm being told because I find I sometimes miss the meaning of something. [genuine assertion]

ARNOLD: I thought I spoke clearly. How do you want me to speak? [considering his words/question]

Now about the last advice: "He's vicious and not worth dealing with. Besides he's dangerous. They should get out fast." In other words, withdraw from the relationship altogether. But do they want to get out of their relationship with Arnold? Given all their options, they may decide that they need Arnold. They may want to break away from Arnold completely but are forced by circumstances to continue in a relationship with him.

Careful use of the nurturing language will give Ann and Richard the best chance of continuing their relationship with Arnold in a way that provides the smallest risk of being punished and hurt. The couple can turn aside Arnold's worst attacks by listening to him without counterattack, and by making genuine assertions. They can make their life easier if not entirely happy.

Ann's Problem

Ann's problem is one of the most difficult an adult child can face with a parent—biological, stepparent, or in-law. Sexual aggression is painful enough between unrelated men and women; the pain sears incredibly in the family. It happens far more often than seems on the surface. Only now do we have evidence for widespread sexual aggression within the family. The exact figures are not available. Some of the larger child-welfare agencies have established programs for the sexually abused young child. Such abuse often continues into adulthood.

Ann could handle Arnold with the nurturing language. Undertaking the task of fending off a father-in-law like Arnold requires practice: role-playing. We would be against asking Richard to role-play his father if Ann has not confided in her husband. The "game" could ignite a powerful anger in Richard. He could turn against her if he feels powerless to be angry with his father. Even if she had told Richard about Arnold's moves, for the same reason Richard would be a dangerous choice as a role-playing partner.

Here are some possible dialogues between Ann and Arnold:

ARNOLD: You really look sexy in those jeans.	[opening signal/ praise]
ANN: Oh.	[wordless listening]
ARNOLD: You have a very nice figure. I can see why my son is attracted to you. In fact, I am, too. Would like to have lunch in my office to-day?	[more praise] [question]
ANN: You want me to have lunch with you today.	[checking listening]
ARNOLD: Yes. I said I was attracted to you.	[repeats feelings]

ANN: You feel attracted to me and that's why you want to have lunch.   [nurturing listening/reflects feelings]

ARNOLD: Sure. I think something nice could happen between us.   [hidden material]

ANN: I'm very upset about the way this conversation is going because it's getting into subjects that I cannot tolerate or even think about!   [genuine assertion]

ARNOLD: Come on! What's the harm in getting to know your father-in-law better?   [defensive/shifting the burden]

ANN: You want to get to know me better.   [checking listening]

ARNOLD: Well, I mean, we know each other. You're married to my son. But I think we should know each other better. Know what I mean? [winks and smiles]   [floundering]

ANN: I really don't understand where this conversation is going. I'm very afraid that it's getting into subjects that horrify me to think about. [Now Ann is visibly upset.] I can't stand it!   [genuine assertion]

ARNOLD: Take it easy! Take it easy! I didn't mean anything.   [backing down]

ANN: You didn't mean anything.   [checking listening]

ARNOLD: No. No. Honest! Just a joke.   [retreat]

ANN: I'm so relieved! I must have misunderstood. I just can't take such jokes.   [genuine assertion]

Let's see what Ann achieved. First, Arnold backed down. Secondly, Ann informed Arnold that a repetition of his advances ("I just can't take such jokes") would be met with the same cry of distress or more. Finally, by not referring to her husband, she gave Arnold nothing to chew on as she did in the original conversation. Recall that when Arnold asked her to have lunch with him, she *answered* his question, saying she had a date with Richard. In effect, she said to Arnold that she preferred Richard to Arnold. He took that as an attack, and counterattacked: "I'm more of a man than he'll ever be." With her new language, Ann short-circuited any attack on her husband.

Throughout the above conversation, Ann scrupulously avoided attack. She did not reject Arnold, but did strongly reject the ideas he proposed. She showed him at every turn that even talking about anything close to what he had on his mind would and did upset her terribly. Her genuine assertions are free of attack; no "you."

She allows him the choice of continuing down the road that will hurt her. In other words, she explicitly is telling him that if he wants to hurt her all he has to do is to continue. Again, few people can keep on hurting when told they are inflicting pain. And they are less likely to injure you the next time.

By checking listening and nurturing listening, both of which reflected Arnold's thoughts and feelings back to him, Ann allowed Arnold to consider what he was really saying and thinking. By hearing it from Ann, he can more objectively evaluate his words, intention, and effect. She reflects it all back to him without an attack, without criticism. All her listening statements were statements, not questions. She is saying: "This is what I heard you say. I hope I have understood you."

In this situation Ann may have society on her side, although not necessarily. Many people, blaming the victim, tend to condemn Ann for wearing "sexy jeans" in Arnold's presence. They see it as a provocation. Perhaps that's why most rapists who are known to the victims are rarely convicted. However, most, if not all, of Arnold's friends and relatives would abhor his behavior because it borders on incest.

By allowing Arnold to consider the meaning of his thoughts, she permits social mores to work on Arnold. It is most difficult for Arnold to persist once he comes to understand that he is doing something rejected by most people he knows.

Overall, by speaking the nurturing language Ann made Arnold feel safe to retreat and to help her in her distress. He felt no need to attack her for her feelings.

Handling a Frank Sexual Approach

Let's see how Ann could handle an outright pass:

ARNOLD: You really look sexy in those jeans.	[opening signal/ praise]
ANN: Oh.	[wordless listening]
ARNOLD: You have a very nice figure. I can see why my son is attracted to you. In fact, I am too. Would you like to have lunch in my office today?	[more praise] [question]
ANN: You want me to have lunch with you.	[checking listening]
ARNOLD: Yes. I said I was attracted to you. I thought we'd have some fun. Something special could happen between us.	[repeats/shows more of his plans]
ANN: You have something specific in mind. [said with interest but not with a smile]	[checking listening]
ARNOLD: Yeah. I thought you and I could get together as man and woman.	[full revelation]
ANN: Oh, my God! I've never heard anything that upset me more! It goes against everything I believe in! I feel totally degraded for having even heard it!	[genuine assertion]

ARNOLD: What's the matter? There are plenty of women who'd give anything to go to bed with me. [defensive/shifting the burden]

ANN: You're saying that because other women would have sex with you that I should. [checking listening]

ARNOLD: They enjoyed it. [more defense]

ANN: They enjoyed it. [reflection]

ARNOLD: Sure did. So would you. [once again]

ANN: I'm really beside myself with this conversation. It goes against everything I believe in; every loyalty. I simply cannot stand it! It horrifies me even to listen to it! I can't listen to it! I won't listen to it! [visibly upset; probably shouting] [genuine assertion/ more feeling]

ARNOLD: Okay, okay. I didn't mean any harm. I was just checking. [defensive]

ANN: You didn't mean any harm. [reflection]

ARNOLD: Nah. I can understand how you feel. [retreat]

ANN: You know what I'm feeling. [checking listening]

ARNOLD: You're upset. You're a good kid. [nurturing]

One might ask: How does Ann do it so smoothly? Role-playing is the answer. It is almost impossible to go into a highly emotional situation without either knowing the nurturing language deeply or having role-played. Psychological therapists know the language, so they can handle themselves in therapy when their patients attack them. However, we have seen psychologists unable to deal with their own relatives in a nurturing way. It is as if they leave their skills behind in the treatment room. Role-playing would help them understand themselves in relation to their own problems. By role-playing in everyday situations, the language skill becomes part of your everyday language.

Some might say: 'Wouldn't it be better if Ann showed some strength and blew the whistle on her father-in-law by telling her husband? Isn't she showing weakness by being "nice" to Arnold?

If Ann wants to end her relationship with Arnold—such as it is—then she should tell her husband. In the process she can also destroy her marriage. Her father-in-law has a bag of tricks he can dump on his son. He can lie. He can blame Ann. He can say she led him on, etc. Her real hope is to cool Arnold and to get him to help her by avoiding hurting her in the way he does.

Some sexual advances include physical handling. However, an advance is almost always preceded by verbal explorations. If Ann issues her cry of pain at the verbal stage, Arnold would probably not advance to the physical. Should he do so anyway, Ann's recourse is again to issue her cry of pain at maximum volume and intensity. Physical struggle may only arouse Arnold's sexual aggression to a higher pitch.

We have shown only two aspects of Arnold's personality: his sexual aggressiveness and his domination of his son. He may have redeeming virtues. He can be very generous to his children. He can be a lot of fun: joking and playing games. He is loyal to his friends. If these traits can be brought into play, then the relationship between the two adult children and Arnold can be rewarding for all.

The Parts of a Cry of Pain

To review: A cry of pain, like a call for help, has three parts:
1. The simple statement of injury or hurt
2. The reason why it hurts
3. The emotional coloring of the statement

The cry of pain—like all genuine assertions—avoids direct attack. So it omits the pronoun "you" and it is never cast in question form.

/ 9 /

Listen First; Then Speak

Phyllis is thirty-five years old. She has just gone through a divorce after six years of a childless marriage. She lives in a suburban apartment a few miles away from her mother, Greta. Greta is fifty-five years old, a widow who stayed home living by herself after her husband died. She has another daughter, three years younger than Phyllis.

Since the divorce, Greta has carried on a campaign to involve herself more deeply in her daughter's life with constant phone calls, surprise visits, advice, and specific orders to do this or that. It is as if Greta has taken on the task of being the parent of a little child again.

The following conversation took place on the telephone.

GRETA: Hello. Are you home? [opening signal]

PHYLLIS: You call my number, I answer, and you ask if I'm home. [mockery]

GRETA: You said you wouldn't be home today, so I called to see if you weren't home. [defensive]

PHYLLIS: Well, I am home.   [mockery]
GRETA: Why are you home when you   [question/attack]
said you wouldn't be? You're not
feeling well.
PHYLLIS: I'm home because I haven't   [answers question]
left yet. And I feel fine.
GRETA: You don't sound fine.   [superiority]
PHYLLIS: This conversation is ridic-   [incomplete
ulous.   assertion]
                                                 [aggressive]
GRETA: Because I call to see if you   [hearing the implied
are okay, you think I am ridiculous.   "you"]
PHYLLIS: I can't believe we're having   [incomplete
this conversation.   assertion]
GRETA: Are you sure you're okay?   [question]
PHYLLIS: Mom, I'm hanging up on   [threat of
you.   withdrawal]
GRETA: Don't you dare hang up on   [authority]
me!
PHYLLIS: You're driving me crazy!   [attacking
                                                 assertion]
GRETA: Sometimes I think when you   [counterattack/
say one thing and do another you   name-calling]
are a little crazy.
PHYLLIS: I don't have to listen to this! [incomplete
                                                 assertion/with-
                                                 drawal threat]
GRETA: Listen to me! I'm your mother! [authority/demand]
PHYLLIS: Does that make you right all   [question/attack]
the time?
GRETA: I have experience; you don't   [superiority]
know anything. If you'd listen to
me, you'd be someone instead of a
nobody . . . looking for who-knows-
what.
PHYLLIS: Don't bait me today! I don't   [withdraws]
have to listen to you! [hangs up]

Whenever Phyllis hangs up on her mother (and she is doing it more and more), she feels, as she says, "lousy." There is a tremendous letdown followed by an acute emptiness and hunger. The phenomenon is well known: Children may not "legally" be angry with their parents. It is not permitted by our social mores. And parents can always withdraw love. So the anger gets turned against the adult child. And anger against one's self is a recipe for depression.

With your knowledge of the nurturing language, you can probably see several places where Phyllis could have turned off her mother's desperate efforts at control. Of course, Greta's motives are mixed:

She is concerned for her daughter: "I called to see if you are okay . . ."

She is checking up: "I called to see if you weren't home."

She wants her advice taken: "If you would listen to me . . ."

She wants to be the mother: "I'm your mother."

She puts her daughter down: "You should be someone instead of a nobody."

And lastly, Greta is lonely. Since her husband died, she misses family, which was important to her as it has been with millions of older parents. Many do not know how to arrange their friends and their lives to fill the voids left by departed children. As we mentioned earlier, older parents find their contemporaries more solicitous and helpful than their own children. Greta has not discovered that—yet.

Our Warring Passions

It is a curiosity of human psychology that, as with Greta, several contradictory motivations can drive us at the same time. We can both hate and love. We can be attracted and repelled. We want to be helpful and we withhold. We work for money and we work for ideals. And we can carry any combination of these without feeling any violation of our emotional consistency. Few of us are single-minded. When we meet a superfocused, one-track person, we are amazed. Psychotherapists recognize these contradictions in their patients. And they know that their task—in part—is to help patients discover their warring hidden passions and to understand how they motivate mixed-up behavior. Modern psychologists pay great attention to the existence of such simultaneous contradictory motivations. Even the ancients understood this quirk of the human condition. The Greek poet Homer spoke of Achilles being of "two minds" in the sense of being undecided as to whether to go out to defend his honor or to stay in his tent. The Greek phrase acknowledges the human ability of holding two opposing ideas in your head at the same time. The American philosopher Emerson turned the notion into a virtue by saying "a foolish consistency is the hobgoblin of small minds."

Moreover, as with Greta, at one moment one motive sways our behavior and in the next moment the opposite. The nurturing language safely reveals to your parents those hidden and conflicting emotions. By listening, you help your parent sort out his or her feelings. If your parent understands the feelings behind what he or she is doing, then he or she is more likely to choose a behavior that is more helpful and less attacking. Not every time but more often than not.

The nurturing language also encourages your parent to listen to you. That idea is the essence of *listening-to-speak*: *People will hear what you say only if they believe that you hear what they say.*

Recall that if you are angry or hurt you will find it difficult to listen to what your parent is saying. You are more concerned with defending yourself against more pain. You want to get back at your parent. So you attack, and that turns off your parent's ear and brain. Nothing you say is heard. That is the sequence in old toxic language, which is structured for attack and counterattack, not mutual aid.

Similarly, your parents will not listen to you if they are primarily concerned with their needs, their pains. They will not listen if they are buffeted by those contradictory feelings. With listening, you can soothe their pains, help them understand their needs, and reveal to them their warring passions. You prepare them to hear what you are about to say. That is why in our discussion of genuine assertions, we pointed out that first you listen, then you assert. Otherwise, your genuine assertion falls on deaf ears or is heard as an attack.

Let's see how listening-to-speak works with Phyllis and Greta:

GRETA: Hello. Are you home? [opening signal]

PHYLLIS: You call my number, I answer, and you ask if I am home. [mockery]

GRETA: You said you wouldn't be home today, so I called to see if you weren't home. [defensive]

PHYLLIS: You were concerned about me. [nurturing listening]

GRETA: Yes, you said you wouldn't be home. Are you okay? [agreeing]

PHYLLIS: You thought something was wrong so you called. [checking listening] [listening-to-speak]

GRETA: You said you wouldn't be home. [defensive]

PHYLLIS: Well, I'm perfectly okay. You caught me on my way out. That's why I answered the phone. And if I don't get going I'll be late for my date with Janice. [genuine assertion]

GRETA: I thought something was wrong. [weak repetition]

PHYLLIS: Hmmm. [wordless listening]

GRETA: I don't want to hold you up. [agreement]

The nurturing language reveals Greta to be concerned about Phyllis and confused about her concern. Greta was caught in a silly trap of her own making: Having been told that her daughter would not be home, she calls anyway. It's hard to say what she was trying to achieve (was she lonely?) except to check up on her daughter in some way. After initial irritation, Phyllis got back on the track. First, she listened: "You were concerned about me." She avoided answering the questions. She eliminated her counterattacking mockery. And then she delivered a complete genuine assertion after listening-to-speak.

She chose an assertion that dealt with the present situation. She could have also said:

"It's very upsetting to me to be checked on so often with telephone calls, especially when I said I wasn't going to be home. It makes me feel as though what I say is not believed."

That would have dealt with the underlying problem. But if Phyllis were in a hurry to leave, the necessary nurturing conversation would be too long for her to finish in the time she had. It is better to handle the quickies well than to leave them entirely unresolved by getting out of them through some trick.

In either case, Phyllis zeroed in on the behavior that was troubling her rather than criticizing her mother directly. If Phyllis had passed judgment in some way, she would have shut off her mother's attention. As it is, the implied "you" goes a long way toward putting people on the defensive, but somehow they find it easier to deal with indirect criticism rather than with a frontal attack. It is as if their behavior were held at a distance from them so they can look at it dispassionately.

By saying "It's very upsetting to me to be checked on so often with telephone calls," Phyllis was including anybody who upsets her in that way. Her mother can then be free to include herself in that group or not. Indeed, Greta could say, defensively: "I don't call you that often," even though she knows better. Or even: "I'm your mother. I can call you as often as I like." Either way, the issue is out in the open so that it can now be examined by both people.

Frequently, divorced adult children find, as Phyllis did

with Greta, that parents reenter their lives in a grand way immediately after the divorce. Parents have been known to mount strong efforts to get the divorced adult child to move back into the family home, even taking the grandchildren. Money is proffered. Or more money demands are made. Old rules are reestablished: curfew, dress, visitation, dating, sex, and work. The parents put on their old cloaks as when the adult children were young. It's as if the divorce meant the end of a temporary adulthood for the adult child.

It is also not unknown for divorced adult children to go running home to momma and poppa, to the nest where they once felt loved and wanted. And why not in a time of trial? But that brings a different sort of interpersonal problem. The parents may not want their prodigal waif; they may have reestablished a comfortable life and can take their adult children only in limited doses. The parents blow heavy winds of rejection toward the anguished child.

Again, if the adult child can sufficiently detach himself or herself to get into the nurturing groove, the adult child and the parents can arrive at a negotiated settlement over where the divorced adult child is going to live. Or if the adult child returns home, he or she can negotiate the conditions of the return.

In addition to such housing problems, we'll deal at length in subsequent chapters on how to achieve negotiated conclusions for the complex issues of visitation, money, nursing home residence, grandchildren, nutrition, medicine, and the larger family.

Back to the Weapons

In Chapter 5 we discussed how listening deflects verbal weapons. Listening reflects back to your parents their verbal assaults. You invite them to judge the judgments, hear the "shoulds," the superiority, the praise, etc. They examine their own acts, their own words. Most often, that examination tells them: "You're attacking." Faced with that, they back off.

Over a long time, listening will create a new environment that changes parental attack habits. However, even though they may attack less, parents (and others) may not consciously realize they are attacking at all, not even when their attacks are reflected back to them by listening. A genuine assertion does label an attack as an attack. It also dramatically displays the painful results of the attack. For the long run genuine assertions can "teach" your parent what hurts. And as your parent "learns" you come closer together in mutuality of feelings and behavior.

In delivering a genuine assertion, you want to be sure that your parent will hear it. And as we said, the best way to do that is with listening-to-speak. Your parent will hear what you say if he or she believes you hear what they say: listening.

Let's see how it works with fending off the weapon of judgment with a conversation from Chapter 5:

PARENT: Susan is not good for you. If you marry her, you'll regret it. [opening signal/ criticism]

YOU-THE-CHILD: Susan is terrific. We get along very well. [defensiveness/ challenging judgment]

PARENT: You say that now. But after you're married, you'll find out what she's really like. [more judgment/ deeper attack]

YOU-THE-CHILD: Look, I know what I'm doing. I'm twenty-eight years old and I have a right to make up my own mind to do what I want without any advice from you. [more defensiveness]

[threat to cut off communication]

PARENT: Yeah. You never were any good at deciding anything. You couldn't tie your shoelaces unless dad or I showed you how. Look [belittlement/ mockery]

what happened to you and Martha.
You bought her a ring and the next
thing you know she's off with somebody else. Same thing is going to
happen again.

YOU-THE-CHILD: Susan is different.   [defensive/on the
Why are you always putting me   ropes]
down? Why isn't anything I do any
good to you?

You're not a mother—at least not   [counterattack]
mine.

Using listening in its various forms, the adult child can re-
direct the conversation so that it is relatively free of attack:

PARENT: Susan is not good for you.   [opening signal/
If you marry her, you'll regret it.   criticism]

YOU-THE-CHILD: I'll be sorry if I   [checking/reflec-
marry her.   tion]

PARENT: She's too flighty and she   [more specific criti-
doesn't seem serious.   cism]

YOU-THE-CHILD: You think she doesn't   [checking/interpre-
really care for me.   tation]

PARENT: I think she likes you well   [backing down]
enough. But I keep thinking about   [expressing fear]
what Martha did to you [taking the
ring and then taking off]. I don't
want to see you hurt again.

YOU-THE-CHILD: It worries you that   [nurturing: reflect-
Susan will hurt me the way Martha   ing parent's fears]
did.

PARENT: I'm not sure she will. She's   [hidden material]
so young—only twenty. It's hard for
me to see her married so young. Of
course, I was married at nineteen.
But times were different then.

Once is not enough. It takes time for your parent to learn that it is painful to you to have you and your friends judged. Repetition and the patience that goes with it brings the reward of having yourself and your feelings understood and taken into account.

Let's look at what a genuine assertion can achieve. We pick up the dialogue after the parent has revealed her concern that her son may repeat her history; i.e., marrying someone "too young."

YOU-THE-CHILD: You think you might have been too young when you married.   [checking listening]   [listening-to-speak]

PARENT: No. It was all right for me. These days, Susan would be too young.   [weak judgment]

YOU-THE-CHILD: I feel as though I'm being treated as a child when I'm told that the woman I love is not good for me and too young. It's very painful to hear.   [genuine assertion]

PARENT: I'm only telling you for your own good.   [defensive]

YOU-THE-CHILD: You're saying that I am unable to judge for myself what's good for me.   [checking listening]

PARENT: You made a mistake before with Martha.   [repeat judgment]

YOU-THE-CHILD: You feel I can't learn from my mistakes.   [checking listening]

PARENT: I wouldn't say that. Only I worry about it.   [backing down/expresses feelings]

YOU-THE-CHILD: Well, it hurts a lot to be told that my judgment is bad and that the woman I love is no good for me. I feel like a baby when I hear that.   [repeat genuine assertion]

PARENT: I don't mean to make you feel bad.	[hearing assertion]
YOU-THE-CHILD: Hmmm.	[wordless listening]
PARENT: You know I love you. I just don't want you to suffer. I guess you're old enough to make up your own mind.	[defensive] [acknowledging assertion]
YOU-THE-CHILD: Okay. I feel better that my judgment about what I'm doing means something. I don't feel like a child.	[genuine assertion]

Note that listening preceded and followed each genuine assertion. Listening-to-speak allows the assertion to enter your parent's consciousness. Listening afterward allows you to understand if your parent heard and understood the assertion. Listening afterward can fend off an attack because of the implied "you." You will feel a powerful urge to defend (i.e., explain) yourself if you are attacked after a genuine assertion. Listening helps you to avoid the urge.

In the dialogue above, the parent could have just as easily replied as follows to the cry of pain:

YOU-THE-CHILD: Well, it hurts a lot to be told that my judgment is bad and that the woman I love is no good for me. I feel like a baby when I hear that.	[genuine assertion]
PARENT: Well, you *are* a baby when it comes to women. You have no sense at all.	[judgment/attack]

It takes a great chunk of courage *not* to say:

A. "You're just wrong. I know what I'm doing. I don't see you doing any too well on the friends you pick."

And to listen instead:

B. "You have no confidence in my judgment in women."

The A response wins little except the satisfaction that you have put your parent down. That is a short-lived reward because later you feel sour for having attacked your mother or father. The sourness can deepen to depression because you are "not allowed to be angry with your mother." Some adult children have become expert at playing the attacking game: They have turned the weapons around. Their success has the bitter edge of having won an empty victory. They do not have a parent as an equal.

The B response, as we have been saying, cannot lose. It opens up your parent to a repetition of your cry of pain. It avoids attacking. It avoids inviting an attack. It listens.

A Show of Pleasure

We now introduce a new idea: a third type of genuine assertion. The first was a call for help; the second a cry of pain. The third, a *show of pleasure*, suggests that the words you hear or the actions you perceive please you. In the dialogue above, there were three assertions. The first stated a cry of pain. The second repeated the cry in slightly altered form. And the third acknowledged that the adult child felt understood—a show of pleasure.

You-the-Child: Okay. I feel better that my judgment about what I'm doing means something. I don't feel like a child.

This show of pleasure contained all three parts of a genuine assertion. It said to the parent: "This is what makes me feel good." It is not a cry of pain or a call for help, but just as important as the other two. In one respect, it is more useful: It is a clincher. It closes a deal between you and your parent.

Just as the cry of pain lets your parents know that you

have been hurt by their words or deeds, the show of pleasure tells them that you have been made to feel good by their words or behavior. And as people normally do not want to hurt others who say they are being hurt, people do want to make others feel good if they can do so safely. The show of pleasure encourages them to make you feel good.

A show of pleasure has three parts:

The simple statement of what makes you feel good: ". . . my judgment about what I'm doing means something."

The reason why: "I don't feel like a baby."

The emotion: "I feel better . . . "

And no "you."

When you air your pleasure as a genuine assertion, you are saying "Thank you" in a special way. You are saying: "Thank you for understanding." You are saying: "I know I was heard." You are saying: "This is what makes me feel good." And the "you" is implied.

In the old toxic language, we have little opportunity to exchange encouragements as expressed in a show of pleasure. We are quick to complain, but slow to compliment. We hold back on what pleases. We can more easily say what's wrong with somebody's behavior toward us (although it is difficult between adult children and parents).

We have saved the explanation of the third genuine assertion for this chapter because it depends critically on listening-to-speak. The force of emotion behind a cry of pain or a call for help can often penetrate your parent's barriers without listening-to-speak. But the emotions behind feeling good do not so easily slide past your parent's priorities. Listening-to-speak will open your parent's ears to the milder show of pleasure. And when it enters your parent's inner world, it can turn things toward you rather than against you.

A show of pleasure enables you to say something nice to your parent without turning it into praise. A show of pleasure compliments behavior or words, not the person.

It says: "This makes me feel good," rather than: "Hey, you're a great person," which can be viewed as a manipulation. Suppose your aging parent has returned to painting pictures and asks you for your opinion. This is tricky because false praise can be just as damaging as destructive criticism:

PARENT: How do you like my painting of the trees? [question]

YOU-THE-CHILD: You want me to make a critical evaluation of your technique. [checking listening] [listening-to-speak]

PARENT: No. I just want to know how you like it as a painting. [clarification]

YOU-THE-CHILD: I like to see painting like this because I can get some sense of how another person sees the same scene as I. I have a feeling for what the painter was feeling. [show of pleasure]

PARENT: I know I'm no Picasso. But I I think I do get some feeling into it. [agreement]

By picking out something about the painting that makes you feel good, you avoid the trap of praise or judgment, particularly after the listening-to-speak revealed that your parent did not want a technical discussion.

Our Five-Point Program of Nurturing

Listening in any form tends to fend off any parental weapon. But it is not enough to insure a long-term result. You need the entire nurturing language sequence:

1. Listening: to slow the present attack; to present to the attacker the meaning of the attack; to search for the hidden agenda.

2. Listening-to-speak: to open the ear-mind of the other person to a coming genuine assertion.

3. Genuine assertion: to issue a cry of pain; to tell the other person's conscious and unconscious mind that you are hurting.

4. Listening-to-speak: to control the urge to defend yourself against an attack stimulated by the implied "you"; to open the ear-mind of the other person for another genuine assertion.

5. Genuine assertion: to repeat the cry of pain if needed; to issue a show of pleasure to clinch the parent's recognition of the behavior that makes you feel good.

Although variations of the sequence won't do much harm, changing the order will prolong the nurturing session. If you make a genuine assertion without listening-to-speak, you can induce a stronger attack than you would get with listening-to-speak. A stronger attack means more post-assertion listening, more exploring, more searching. The attack could trigger enough anger in you so that you can lose the thread of nurturing entirely, and it takes a long, long time to get back.

We would be concerned about a lesser result. If the sequence is changed, you will not see the quick changes in your parent's behavior that you were looking for. Your effort to change your language will not be rewarded. You may think that the nurturing language is not working and abandon it. We would like to have your efforts bring some success to encourage you to continue. So in that respect adhering to the specific order can be crucial.

Stopping the Question Barrage

Listening can slow the flow of questions from an addict questioner. However, listening alone may not stop future bombardments from the addict. To change the addict's behavior you need the nurturing language's five steps. These help you infiltrate behind the parental defenses to demonstrate to the parent that questions are painful.

Let's return to a previous example:

PARENT: How are you?
YOU-THE-CHILD: Not bad. And you?
PARENT: Fine. Fine. How is Emily?
YOU-THE-CHILD: She's okay.
PARENT: And your job? What's happening at work?
YOU-THE-CHILD: Everything's all right.
PARENT: Where are you going on vacation this year?
YOU-THE-CHILD: I don't know.
PARENT: And how's Emily?
YOU-THE-CHILD: I told you. Emily's fine.
PARENT: I just wanted to know how she was. Are you going out tonight?
YOU-THE-CHILD: Probably.
PARENT: Where are you going?
YOU-THE-CHILD: I don't know.
ETC.

This is, of course, the typical zigzag questioner striving mightily to breach her son's indifference. As the son *answers* each question with the least possible commitment, the parent tries harder with more questions. Now for a complete effort with the nurturing language:

PARENT: How are you?	[opening signal]
YOU-THE-CHILD: Not bad. And you?	[answers/asks question]
PARENT: Fine. Fine. How is Emily?	[question]
YOU-THE-CHILD: She's okay.	[answers]
PARENT: And your job? What's happening at work?	[question]
YOU-THE-CHILD: You have something in mind.	[*Step 1*] [checking listening]
PARENT: No. I just want to know what's going on.	[reveals aimlessness of question]

You-the-Child: You just want to know what's going on.

[*Step 2*]
[listening-to-speak]

Parent: I'm interested in what you do. There's nothing wrong with that.

[defensive]

You-the-Child: It makes me very unhappy to be asked one question after another. I feel I'm being cross-examined and I don't get a chance to talk about anything important.

[*Step 3*]
[genuine assertion]

Parent: I just ask questions because I take an interest in what you do. Besides, I don't know any other way except to ask questions. You won't tell me on your own. You ignore me.

[defensive]

[attacking]

You-the-Child: You feel I should volunteer what I'm doing because otherwise you feel ignored.

[*Step 4*]
[listening-to-speak]
[nurturing listening]

Parent: Yes. I ask the questions and you give me short answers as if you want to get away from me.

[reveals feelings]

You-the-Child: You think I'm not interested in you.

[nurturing listening]

Parent: I think you are. You just don't show it.

[backing off]

You-the-Child: When I feel I'm being cross-examined I really don't feel like talking. When one question follows another, it gives me no time to give good answers or take an interest in what's being said.

[genuine assertion]

Parent: I like the way we're talking. I feel I'm being listened to.

[genuine assertion]

YOU-THE-CHILD: You feel good that   [nurturing listening]
we can talk and that you're being
listened to.

PARENT: Very good!

YOU-THE-CHILD: Yes. I feel very warm   [*Step 5*]
when we talk and really exchange   [show of pleasure]
ideas and feelings without too many   [the clincher]
questions.

The dialogue continued beyond the second genuine assertion because the adult child had to "clinch" the conversation with the statement of pleasure. It is important to continue until you reach the clincher. Listening provides a reward to the parent, but it is not as explicit as the information that you are pleased with the behavior or the help or the feelings your parent has offered to you.

After only one "training" period, the parent will probably cut back on the questions. In fact, parents often pick up the idea of the genuine assertion to reveal their own hurts, needs, and good feelings. In psychology we call that feedback.

You do something. You assert. Your parent asserts back to you. Your behavior changes—you become more nurturing—because of your parent's feedback behavior. The feedback effect—when it occurs—rapidly encourages use of the nurturing language and mutual support and decreases the weaponry.

As an exercise, see how you would handle the following zigzag questioner who darts in and out of intimate areas.

PARENT: How are you and Mildred getting along?

YOU-THE-CHILD: Not bad.

PARENT: And Mildred's leg? Is it healing?

YOU-THE-CHILD: It seems to be getting better.

PARENT: Are you happier in your job?

YOU-THE-CHILD: Oh, yes. Things are fine.

166

PARENT: Did you talk to your father? [The parents are divorced.]

YOU-THE-CHILD: Just last week.

The Most Terrible Word

Now we deal with the most terrible word in the English language: "should." It *should* be banned. Which is about as far as we'll go in using the word. "Should" hurts most of all because it implies that somehow you are incompetent— emotionally, intellectually, or physically. The user suggests he or she knows better and, of course, mother or father "knows best."

Listening-to-speak becomes especially important in holding back the "shoulds" and their cousins, "ought," "must," "have to," etc. Listening-to-speak establishes a firm platform from which to launch your complete assertion that you find unwanted advice painful. Here's a conversation that would be amusing if it did not have such tragic undertones.

Barbara, who is married and has two children, lives four hundred miles away from her parents, Henryk and Lettie. The parents, planning a visit, offered to take Barbara and her family to a basketball game at Barbara's alma mater. The daughter is not a basketball fan, but thinks the outing will be fun for everybody. This is a telephone call:

BARBARA: I got a schedule of the games. There are no tickets to the big game [the one Henryk wants]. I checked the other games. I'll only be in town for a few of them. Maybe we can decide which one you can come up for.   [information]

  [offers choice]

HENRYK: You ought to be able to get tickets through the alumni association. Do you belong to your town association?   ["should"]

BARBARA: I belong to the national.	[answers]
HENRYK: But do you belong to the one in your town? You ought to join it. If you go to the basketball games you might meet someone from the university. They would find you a job. After all, that's why we paid for you to attend a prestigious school. So you can make contacts.	[repeats question/ "should"] [motive]
BARBARA (impatiently): Do you want to go to the game or not?	[counterattack]
HENRYK: You really hurt us when you talk like that. We hardly ever see you. We just aren't communicating. You don't *know* me anymore.	[aggressive]

Henryk's final plaint has all the ingredients of a genuine assertion except that it contains three "yous" and they convert this assertion into aggression. Barbara's counterattack arises from Henryk's attempt to direct his daughter's life one more time. Instead of a counterattack, Barbara could take a different path:

BARBARA: You say I should go to basketball games to get a job.	[checking listening] [listening-to-speak]
HENRYK: High-powered people go there. You could use a push from them.	[repeating]
BARBARA: I get very upset when I'm told how to get a job or run my life. I get the feeling that I don't know what I'm doing.	[genuine assertion]
HENRYK: Everybody can use a little advice.	[defensive]
BARBARA: You think I don't know what to do.	[checking listening]

HENRYK: You're doing all right. I just want you to do better. [backing down]

BARBARA: I don't know what we're going to do about the game. I'm out of town for most of the games and I'd be disappointed if the kids didn't get to go. [allowing choice/ call for help]

HENRYK: Mom and I were going to come up and take the kids even if you couldn't make it. [offer to help]

BARBARA: That would be very nice. They'd like that because they've never been to a game before and I'd feel as though I had spoiled their chance if we canceled. [show of pleasure]

Each time the sequence remains the same with the same five steps: listening, listening-to-speak, complete genuine assertion, listening, another assertion and so on. And Barbara didn't forget her clincher. If the series is repeated over and over on many different days you can change your parents' habits of using weapons and withholding help, affection and even love. The nurturing language is made to order for eliciting love and affection. We would rather hold off on how that works until the next chapter, in which we discuss your feelings about your parents. It is difficult to get love if you do not love. And we'll show you how that works.

How can you remember all this in the heat of a confrontation? The best way is to role-play. If you play it many times with a friendly person, your statements will sound natural (as they eventually will be as you learn to speak the nurturing language fluently). You will not get flustered when your parent speaks. You will be ready for the unforeseen remark. Your anger will be less when your parent attacks after an implied or a spoken "you." Role-playing, simply put, increases your chance of success.

A Reprise

Remember the five steps. We examined listening-to-speak as an essential move before making your genuine assertion. We showed how listening after the genuine assertion cools tempers that may rise on hearing the implied "you." And then came the third kind of genuine assertion: the show of pleasure. In essence, you are praising the behavior, not the person. You are stimulating more of the same "good" behavior because you are rewarding your parent—reaching out to say "Thanks." And you are sealing the implied bargain: "I won't be hurt if you don't do that."

/ 10 /

Loving, Hating, and In-Between

"I hate my father. I don't even want to make the slightest effort to get close to him again. Ever."

"My husband and I talk to his folks about once in three months. They live only a few miles away. We just have nothing in common."

"I love my mother. But I cannot get her to do any of the things she should do for her health. If she doesn't go to a doctor soon . . ."

"I just wish I didn't have to look after my father. He hasn't worked in years. He needs money all the time. He's not a bad person. It's just that he takes up so much of my time and energy. And he's no fun."

"I like my parents. We have dinner or breakfast or lunch about once a month. But we never talk about anything that really matters . . . what we're thinking and feeling."

"My wife just cannot live without talking to her mother once a day either in person or on the phone. Just let one of them feel bad or need help and the other goes running to be there."

We can love our parents. We can hate them. We can harbor feelings between the two extremes. A lifetime of give-and-take has shaped our feelings toward them and theirs toward us. Just as important, our reaction to them and theirs to us is like a ritualistic dance; we move and countermove to some mutually acknowledged inner, silent music composed long ago. In the parent–adult child relationship, feelings and behavior seem fixed as if by strong habit. Indeed, moves to change hurtful behavior or feelings may make us feel uncomfortable, for some of us have grown to look forward to the punishments, and if they are not forthcoming we miss them. An absence of punishment may feel like an absence of attention and, in some twisted way, an absence of love. Each of us has a different story to tell.

Up to this point, the nurturing language has dealt with the outer form of communication: the words, the sentences, listenings, choices, assertions, and the rest. But all that would be meaningless, mechanical, even damaging if the nurturing language did not communicate your true feelings. Your parent would soon interpret your sentences as clever manipulations that he or she did not quite understand.

On the other hand, your parents may know from reading or from having been in psychological treatment or by other means that you are "using" something psychological on them. Your whole effort would be undermined.

Even those who understand the nurturing language sometimes regard it as a manipulation because it is so different from the way most people relate to one another. But a lack of true feeling would destroy most of the effect of your new attempt to reach the inner world of your parent.

The Apostle Paul in his Epistle to the Corinthians expresses a much broader idea:

Though I speak with the tongues of men and of angels, and have not love, I am become as sounding brass, or a tinkling cymbal.

—I Corinthians 13:1

In this verse, Paul uses the word "love" (or, as in the King James version, "charity") to mean a love of mankind in the Christian sense: a divine love. Modern psychology tells us that a similar phenomenon exists in interpersonal relationships. If we do not have a *loving regard* for the other person we become, to them, "as sounding brass, or a tinkling cymbal." We are unheard.

A loving regard. We are not talking of love, per se, though love is not excluded. To us, a loving regard means that we can hate or dislike the other person's behavior or words and still accept him or her as a fellow human being.

Acceptance. A difficult concept, too often misused to mean that we should neither notice nor respond to the other person's hurtful behavior. No. Acceptance means that regardless of the behavior or words, we accept that the other person possesses the capacity to act humanly; we do not abandon that person. We are quite close to Paul's conception of charity, of caring.

To have a loving regard for (and to accept) a person who has hurt us again and again requires courage to face more possible hurt and deep faith that changes are possible. Many of us are willing to face more pain because we feel that we want to rebuild a damaged relationship with an aging parent. We want to recapture a part of the feelings we had for our parents when we were young children. Most of all, we want them to love us as we believe they once did. And perhaps still do, though they cannot express that love.

Up to now we have emphasized the utility of the nurturing language to ward off assault, to soften another's aggressiveness toward you, to elicit the help you need. Now we show another dimension. Only through your speaking the nurturing language and speaking it with a loving regard can you hope to rebuild your damaged or destroyed relationships. Through the language you can examine common problems, negotiate their solutions creatively, and take action to re-establish the trust and love you need and want.

Manipulations and Other Red Herrings

It is loving regard that makes the nurturing language genuine, sincere, and openhanded. Without the acceptance of the other human being, without risking the potential for pain, the nurturing language becomes a tricky device and sounds like it. Oh, your newly found vocabulary will "work," in the sense that you will fend off weapons and will get your parent to reveal more hidden feelings and agenda. But you will probably not get beyond that. You will remain on the level of a parlor game and not reach the heart of the parent-child relationship.

You will indeed be fielding a manipulation: You will be taking unfair advantage of your parent to achieve a goal that is mostly to your benefit. You will be unfair because you will be using elements of the nurturing language, elements that you understand and your parent doesn't; elements of psychological science that you will have appropriated to take advantage of your parent.

That's what we mean when we say that someone is manipulative: That person is employing unfair methods to take advantage of another. The unfairness arises from methods that violate spoken and unspoken rules of human dealing.

Here are some unfair ploys:

Lying is an unfair method because we expect people to tell the truth.

"I have no money left at all. My bills are unpaid and I don't know where to turn."

Unfair, because the person speaking has twenty thousand dollars in a safe-deposit box.

Breaking a confidence is unfair because we ask people to keep our secrets.

"Beverly says her husband is seeing other women. I wonder what she will do."

Unfair, because Beverly told her secret to get some support or advice. Now her problem has expanded to handle gossip or the possibility that her husband may hear about her fears.

Promising one thing and doing another leads us astray because we rely on people's promises.

"You said you'd lend me the car to go shopping. If I can't have it, I'll have a terrible job getting all the stuff together for my party."

Clearly unfair. The person who offered the car is now in the position to extract some extra "payment" that the borrower had not anticipated.

Acting on information that only you have allows you freedom denied the other.

"I didn't know that you were invited to a birthday party for Jeff next Tuesday. Had I known, I'd have made different plans for that night."

Withholding information is always unfair because it leads others to do things they would not have done or not to do things that they would have wanted to do. (Withholding information may also be illegal: If you buy or sell stock because as a director of a corporation you have data that the public doesn't, you can go to jail. Those who bought stock when you sold can sue you for any losses they incurred.)

If you act openly in defying another person's clearly expressed rules, you are forcing the other to defend himself against an act already done.

"We don't give our children candy. They know it. And now you've given them a whole chocolate bar."

The rule-maker—the parent in this case—has his rule challenged by someone he cannot control. His children take his rule less seriously. He is made to feel foolish and ineffectual. This is at the core of the good-guy/bad-guy confrontations in many families. One person is cast in the role of the denier; the other as the giver. The giver always wins because once given, the thing cannot usually be taken away. The denied thing can always be given at some future date.

"We agreed—no movies this week, and you let the kids go."

"Dad is not supposed to eat red meat because of his high blood pressure and you go ahead and cook it."

"I thought we said we were going to keep mom in the nursing home despite her complaints."

All unfair. Each puts the giver at an advantage that the denier does not have.

A particularly underhanded manipulation is to send a third party to do your dirty work or to be a witness to your needs.

"I thought that as long as John was going past your house I'd ask him to stop by and pick up the check."

"Now, Margie, tell us the truth, don't you think Al ought to pay at least half the bill for dad? After all, he's got the money."

When a third person comes on the scene, it prevents you from being a "bad guy," i.e., saying no when you feel you must.

This repertoire of unfair practices is enlarged by the verbal weapons armory. Those weapons provoke guilt, the feeling that you are doing something wrong. They instill inferiority, the feeling that you are no good or incompetent. And, as in the case of a torrent of questions, they block the expression of your thoughts, feelings, and needs.

Just as the nurturing language diverts verbal weaponry, so it can be employed to counter manipulations. Unfortunately, in most cases the manipulations are complete before you can move against them. All that is left to you is to insure that they do not happen again. Therefore, you employ a cry of pain when you are a victim of a manipulation. We are contrasting the old toxic responses with the new, nurturing ones.

Lying:

TOXIC: "You lied to me. You told me you had no money. And now I find out that you have twenty thousand dollars in your safe-deposit box. How could you do that?"

NURTURING: "When I'm told that there's no more money and I find out that there's quite a good deal left, I feel as though I've been taken advantage of. It just frustrates me in dealing with this problem."

Breaking a confidence:

TOXIC: "Damn you. I tell you my secrets and then you go ahead and blab to everybody. I can't face Eugenie. And God knows what Dennis will think."

NURTURING: "I was so embarrassed to find out that what I said about Dennis in secret is now known to Eugenie. I don't know how I can face her."

Broken promises:

TOXIC: "You promised me the car so I could go shopping. And now you've backed out. I can never rely on your word. Your promises mean nothing."

NURTURING: "I'm really in a terrible bind. I was promised the car to go shopping today for my party. And now that I can't have it I don't know how I'm going to get everything done."

Secret information:

TOXIC: "Why didn't you tell me you were invited to Jeff's party? After all the arrangements I made to take you to the country? Now what am I supposed to do? You're so inconsiderate."

NURTURING: "I made all the plans to take you to the country next Tuesday. Now that there's Jeff's party and your invitation, I'm left hanging for the whole day. Had I known, I would have made different plans."

(The "you" is hard to avoid in this situation. But it is given with the sense of information and the least aggressiveness.)

Subversion:

TOXIC: "There you go spoiling the kids and undermining my authority. I'm going to forbid you to visit if you keep giving them candy when I say no."

NURTURING: "When we have agreed not to give the kids candy and then they get candy, it makes me look like a fool or a tyrant. It frustrates me as a parent."

Third-party warriors:

TOXIC: "What a manipulative person you are! You know I wanted to discuss your check with you this week. And then you send John to pick it up. How tricky! I can't believe it. I feel like not giving you any money at all."

NURTURING: "When John arrived at my house to pick up the check I was nonplussed. I didn't know what to tell him because I wasn't ready to make it out for the amount he asked for. It put me in a situation where I couldn't get out. I thought we were going to discuss the check before I had to make it out. What an embarrassment!"

Of course, you can expect counterattacks even with the nurturing response because of the implied "you." No one likes to be caught in a manipulation, much less called on it. Therefore, the cry of pain will be preceded and followed by a good deal of listening. Otherwise, your effort to stop manipulations will go for naught.

All the unfair methods and verbal weapons come with the old toxic language. The nurturing language evokes the opposite responses in the speaker and the hearer: warm, safe feelings. Open communication. Revelation of the underlying agenda. Free choice. Support of your competence and your true feelings.

Why then do some people see the nurturing language as a manipulation? We believe that stems first from its novelty. Newness makes it seem strange, awkward, foreign, all of which confuses nurturing with unfairness.

Secondly, the situation seems unfair: You have a method—the new language—that the other, your parent, does not. Seems unfair. It would be unfair only if you employed the nurturing language to gain some advantage over your parent. What you want is to grow closer to your parent, make him or her feel safe to reveal the inner world and you to be safe with your parent. You want mutuality. The nurturing language opens up those possibilities. In time, with your persistence, you will find your parent beginning to speak the language, and the one-sided character of the exchange will evaporate.

The third reason, to which we have already alluded, is most important of all. People will see your attempt to speak differently as a manipulation if there is false feeling behind it. And there lies the greatest dilemma of learning and speaking the new tongue.

Choosing Your Feelings

The dilemma stems from the need in speaking the nurturing language on the one hand to be genuine (to express real feeling) and on the other hand to avoid aggression. For if your feelings toward your parents are strongly negative—hate, fear, disgust, fury—no matter what your words, you will communicate an attack.

PARENT: You never call me anymore. Why don't you call me?
YOU-THE-CHILD: You want to hear from me more often.

On paper, your response seems like a standard checking listening. The words are there. But if you said them with anger or mockery in your voice, in your facial expression or the stance of your body, you will communicate just the opposite. Rather than encouraging your parent to explore the hidden agenda, you will close down your parent's desire to talk. Try out the above checking listening response and speak out loud, emphasizing each word angrily, and you will understand what we mean. To suppress the anger, however, will make the response sound false.

You are facing what seems like an impossible trap. Express the anger and you sound aggressive; suppress it and you sound false. However, recall that as human beings we are capable of holding simultaneously more than one contradictory feeling. Confronted by a parent who attacks us, we may be not only angry, but curious, impatient, sad, bored. There is no rule or requirement that we must only display the emotion that is strongest. We can, to some extent, choose the emotion we wish to display. We do it all the time with strangers or casual acquaintances.

If, for example, somebody bumps into us walking on the street, we do not necessarily flare with anger, although we may feel angry at what we believe to be carelessness. Instead, we take a pause—a beat—and wait to examine the other person's reaction. Is he apologetic? Will he turn to see if he has done any damage? Will he offer to help? Or will he simply brush by us without a backward glance? Our first response, then, is curiosity. We want to know the meaning of his bump into us before we allow the display of our angry feelings over being bumped. We choose curiosity, momentarily, over anger.

Unfortunately, in situations with people close to us, we fail to pause for the beat. We plunge ahead and explode with anger and other strong emotion. The closer the relationship, the freer we feel to indulge our strongest emotions. That's because we know intuitively that it takes powerful forces to disrupt a close bond—parent/child, wife/husband, lover/

lover, friend/friend. We know "they can take it." We also know they often have to "take it."

But we step cautiously in weak relationships—colleague/colleague, social acquaintances—or where the power lies on the other side—boss/you, bureaucrat/you, customer/you. We understand that these are fragile connections and we do not display strong emotions if we can help it. We fear disruptions and responses we cannot control. Talking back to a boss or a bureaucrat can be a disaster.

Imagine you are a homemaker. Your spouse brings the boss home for dinner. You have a new white linen tablecloth. The boss tips over a glass of red wine. What is your reaction?

Now, again, the same scene. This time your spouse dumps the wine. Your reaction?

Yet, in a real sense, being careful with feelings of those close to us may be more important in our lives than being considerate of strangers. If we nurture those around us they will pay us back with nurturing behavior. And because they belong in our lives more than do strangers, the payoff continues.

You can choose your feelings. Let's see how.

Bringing Your Inside Outside

You have the best chance of getting your parent to hear your nurturing words if you attach positive feelings to them, or at least avoid the negative ones. We are speaking mostly of listening: wordless, checking, or nurturing. When you are issuing assertions, it's okay to express strong emotions to give the assertion validity. But when you are searching, trying to understand what your parent is saying, thinking, or feeling, then strong emotions block transmission.

"But I hate my father. I can't bring myself *not* to be angry or disgusted or wanting to run away. When I face him I just can't be cool."

This from a young woman who one day was served with an

eviction notice from her apartment. In a panic, she called her father at about 10:30 P.M. His reply: "I don't take calls after ten o'clock." And he hung up.

Very harsh. Difficult to overcome one's upwelling feelings under such circumstances. Yet you can learn to choose your feelings even under such duress. It does take some role-playing to achieve the calmness to do it. And it takes an understanding of how to choose. To explain that we have to take a short digression into acting.

Actors Who Really Have Feelings

Actors on a stage do express emotion. A good actor does it so realistically that we believe he actually feels anger, rage, love, sadness, etc. Many do feel those feelings. There is a school of acting, called method acting, that holds that unless the actor harbors those emotions as his own at the time he is acting the performance will ring false. A great deal of effort then goes into the actor's assuming the persona of the character he is playing so that he is the betrayed king, the eager lover, the harsh businessman, etc.

To achieve that result actors frequently create images in their minds, images of themselves as the betrayed king, the eager lover, etc. And then as they say the words, the images guide the emotional tone of the words. They feel "themselves" to be angry, sad, happy. And out come the appropriate emotions.

In an older acting tradition, the actor learned a repertoire of facial expressions and body movements that symbolized the emotion and cued the audience; the back of the hand across the forehead to express dismay, the open mouth for horror, the glancing eyes for suspicion. To the audience it was like reading a book: They had only to be able to read the "vocabulary" of gestures to understand. Today, we find those old acting gestures funny and unreal. We regard them as mechanical.

In the same way, if you try to express emotion by attaching symbolic gestures to the nurturing language, you will seem unreal, perhaps funny. The better way to express the real emotion is to conjure an image in your mind of what emotion you want to choose. In modern psychological terms, you are relying on a hidden thought to choose your feelings.

A Ladder of Images

Going back to the young woman who hates her father (he hung up on her in time of need): We assume for the moment that she wants or needs to have some relationship with him. What positive emotion could she possibly bring out in the face of his hostility? Here it is.

I will listen to you.

That statement expresses the minimal amount of *positive* regard that one human being can have for another. It says that you will hear your parent's words, feelings, and needs regardless of your other feelings about him or her. If you can make that statement to your mind's ear, then when you listen, your listening will appear genuine. The image in your mind's eye can be one of you earnestly listening to your parent. Other emotions may leak out in small doses, but the predominant feeling will be: "I will listen."

In our earlier example, it would go like this:

Person	Inner Statement	Inner Image	Spoken Words
Parent	???	???	Why don't you call?
You-the-Child	I will listen	You listening	You want to hear from me more often.

If you concentrate on the sentence "I will listen to you" and hold the image in your mind, you cannot help but have your checking listening come out genuine. If you cannot say the "I will listen," then it may be that your negative feelings are so great that they simply paralyze you. Again, role-playing will make it possible for you to choose your emotions even on this simple level.

"I will listen" promises nothing to your parent or to yourself beyond listening. It is a gentle knock at the door. It gives you the courage to knock. It expresses a mild emotion on your part even though you despise the person you are talking to.

With role-playing you will find that the choice of emotion becomes almost automatic: You are attacked; you think "I will listen"; your mind's eye sees yourself listening; you give the listening response.

With "I will listen" you are giving very little. You are giving so small a piece of yourself because you are afraid. Your experience tells you that when you give something more of yourself you regret it: You are rejected or attacked or both. But suppose you want to give something a bit more. You do not hate your parent so passionately as our example. Then:

I am *interested* in what you have to say.

Now you make an additional commitment. Not only will you listen; you will be interested. The image: yourself listening with interest. The feeling tone is raised. Even though you may be in an unpleasant situation—your parent is cross-examining you on your love life—you can still muster enough emotional energy to squeeze out "interest" while you are disgusted and distraught with your parent's behavior. You can still be interested in what he or she has to say.

Why will you want to promise more? Why not stick with "I will listen"? If you express more positive emotion, you will more likely be heard. Your listening responses will be more stimulating to produce more hidden thoughts, feelings, and needs. Your assertions that follow will be more seriously attended to. So you want as much positive regard as you can muster. We are providing a way of mobilizing that regard under adverse conditions.

Listening and interest are the first two rungs of a ladder of feelings that increase in power and commitment. You can decide ahead of time the degree of commitment and the inner statement and image you wish to adopt in giving your nurturing language a genuine feeling tone.

The Ladder of Emotion

1. I will listen to you.
2. I am interested in what you have to say.
3. I like you and I am interested in what you have to say.
4. I like you and I want to help you.
5. I care for you and I am interested in what you have to say.
6. I care for you and I want to help you.
7. I love you and I am interested in what you have to say.
8. I love you and I want to help you.

Eight rungs on a ladder of emotion. They are silent signs to yourself to choose one feeling out of many that you may harbor toward your parents. You don't have to say them out loud. They are meant for you. They provide you with an image to choose your feelings. And they are meant to be used mainly with listening.

FATHER-IN-LAW: You have a very nice figure. I can see why my son is attracted to you. In fact, I am, too. [opening signal]
Would you like to have lunch in my office today? [question]
DAUGHTER-IN-LAW: You want me to have lunch with you today. [checking listening] [thinks: I will listen]

The minimal emotional response that the daughter-in-law can bring herself to give is "I will listen to you." She must make sure that she is hearing sexual aggression and not something else. If her father-in-law were a stranger, she would be careful to make the search first. Only when she is sure does she emit her cry of pain. It is accompanied by anger or fear or bewilderment. At that moment, her true feelings about what she has heard can be safely emitted; safely in the sense that she will get her father-in-law to listen and to help her.

MOTHER: Where are you going on vacation this summer?
[opening signal]
[question]

SON: You have some reason for asking.
[checking listening]
[thinks: I am interested in what you have to say]

Vacations bring mother and son into conflict. She wants to go with his family; he is unable to make arrangements to accommodate her. In the past, they have ended with screaming fights. He is feeling anxiety, anger, and combatativeness because she is starting her campaign. Instead, he chooses "I am interested" as his emotional image. It will give him some breathing space in his search for his mother's hidden agenda.

MOTHER: I do like your new living room furniture. You have such good taste.
[judgment]

DAUGHTER: You like my taste.
[checking]
[thinks: I like you and I am interested in what you have to say]

Praise can be a verbal weapon. The daughter starts her search with checking listening. Her image is "I like you and I am interested." Later when the nature of the praise becomes clear she can give vent to other emotions.

FATHER: How are you going to get to [question]
the wedding?
SON: You think you might need a lift. [checking listening]
[thinks: I like you
and I want to help
you]

The son may be annoyed because he believes his father at
a later date is going to ask for transportation. But he wants
to make sure. So he searches. And he keeps his annoyance
in check while he activates a milder emotion, thanks to the
image.

Beyond Merely Liking

The next four rungs of our ladder of feelings allow much
deeper commitments: "I care for you." "I love you." We
make the differentiation because many people have difficulty
even thinking the word "love" when they have had substantial troubles with another person. Outside of the richer
connotation of the word "love" and its somewhat deeper
attachment, the two words "care" and "love" are interchange-
able in the nurturing language. They allow you to approach
your parent warmly.

They are used when your parent needs help and you are
doing a lot of nurturing listening. For example, your parent
has symptoms. He has failed to consult a physician. He resists advice to go. Yet, he complains.

FATHER: I am so tired these days. [opening signal]
And my head hurts so much I can
hardly read.
DAUGHTER: Your head hurts a lot. You [nurturing listen-
must be in agony. ing]
[thinks: I care; I am
interested]

FATHER: Yes. And the doctors don't   [more data]
know anything. They're a waste of
time and money.
DAUGHTER: You don't think a doctor   [checking listening]
can help at all.   [same image]
FATHER: I'd try one if I thought one   [admission]
could.

As long as the daughter remains caring and ready to help, the father will continue to explore his feelings about doctors. Had the daughter minimized the father's symptoms ("Oh, you're always belly-aching; it's probably just a cold in your head") or pushed advice on him ("You must see a doctor; you're just a baby if you don't"), the father would have withdrawn entirely.

If you minimize the feelings of the other person ("Oh, it's nothing") he is made to feel inadequate and foolish. He becomes closed to you and he feels unsafe. If you give advice you are employing the worst word in the toxic language— "should." And you know the consequences of that.

Emotions and Assertions

When you are making your genuine assertion you can let your feelings flow freely. No holding back. Remember, your feelings are what make your assertions genuine. Then you can show your joy, anger, desire, fear, sorrow, or whatever. It's okay to let your parent know what makes you angry when you issue your cry of pain:

"When I'm told that I have to check in every day, even when I'm out of town, it makes me feel as though I were still a kid. And that makes me angry."

You are angry with the requirement, not your parent. Your parent may read the implied "you." But if you consistently separate the behavior you dislike from the person whose behavior it is, the separation will be clear. And you can give full vent to your feelings.

Putting the feeling into a call for help is just as important, as we have mentioned. If the call for help is given matter-of-factly, it will not necessarily be heard. And it is important to remember that a second call for help may have to be accompanied by the escalated emotion you feel at not being helped.

And then your show of pleasure: Just saying that you're pleased or happy that you are understood, heard, or helped does not carry the same influence that it would if accompanied with the strong feeling you have at the moment.

Unfortunately, many people have been hurt when they expressed their real emotions because they used the old toxic language. To make their verbal weapons more telling they have sharpened them with anger, mocking tones, bitterness, irony, or whatever they are feeling. Because emotions do sharpen weapons, they and the reaction to them become more powerful, and the punished person punishes back harder. And if you've been hurt either way, you tend to bottle up your emotions to avoid being hurt again.

In the nurturing language you can let your emotions flow with genuine assertions, and you choose them with listening. With genuine assertions you want to be heard. With listening you want to hear. Powerful emotions attending assertions help the assertion carry through to the other person. Powerful emotions accompanying listening tend to block the other person from speaking or from preparing to hear what you have to say.

In sum, it's okay to feel. It's okay to express those feelings. At the right time.

/ 11 /

Looking for Mother;
Looking for Father

The story of a lost child searching, in adulthood, for its father recurs again and again in Western literature. An early myth tells of Telemachus, a Greek youth seeking his father, Odysseus, who had gone off to fight the Trojan Wars. The tale was taken up by James Joyce in *Ulysses*, a modern story of Stephen Dedalus, an Irish youth, groping toward his spiritual father. And now we have the true-life stories of adopted children who are driven to discover their biological parents.

Having a parent seems, in our culture and in our time, to be central to our psychological lives. Often, no matter how badly a parent has treated a child, the child returns again and again to the parent, seeking—what?—love, support, acknowledgment. It is a common observation that abused children cling desperately to the mother or father who abuses them. The child who has received unstinting loving regard—in our sense—builds an unbreakable bond with the parent.

Linda is now thirty-two years old. She has a sister and a

brother. Their parents, Cindy and Bob, are ranchers in Texas. Linda has gone off to be a fashion designer in New York, her brother is in business in Chicago, and the sister is at the University of California at Berkeley.

"My main desire while growing up was to please my parents," Linda says. "Now I have my own motivations for doing things. My relationship with them is very pleasant. They never nag, never tell me what to do, or tell me that I made a mistake. They never are judgmental. We've never had a cross word.

"I consider them my best friends. I can count on them in a crisis to help me get out of a bad position. When I was in terrible trouble last year, my mother wanted to come to New York, but I did not want her to see me on the bottom.

"I helped my father financially in 1970. He was having nightmares about committing suicide. So I just sent him my paychecks. That kept my brother and sister in school. I felt I bought my father's life back."

How did this come about, this bonding between Linda and her parents, and, as she reports, between her parents and the other two adult children?

"Growing up," Linda says, "we had a lot of freedom to make choices. I had to come home at a given time, but all the other choices—where to go to school, how to do my homework—were left up to me. I was never *told* to do anything. I became self-motivated.

"When I brought home a boyfriend they didn't like, they tried to be polite. They never criticized him.

"My main desire, then, was to please them. I don't know how they did it except that I felt I was on my own but could count on them if I needed help."

To us, Linda's story demonstrates the powerful effects of the nurturing language. Somewhere along the way, Cindy and Bob picked it up, learned it, made it their own. Their rewards in having loving children have been incalculable. It is as if they had long ago read Dr. Thomas Gordon's *Parent*

Effectiveness Training and followed it in spirit and letter. They produced independent loving children.

Each of us in some way seeks this same relationship with our parents. We want them to understand us, to be there, to help us when we need help, to leave us free to make choices, to be affectionate, to support us emotionally, and to accept our help, our love, and our understanding. At the same time, the gulf of years stands between us and our parents. It is a gulf often filled with misunderstanding, withheld help and love, persistent directive advice, attacks and manipulation.

From reading this book, one might conclude that all parents are horrors, using weapons and manipulations to achieve domination over their adult children. Our story of Linda and her parents shows that there are parents who have done a good job. Indeed, we believe that a huge majority would win stars in any competition on parenting. But this book concerns the problems between adult children and their parents. We have emphasized the problem parents.

The Meaning of Relationship

The oldest meaning of "relation" is that of "kin," of "blood relative." The word comes from the Latin, meaning to carry back. In the modern use, we take relationship as a social and psychological connection between people. Unfortunately, it has also been overused as a synonym for "love affair." You often hear young people complaining that "Bonnie is afraid of a relationship." More correctly, Bonnie fears a close connection with its implication for commitment. Relationship, by itself, does not (yet) imply emotional closeness, although in common speech it is coming to mean that.

We have used the word throughout this book to suggest closeness, although we were careful to leave open the degree of closeness. We believe that just as there is a ladder of emotions, there is a ladder of relationship. It is an important concept because while many of us hunger for the kind of connection Linda has with Cindy and Bob, we may not be able to attain it, at least not quickly. We have to settle for something less so we can build up to something better.

"I hate my father. I do not want to make the slightest effort to get close to him again. Ever!"

These words in our last chapter were spoken by a young woman, Carrie, whose father told her in a time of severe trial, "I don't take calls after ten o'clock." Her feelings are now so strong that while she is inviting him to her wedding she refuses to have him walk down the aisle with her. At this writing we do not know if the daughter will relent or if the father will even attend the nuptials.

The gulf between them seems unbridgeable. Furthermore, when Carrie—in her Telemachian searching for a parent— tries to nurture her father, she finds it impossible: "I can't bring myself not to be angry or disgusted or wanting to run away. When I face him, I can't be cool. He's just a bastard."

Using Distance to Get Close

There are thousands like Carrie. They cannot approach their parents because they long so earnestly for the loving relationship they never had. They hunger for parental love, so much so that when a parent rejects their yearning, they often react violently. For us, most importantly, the adult child, face to face with a hateful parent, loses his or her grip on the nurturing language. Confronted with a weapon wielded by a rejecting parent, such an adult child, seeking love from the hated parent, finds it almost impossible not to strike back or to withdraw. Listening is forgotten. Assertions automatically turn into aggressions.

It's much the same when the child, rather than hating, does not *like* the parent. After many years, the parent's repeated behavior—nagging, stinginess, whining, intellectual narrowness, emotional flatness—may have turned the parent into an unlikable person. The adult child no longer seeks the parent's company. "We have nothing in common" is what we often hear. Such adult children also find it difficult to stick with the nurturing language. They, too, strike back. Or more often, they withdraw.

"What will I get out of it?" they ask. "If I make the effort I will get close to a person I really don't like. It's better we keep apart."

Again, there is often a contradiction. The undesirable parent is still a parent. The adult child, in spite of the dislike, still yearns to have a real, likable parent. The clash of feelings leads to extreme discomfort in many adult children. They often hear the voice of conscience—the voice of society—say they "should" be better children. In susceptible individuals the anger toward the unliked parent, turning inward, becomes depression.

We offer a way out of this dilemma. Just as you can—to a degree—choose emotions, so you can select the kind of relationship you want with your parent. By narrowing the choice, you put some emotional distance between yourself and your parent. You close the gap between your longings and reality. If Carrie hates her father and yearns for his love, she cannot bridge the wide opening between her conflicted feelings and the relationship as it exists.

But suppose Carrie chooses a different relationship. She says: "For now, I want only to be able to talk to him without hostility." That choice immediately narrows the gulf between Carrie's desires and the reality. And she puts emotional distance between herself and her father. She can be cool in the face of provocation. She can hold on to the nurturing language. The relationship she has chosen can work for both parent and adult child and form the basis for moving to a closer relationship, one that has more satisfactions.

The Ladder of Relationship

What is the least involving connection you can have with another person and still call it a relationship? We express it this way:

I want only a dialogue.

I want to be able to speak to the other, to hear and to be heard.

I want little or no hostility.

We call this a *minimal relationship*. If you cannot achieve this level of connection, then the feelings are perhaps damaged beyond repair. But if someone like Carrie can express the minimal relationship to herself and choose to seek it, then the nurturing language can help. Emotional distance allows the skill to be acquired and displayed to the parents.

If Carrie adopts this position, she would not call her father when she is in trouble. She avoids rejection. She wants only dialogue, not help, not emotional support, not love. She would not leave herself open or as a target for weaponry. But she will be able to talk to her father. Whatever weapons come her way can easily be turned aside by the nurturing language. She can be cool because he does not withhold from her anything she wants.

To many, such a relationship seems empty and unnecessary. They would not even try to have any connection with a parent if they could not have the love, trust, help, support they expect. Except, except . . . in cases like Carrie's, the need for some connection with a parent is so strong that it will not be denied. Further, by accepting the minimal bond, Carrie can connect with her father, however devoid of the usual love the tie might be.

There is another reason for seeking even such a tenuous tie. If Carrie can handle this, she may be able to build on it to include some of the characteristics of a stronger, more rewarding link. Her nurturing language will be practiced and natural. Once the dialogue of low hostility is open and running, then it is possible to reach the *moderate relationship:*

I want mutual emotional support.

I am willing to give emotional support if needed.

I am willing to accept emotional support if offered.

The moderate relationship includes the elements of the minimal relationship. There is dialogue, hearing and being heard, and low hostility. You now add the desire for emotional support and a willingness to give and to receive it. The connections are more complex and stronger, the rewards greater.

In an emotionally supportive relationship, the weapons are mostly sheathed. There is more listening to the other's hurts and needs. And more nurturing listening than would happen by chance. By providing nurturing listening, the adult child induces it in the parent. There is no mockery, belittlement, or trivialization of feelings.

PARENT: I just got the most terrible news! Anthony [a close cousin] died.   [opening signal]

YOU-THE-CHILD: You must feel awful! You were so close.   [nurturing listening]

PARENT: Yes. He was not young. Seventy-five. But he was so vigorous. And so much fun.   [information/feeling]

YOU-THE-CHILD: You're going to miss him.   [nurturing listening]

PARENT: We all will. You, too, I think. He liked you a lot. You seem struck by the news also. I didn't notice till now. I was so upset.   [nurturing]

YOU-THE-CHILD: It's quite a blow. I considered him my friend. And he was always willing to help. And fun to be with. I will miss him.   [genuine assertion]

PARENT: It does hurt. But when the time comes . . .   [sympathetic]

Notice that when you nurture your parent's feelings, your parent will return the favor. It's not exactly the nurturing language, but the feelings are there and the dialogue is free of recrimination or hostility. In the absence of nurturing, the conversation could easily have gone like this:

PARENT: I just got the most terrible news! Anthony [a close cousin] died.   [opening signal]

YOU-THE-CHILD: Oh, my God! Anthony! I can't believe it. He was so much fun. You don't know what this does to me. I'm going to miss him.   [aggressive/self-centered]

PARENT: If you miss him so much, how come you hardly ever visited him?   [attack]

YOU-THE-CHILD: You don't know how busy I've been. I did call him on the phone.   [defensive]

PARENT: It's not the same thing. I know he wanted to see you, especially when he was in the hospital.   [bearing down]

YOU-THE-CHILD: I don't have the time you have.   [more defense]

Hardly supportive. And not mutually supportive at all. The parental attack arose from the adult child's failure to listen before asserting. Somehow, in making an aggressive and self-centered statement about grief, the adult child touched off the same aggressiveness in the parent.

The goal of the moderate relationship is to provide mutual emotional support *if needed.* So the first step is to search, to find out if the parent needs emotional support. And you accomplish that with nurturing listening. The nurturing listening by itself gives your parent the support he or she is looking for.

The second step is to ask for the support you need. You accomplish that with a genuine assertion, preceded, of course, with listening-to-speak. If you have adequately completed your search and provided the emotional support your parent requires, then you will have also done your listening-to-speak. Notice how it works in the first dialogue above and how the failure occurs in the second.

The next rung of our ladder is called *strong relationship:*

I want a mutual helping relationship.
I am willing to provide help if needed.
I am willing to accept help if offered.

This category includes the previous two: the dialogue and the mutual emotional support. This level of connection is quite complex. To support such a bond requires high commitment on both sides. Because the adult child will be the possessor, at first, of the nurturing language, the burden falls on the adult child to sustain the nurturing communication.

It may seem at first that emotional support may be more difficult to achieve than help, i.e., financial, physical, or other. To some it may seem that we have our categories reversed, that mutual emotional support represents a stronger tie than mutual help. Our experience is that to provide emotional support requires mostly words. But help needs deeper commitment of other resources.

We feel that it's up to the speaker of the nurturing language to decide which represents the stronger link. Our point is that the selection be made, on whatever basis that is comfortable. Once selected, the bond description will serve as a goal for action. And that is the important issue. Select the relationship goal that is achievable; the rest will follow.

In dealing in the strong relationship, the adult child follows the same pattern of communication as in the moderate relationship:

PARENT: Everything is so expensive   [opening signal]
    these days.
YOU-THE-CHILD: You're finding it hard   [checking listening]
    to make ends meet.

PARENT: My Social Security check seems smaller every month. [more information]

YOU-THE-CHILD: You're finding that, with inflation, you need more money. [checking listening]

PARENT: Oh, I don't want to be a burden to anybody. You have your own family to take care of. [feelings coming up]

YOU-THE-CHILD: You feel that if I helped you out I'd deprive my family in some way. [nurturing listening]

PARENT: Actually, I don't need much. Probably twenty dollars a week would not make me feel so pinched. You know I don't go to the movies anymore. [more information]

YOU-THE-CHILD: You think that twenty dollars a week would be enough for you. [checking listening]

PARENT: Yes. But I don't want to deprive your family. [repeat]

YOU-THE-CHILD: I wouldn't find it a deprivation to help out with twenty dollars a week. In fact, it would make me feel easier if I knew my mother was comfortable and didn't have to scrape along. [genuine assertion]

PARENT: That makes me feel very good. I'm glad you can manage it. And I do feel okay taking the money. I didn't know how I was going to ask you. [genuine assertion]

This mother felt unhappy about approaching her son for money. She needed help and did not know how to ask. So she began with a coded message, an opening signal. Had that signal been rejected or ignored, she would have held back her real needs. And the adult child would not have been in a position to offer the help the parent really needed.

Although it seems more common for aging parents to demand help from their adult children, the opposite is more frequent than is realized: parents in difficulty who are afraid to ask their children for help. The nurturing language gives you the tools to find out and to help.

To get help from a parent, you approach in a step-by-step way: an opening signal, listening-to-speak, a call for help, more listening, a repeat call for help if necessary.

YOU-THE-CHILD: We're going upstate this weekend to look for a summer place. [opening signal]

PARENT: Aren't you going back to Lake George? [question]

YOU-THE-CHILD: You liked the lake. [listening-to-speak]

PARENT: Oh, it was great! The children had such a good time. And so did I the week I was there. [reveals opinion]

YOU-THE-CHILD: We like the lake, but we found the cottage too small. That's why we're going there this weekend. We want a bigger place. And we have a terrible problem. Our car is being repaired and we won't be able to have it until Monday. We're stuck. We don't know what to do. [genuine assertion]

PARENT: Why not rent a car? [question]

YOU-THE-CHILD: You know where to rent a car this late in the week? [checking listening]

PARENT: No. I just thought you could. [no solution]

YOU-THE-CHILD: We've tried and everything's reserved. We're afraid that all the good places will be [genuine assertion]

200

rented if we don't get up there this
weekend.

PARENT: I'd lend you my car but I [moving toward
was thinking of driving over to   solution]
Roger's Sunday night.

YOU-THE-CHILD: You have some spec-   [checking listening]
ial reason for going over to Roger's.

PARENT: He's invited me to dinner. I [creative solution]
guess I could take the bus or if you
got home before six o'clock Sunday,
I could still get over there in time.

YOU-THE-CHILD: We could leave Fri-   [genuine assertion/
day night, stay over Saturday and   show of pleasure]
leave Sunday before noon and get
back by six. It would certainly be a
relief to be able to get the summer
organized.

PARENT: The lake is great. I'm glad I [show of pleasure]
could help.

Some people might say: "Why beat around the bush? Why
not come right out and tell your father that you need the
car? Why *manipulate* him into giving you the car?"

First, without a chance to put his creative skills to work,
the parent could easily have weighed his need to drive to
Roger's as more important than lending the automobile. Unless the adult child provides enough factual and emotional
information (via the genuine assertion) about the need for
the car, the parent has no way of knowing that the adult
child's need could take priority over his.

Second, the nurturing language provides that a call for
help offers the potential helper choices about helping and the
way in which the help is offered. Denied a choice, a person
tends to say no before putting his or her creative abilities into
gear. With a choice, the parent figured out a way to offer the
car and still get to Roger's on time.

Third, it is more manipulating to be blunt in the strong relationship because the demand for the car appeals to parental conscience rather than to a weighing of the relative needs. Constant calls to that conscience can only weaken the strong relationship because the parent may think "This relationship is important only in times of need."

Choice cultivates the strong bond because choice cultivates the creativity of both parent and adult child.

The Strongest Tie

Many people crave a relationship with their parents that they have only seen in others. It includes the low-hostility dialogue, the mutual emotional support, and the mutual aid. The strongest relationship of all, it is marked by:

I want a trusting, loving relationship.

I want to feel safe when I reveal my inner needs, thoughts, and feelings.

I want to offer safety for the other's inner needs, thoughts, and feelings.

I want and will give comfort.

It is the kind of bond between Linda and her parents. No secrets. No barred conversation. No effort too great. "I bought back my father's life," Linda said. She did it not out of duty but because she loved and trusted him.

Such relationships do not come into being overnight. It took years for Linda's parents—using their form of the nurturing language—to imbue Linda with the love and trust she felt toward them and to convince her that they, in turn, loved and trusted her.

Can a tattered relationship marked by years of hostility, punch, and counterpunch be rebuilt to the level of the strongest tie? We believe it can, but it will take a long time. The reconstruction passes through each stage before moving to the next. If you can achieve and maintain the low-hostility dialogue for several weeks or months, then slowly you can move to the area of mutual emotional support.

When it is clear that both sides can be mutually supportive, you can move up to the stage of mutual help. And from there to the strongest bond of love and trust. We think that with hard work the entire voyage can be taken in less than a year. All of which is not to say that there are no rewards on the way. Each stage pays off handsomely.

Achieving the low-hostility dialogue means that if you were not talking to your parent, you will now at least have a pleasant relationship. You will be able to talk about things of common interest. You will no longer suffer the pangs of pain inflicted by broadsides of verbal weapons or manipulations.

Achieving mutual emotional support brings you someone to whom you can turn for succor, and someone who turns to you. And mutual help gives you the chance to help an aging parent: with money, with medical help, with housing, with social life. And get help back.

Sick Relationships

In this real world we sometimes come up against a person who operates largely within twisted relationships. Such a parent has been rewarded emotionally again and again by the adult child's angry or defeated responses to manipulations and verbal weapons. The parent, so rewarded, cannot give up the instruments of his pleasure and domination.

James is such a person. He is now sixty-eight years old. A handsome and physically fit man who operates a large trucking business, James dominated his wife and three children for forty years. He barked orders to them as if they were his truck drivers. Witty, he turned his wit to sarcasm against James Jr., his oldest son, who works for him. His daughter, Irene, tried to escape from his sexual teasing into a marriage that was and continues to be difficult for her. And his younger son, Gary, took to the road as a flower child and now lives quietly in a commune in Oregon. Father and son have not spoken in years.

Now James is widowed. He has tightened his grip on James Jr. and frequently visits Irene, stirring trouble in troubled waters. For forty years James has tasted the sweetness of absolute control. He loves to make James Jr. cower before him. He seeks now in Irene a replacement for his lost wife, a wife who played servant to him.

Neither Irene nor James Jr. seems to be able to make a move; to "stand up" to him. In fact, Irene—when she is honest with herself—welcomes her father's troublemaking because it gives her a weapon against her husband. And James Jr., so long under his father's thumb, feels acutely uncomfortable when James Sr. is away. He is confused about what to do. He wants his father to take over. For Irene and James Jr., then, there are rewards as well as pain from their father's controlling tactics.

However, it is not all emotional profit for James Sr. The more he dominates his older son, the worse he feels that he does not have a "real man" for a son. His other employees see the father making a flabby puppet out of the son and they smirk. James Sr. knows that they laugh at him for that, and it hurts him to be demeaned by his employees.

With Irene, he sees a reflection of his own marriage in hers. But she puts up a fight against her husband as James Sr.'s wife never did. And observing Irene he realizes how one-sided his marriage was. That's why he visits her so often now. He wants to fix things up. But he is too controlling and interfering and he knows he makes matters worse.

And finally he has lost Gary completely.

Such relationships can only be characterized as "sick."

They are sick because the parties are both punished and rewarded by their own acts and the acts of the others. James Sr. behaves emotionally like an alcoholic toward alcohol. He hates himself when he controls his children; but the rewards of control are so great that he cannot avoid an opportunity to exercise control.

James Jr. bears the cross of his father's domination. At every turn he is thwarted. He does not know how to deal with women because he has taken his father as a model and cannot succeed in mimicking his father's manipulations. Yet, he is at a loss when his father does not intervene. It is as if he is always looking over his shoulder expecting the barked command.

Irene in her way feels both pain and enjoyment in her father's interventions. She would like to give up the pain but does not want to give up the pleasure.

All three are living in a world of their making in which they want and do not want the bond. They are damned if they do and damned if they don't. The harder they struggle, the tighter they are caught by the web of their unconscious design.

Such relationships between adult children and their parents are far more common than we imagine. Incidentally, there are many such relationships in which the adult child rather than the parent is the key dominating agent. In such situations, the adult child has turned the power structure around. But the bonds are no less sick.

Nor do sick relationships owe their existence only to a domineering, controlling parent or adult child. In fact, the star player can be of an opposite cast: someone who acts completely dependent.

Theresa has arthritis of the hip and knees. The disease has frozen her joints so that for ten years she had been hobbling around with a walker; now she is in a wheelchair. She is close to seventy and lives with her daughter, Jill, and Jill's husband, Andy. Both Jill and Andy work; their children are grown and on their own.

For three months, Theresa was in a nursing home where Jill and Andy hoped she would get some rehabilitation treatment and also have some company during the day. But they have brought her back to their house because Theresa could not "adjust." Theresa wept constantly, refused to do her physical therapy exercises, stopped eating, and would not socialize with the other people.

"They are old and sick," she would say. "I have nothing to say to them."

For their part, Jill and Andy tried to help Theresa adjust; or they thought they were helping. They visited her every day so she would not be lonely. The cajoled the staff into giving Theresa special care. They would harangue Theresa about her eating, her physical therapy, and her refusal to socialize.

Why is this relationship sick? Jill and Andy believed they were acting like "good children." The adult children felt guilty—i.e., that they had done something wrong—about giving their mother up to a nursing home. Yet they also knew that Theresa would get care there that they could not give. Torn between between guilt and reason, they feed Theresa's dependency so that eventually the nursing home fails. The failure both rewards and punishes them: rewards them by assuaging their guilt over having put Theresa there in the first place; punishes them because they know the nursing home is better than at home.

The relationship also rewards and punishes Theresa. She knows that because Jill and Andy both work, her being at home places a great strain on them. During the day, they have to get a nurse for her. But they cannot leave her alone at night. And their weekends are tied up, too. When they should be enjoying the fruits of a life together, they are trapped by an invalid mother.

Theresa knows that, but she also is afraid of dying away from her family. She prefers—she thinks—their company to that of her peers. She also feels rejected by them but knows also that the nursing home could do her some good. So she simply goes limp, emotionally, foisting greater dependency on Jill and Andy. And the nursing home failure punishes and rewards her in the same way it does the adult children.

Sick relationships are also created by individuals who consistently reject their adult children or their parents. By rejection, we mean that at every opportunity they deny the adult child or the parent access to their love, affection, help, support, or even presence. Because we have been brought up to expect acceptance from parents and children, we never quite believe we have been rejected. We try again and again by every means to win our parent's or children's love, help, and support. You can easily see how this bond by rejection deteriorates into sickness.

Adult children trapped in this relationship seem especially poignant because it is true that some parents have never learned to love their children: No matter how hard the adult child tries, he or she can never succeed in winning that love by simply doing what the parent wants.

Seduction, physical or emotional, also breeds sick relationships. By seduction we mean unremitting parental offers of caressing, affection, or love as a reward for doing what the parent wants. The adult child who learns to expect to be loved or caressed for being "good" loses his or her ability to separate from the parent's needs. If such an adult child fails to meet the parent's needs the adult child feels extreme punishment. Constant seduction by the parent of the opposite sex impairs an adult child's emotional or sexual ties with persons of the opposite sex.

Sometimes parents have distorted views of reality. And they pass all their thoughts, needs, and feelings through that distortion. It governs what they hear you say. For example, a parent may feel on the verge of starvation but have a substantial savings account. We have all heard in the extreme cases of old people dying alone in a hovel with tens of thousands of dollars in a mattress. They may also twist their perceptions of their health, their sexuality, their grandchildren, their friends, the place where they live, of your acts and of you.

Parents who suffer from distortion of reality also build

sick relationships. Their adult children, often unaware of the thought-warp, feed the parent materials that reinforce the twisted thoughts.

The parent in the following dialogue has ten thousand dollars in savings.

YOU-THE-CHILD: We looked for you at the church social last night.   [opening signal]

PARENT: I didn't have the bus fare.   [distortion: parent did not want to spend]

YOU-THE-CHILD: Why didn't you call me? I would have picked you up.   [question]

PARENT: I hate to run up phone bills.

YOU-THE-CHILD: You should have borrowed some money from Alice.   ["should"]

PARENT: I don't like to borrow money from Alice because then she asks me for money.   [more distortion: Alice hardly ever borrows]

YOU-THE-CHILD: What happened to your Social Security check?   [question]

PARENT: Everything is so expensive. It just disappears before I know it. I just never have enough money. Other parents get help from their children.   [guilt induction]

YOU-THE-CHILD: But I already give you fifty dollars a week.   [defensive]

PARENT: If you think it's enough, then it's enough.   [more guilt]

And the sick relationship continues. If the adult child recognizes the reality-warp, then the nurturing language can reveal the distorted perceptions to the parent and you can step toward freeing yourself from the unhealthy bonds.

Getting Out of the Trap

First you have to know you are in a sick relationship to get out of one. Here is a checklist to figure out if the tie that binds is sick:

1. I let my parent have his or her way even though I know it's wrong. —Yes —No
2. Whenever I do something my parent disapproves, I feel very guilty. —Yes —No
3. No matter what I do I cannot get my parent to see what my problems are. —Yes —No
4. I try to anticipate every need that my parent might have. —Yes —No
5. I'm always fighting with my parent, but I know we love each other. —Yes —No
6. I wish that my parent would think about me sometimes instead of him-(her)self. —Yes —No
7. I know that if I do what my parent wants, he(she) will be very good to me. —Yes —No
8. I know that my parent orders me around, but it's really for my own good. —Yes —No

If you answered yes to as few as two of the above statements, it is likely that the relationship between you and your parent may be a snare for you both. If you answered yes to even one of the above, you may want to think very carefully about how you and your parent relate to each other and if indeed you are free of the reward/punish conflict of a sick bond.

The nurturing language is highly effective in releasing the

prisoners of a sick relationship. By blunting the use of weapons and manipulations on both sides, our new language removes the rewards for those parents who rely on weapons and manipulations to control their adult children. Through listening-to-speak and genuine assertions, the adult child—safe from retaliation—establishes his or her own needs, thoughts, and feelings. Domination is weakened.

Searching through listening discovers distortions that the parent may hold about money, health, housing, fears, etc. When listening reveals the thought-warps, the adult child can avoid feeding into them.

Let us see how the nurturing language helps both parent and adult child discover twisted ideas. The dialogue below starts out the same as in our previous visit with this mother and her son. The parent has ten thousand dollars in a savings account.

YOU-THE-CHILD: We looked for you at the church social last night. [opening signal]

PARENT: I didn't have the bus fare. [distortion: parent did not want to spend]

YOU-THE-CHILD: Why didn't you call me? I would have picked you up. [question]

PARENT: I hate to run up phone bills.

YOU-THE-CHILD: You're saying you're so strapped for money that you're afraid to make a phone call. [checking listening]

PARENT: My phone bills are much too big. Last month, I spent ten dollars on the phone. When your father was alive it never went above five dollars. [defensive]

YOU-THE-CHILD: You feel you don't want to pay any more for the phone than you did twenty years ago. [checking listening]

PARENT: Oh, I know things have gone up. I just see money running through my fingers. Soon I won't have any left. [seeing distortion]

YOU-THE-CHILD: You feel you're spending too much and soon your savings will be gone and you're scared nobody will take care of you. [nurturing listening]

PARENT: No. I'm not worried about that. I know you will. You already are. The money's going too fast. [sees distortion]

YOU-THE-CHILD: It's going too fast. [checking listening]

PARENT: Five years ago, I had twelve thousand dollars in the bank. Now it's down to ten thousand dollars. [reveals hidden fact]

YOU-THE-CHILD: So you're worried that in fifteen years you'll have nothing left. [checking listening] [listening-to-speak]

PARENT: It does seem silly, doesn't it? [full understanding]

YOU-THE-CHILD: I can understand how you'd be worried about money. Almost everybody is. And when you're dependent on pension income it's scary. [nurturing listening]

PARENT: I guess I shouldn't scrimp. A few bus fares won't bankrupt me. [creative solution]

It takes a good deal of patience not to break in and say: "You damn fool! A dime phone call won't make you starve!" Only by working through the distortions by herself could this parent come to realize how twisted her thoughts were.

In the same way, the adult child can offer the parent help without creating dependency in the parent. The nurturing language does not foster dependency because before help is offered listening uncovers true need and allows the parent first to solve his or her own problem.

Because praise is tantamount to judgment, the adult child can be wary of seduction. Effusive use of honeyed words and caresses can be examined with the parent.

A sick relationship requires constant application of the nurturing language. The adult child also has to see that the relationship is sick; that although it is punishing there are rewards in it as well. Therefore, it requires a conscious effort to trade the sick rewards for healthy ones: rewards that do not carry a freight of punishment.

In a sense, giving up a sick relationship is like losing weight or giving up cigarette smoking or alcohol. You know the sick bond is no good for you, but you are getting sufficient reward out of it to make the sick relationship a habit.

/ 12 /

Getting Along Great Even
with Real Problems: I

We now show—very pointedly—how the nurturing language can help you and your parent erase some of the thorny dilemmas of living.

There can be no general formula because the exact way out of each person's difficulty depends on the people involved and the history they have created together. Instead, here are case studies to illustrate the principles of how to apply the nurturing language in real-life situations.

Some will parallel your situation. Others will be totally alien to you. But by following the accounts you may acquire more insight into how the nurturing language works and then apply it in your own life with your parent. Even when you cannot solve your problem completely, the nurturing language will strengthen the bond with your parent because you will have approached the mutual trouble with dignity and concern.

As we grow older, we face and experience the inexorable ravages of time. We mentioned this in Chapter 2, where we discussed what your parents might really have on their minds. They do carry the statistics in their heads: They know older people get sick more often, have more surgery, have more mental problems, more money worries and troubles, housing difficulties, and, of course, more bitter exchanges with their adult children. And they feel they are losing their lifelong control over their family. Each statistic generates its peculiar breed of problem.

Parents often turn to their adult children for money, comfort, transportation, company, advice. Sometimes they need the help and won't ask for it for a variety of reasons, none easy to understand, no matter how well we think we know our parents and what they think. So we have a second task: to search out our parents' true needs. We do want to give that help, but we must give it carefully, lovingly, else we end up hurting, not helping.

The Perils of Advice

Advice is seldom welcome; and those who want it most always like it least.

—Earl of Chesterfield

Chesterfield was not the only clever fellow to note the futility of advice. In the first century B.C. we have:

Many receive advice, few profit by it.

—Publius Syrus

Seventeen hundred years later:

We may give advice, but we do not inspire conduct.

—La Rochefoucauld

These intelligent men, however, expressed only one aspect of the taint of advice. The nurturing language tells us why people do not take advice, no matter how "good": It is full of "shoulds," "oughts," and their ilk.

"You should really see a doctor about that cough."

"I would put my money into city bonds."

"You ought to see your daughter more often."

We know now that "should" undermines the person to whom it is directed. Rather than be undermined, the target of the "should"-laden advice rejects it. The giver of the advice feels the rejection personally: Has he not acted from the highest motives? He sees the other person as acting stupidly, and soon the advice turns to recrimination. And that sows discord into the relationship.

Carl Rogers discovered another unhappy side effect of advice: It creates dependency, especially when the advice is "good" and is taken. He tells the story of a counselor whose client would not make peace with his mother-in-law. By a subterfuge, the counselor tricked the young man into writing a conciliatory letter to his mother-in-law. The woman responded helpfully. And the young man, amazed, patched up his differences with her.

But afterward, the counselor found the young man on her doorstep for every little problem he faced. He had become dependent on the counselor. Dr. Rogers tells this story to reinforce his idea that the role of a counselor is to provide a psychological environment in which the client solves his or her own problem. The nurturing language has the same goal: to support parental independence and creativity in solving individual or mutual problems.

Dependency sucks the marrow out of a relationship because it destroys equality. The giver is one-up on the taker, who "ought" to feel grateful. Dependency dries up creativity in problem-solving. In the dependent person, dependency fosters the use of "tricks" to deepen the dependency: forgetfulness, helplessness, carelessness, loss of things, and increased sensitivity to pain and to insult.

Advice alone does not bring about dependency. Unasked-for help stimulates dependent behavior. Help too quickly given also provides opportunity for dependency. Too generous help acts the same way. A powerful, dogmatic person can attract dependent persons.

If you find your parent plaguing you with endless questions because he or she "doesn't remember," that is a clue to a dependent relationship. "I can't remember" is the hallmark of a dependent person. People fail to remember important items when they know that somebody will do their remembering for them; they cultivate forgetfulness. It gives them a chance to test you to see if they can "depend" on you.

Helplessness increases as you try to help. Parents often incapacitate their children by overwhelming them with help. You can see "help" do its dirty work on disabled children. A palsied child who cannot eat with knife and fork miraculously learns to do so when taken away from the "helpful" parents.

Adult children often turn the relationship around, becoming the smothering parent to the parent. If a parent comes to understand that help will come from you, they try less to solve problems on their own. They become like children. Indeed, one often sees adult children treating their old parents as children. The adult children who parent their parents often adopt the same attitudes that their parents had toward them. The adult children address them in that high-pitched sing-song tone reserved for very small boys and girls. The adult children talk to strangers in the presence of their parents as if the parents were not there. They use the third person pronouns, "she" and "he," as if the parent cannot understand what is going on. "He doesn't like cereal." "She will take her medicine if you put it in a small spoon." They make decisions about what the old person will wear or eat without consulting the parent. Such adult children have made dependent children out of their parents.

Carelessness and accidents often increase among dependent parents. It is as if the parent thought: "Nothing can happen to me. My son (daughter) will take care of everything." Such people tend to lose things, apparently believing that if they do not keep track of things, somebody else (you) will replace the lost items.

Finally, they suffer increased sensitivity to pain and insult. The dependent parent attempts to attract the adult child's help by issuing fake cries of pain. The adult child has, then, a whiny parent, constantly complaining about everything. If the nongenuine cries consistently bring the adult child running, the parent, in time, no longer distinguishes between real and imagined pain. To the parent, the cry is no longer fake. And that makes the adult child respond to it even more readily because it sounds real. As the adult child struggles to get out of the dependency trap by being a "good child," the trap tightens.

Parents in old-age or nursing homes report insults and mishandling by the staff and by other residents. While some are based on truth, others are exaggerated to attract the adult child's attention. And when the adult child responds, the parent learns to search out insults to report. Further, the parent abandons all attempts to handle the problem and waits dutifully for the child to take it up with the administration.

How to Lose Your Parent's Love

Modern psychological research has revealed that the more you do for a person to gain that person's love the less love you gain. That finding conforms to common sense: We have all known young men who shower gifts on a beloved only to have the object of their adoration reject the love (and keep the gifts). Wives who adore their husbands and will do anything for them find a failing of love from the spouse. They even submerge their own personalities to hold their husbands' love. How many devoted wives have found their husbands unfaithful with another woman "who doesn't do half as much for him as I did and do"?

When we create dependency in our parents, we are "doing"

for them to keep the love we think we have or to win the love we never had. In essence, by giving unasked-for advice, by being too quick to help, or by overhelping, we risk losing what love our parents have for us.

There are adult children whose parents were and are incapable of love. Such children, desperate even as adults to win that love, will shower their parents with gifts and services in the futile effort to extract that love. To no avail, they are trying to bring a garden from a stone. All their efforts have just the opposite effect.

Research shows that if we do things for people because we like to, we can gain and keep the love of those who benefit. The difference is subtle. If a man takes pride in his wife's beauty because he enjoys beauty, he can hold his wife's love. If he takes pride in his wife's beauty because her good looks are an adornment to his status, he may lose her love. Another example: If we give our parents money to gain their love, we can lose that love. If we give our parents money because we like to see them well cared for, we can win their love. The problem lies in making the distinction clear to our parents.

You can do that with the nurturing language. Only through searching (listening) will you be able to grasp what a gift of money (or anything else) means to a parent. Only through a genuine assertion can you make clear to your parents why you are giving the money. And the assertion has to be sincere. It has to say, unambiguously, why you are giving the money.

If you avoid the dependency trap through the nurturing language you gain in two ways: avoiding the dependency and keeping or gaining your parents' love.

Avoiding the Dependency Trap

It is easy to see how the nurturing language avoids the dependency trap. Searching establishes the true needs of the parent. As parents are led by listening to consider and reveal their true needs, the adult child can then measure accurately the help to be delivered. The adult child escapes the pitfall of being overly helpful.

Listening-to-speak allows the parent to put his or her own creativity in gear, gives the parent a chance to solve the problem without help. The adult child's genuine assertions establish to the parent how much help the adult child can comfortably give. The parent, then, has a chance to weigh his or her needs against the adult child's ability to meet them. The language as a whole gives the parent a choice of the kind of help that is wanted. And when there is choice, the parent tends to solve his or her own problems.

"But I want to help my parents. They helped me as a child and I should return what they gave me. I don't want them to beg me for help."

True enough; provided the help is what the parent really needs, not what the parent first *says* is needed, not what the adult child *thinks* is needed. Two adults are negotiating. And in a true negotiation neither party begs. There is equality. Otherwise, the adult child can turn the parent into an emotional cripple as surely as a smothering mother converts a disabled child into a helpless one.

The nurturing language uses three axioms about advice and help:

Don't give advice; don't take it. The danger of advice works in both directions: Taking your parent's advice can create dependency on the parent with all the same burdens on you and on the parent. Oscar Wilde remarked that to take any advice was dangerous and to take good advice could be fatal. Taking advice means relying on others to do your thinking for you. Better to use another as a sounding board, or as a resource to bring up issues that you may overlook, but the final thinking through can only be yours. By now you can see how the nurturing language allows you to ward off the "should"-laden advice and to depend on your own problem-solving creativity.

Don't offer to help; help only if asked, and then only after checking for the true needs. Remember the possibility of dependency. Remember, too, that your parents' unasked-for, overly generous help can have the same effects on you as your help can have on them.

Give your parent a choice of the kind of help he or she wants. We have said enough about choice to suggest that by offering choice you have the best chance of getting your parent to help himself or herself. And both of you escape dependency.

If Your Mom or Dad Is Sick

When a young person is ill, we have high confidence for recovery except in the gravest disease. When sickness strikes an older person, the potential for disaster runs high. One has only to glance at the mortality and sickness statistics to observe the truth. To anyone over fifty, illness represents the first knock at the door of eternity. And for a parent of advancing age, the symbol—sickness—stands out vividly as foreshadowing things to come.

It would be well to keep this older person's view of disease and symptoms in mind. It colors that person's attitudes and behavior toward his or her own health and the health of close relatives or friends. You may, for instance, hear what sound like exaggerations of minor aches. Or in the face of serious debility, the parent may issue a complete denial that anything at all is wrong.

In dealing with your parent's health, the major principle is:

Nurture rather than minimize.

Confronted with a complaining parent, we tend to say:

"Don't worry, you'll be out of the hospital in a week. You're strong as a bull."

"It's only a cold. Why are you getting so upset?"

"You've had arthritis for thirty years. And you're always bitching. By now you should know it won't go away. Be a little brave."

In effect, the adult child is hurling verbal weapons at the

parent. Instead of comforting the parent, the child makes the the parent feel foolish, mean-minded, and selfish. The parent begins to doubt the reality of his own feelings. And rather than deal realistically with the health issues, the parent exaggerates or denies.

It is easy to nurture sick people and make them feel better without cracking jokes or using false cheeriness. Listen to this telephone conversation:

YOU-THE-CHILD: I just heard about your operation. [opening signal]

PARENT: Yes.

YOU-THE-CHILD: Guess you're not having an easy time. [nurturing]

PARENT: I hate hospitals. [expresses feelings]

YOU-THE-CHILD: I remember when you "escaped" from the hospital after you had your appendix out. [nurturing listening] [reflecting thoughts]

PARENT: Yeah. It's not so easy to escape from this time. [understanding]

YOU-THE-CHILD: This time it's more difficult. [checking listening]

PARENT: Yes. I'm in a lot of pain. [reveals reason]

YOU-THE-CHILD: I'm sorry to hear that. [sympathy]

PARENT: Well, the painkillers are starting to work a little and they say I'll be all healed in a month. [understanding]

Let us look now at a deceptively simple problem: taking medicine. A person over sixty-five is likely to be taking—on average—six different pills several times a day. Typical ones include drugs for arthritis, heart pain, high blood pressure, diabetes, gout, kidney or urinary infection, and one or more of a host of tranquilizers. The medicines available today are extraordinarily powerful. They do relieve symptoms. They do prevent recurrences of disease, and in some instances—high blood pressure, for example—prolong life.

Yet medical studies show that up to 50 percent of persons do not take the medicine as the doctor prescribed. In some instances, the drugs are life-saving. It is an astonishing discovery that so many ignore the doctor's advice. Ah! There it is: advice. Even a doctor's prescription has its built-in "should." So powerful is our reaction to "should" that we even reject life-saving medicine to avoid being undermined. Too simple? We have yet to find a better explanation.

In a seminar among medical students, we role-played a male patient for a young doctor who prescribed a high-blood-pressure drug. Although the young doctor spoke with a kind voice, she rode roughshod over the "patient's" fears, ignorance, and insecurity.

PATIENT: I hear these drugs make you impotent.
DOCTOR: Don't worry about it. It sometimes happens, but it's rare. Believe me, it won't happen to you.
PATIENT: But I heard that . . .
DOCTOR: If it happens, we can fix it.

The doctor was minimizing, not nurturing. Rather than be reassuring, the dialogue raised the "patient's" apprehensions. We then reversed the role-playing with the doctor as "patient."

PATIENT: I hear these drugs make you impotent.	[opening signal: fear]
DOCTOR: You're concerned that the medicine will make you unable to have sex.	[nurturing listening]
PATIENT: Yes. I heard that it's a side effect. I don't want to lose my sex.	[expressing more fear]
DOCTOR: Sex is very important to you.	[nurturing listening]
PATIENT: You bet. My wife is worried enough about my high blood pressure and I don't want to give her a husband who is a cripple.	[more hidden material]

DOCTOR: You would feel better if we could do something about the side effects.   [nurturing listening]

PATIENT: Can you really do that?   [question]

DOCTOR: You think that the side effects cannot be controlled.   [checking listening]

PATIENT: I didn't know that they could. I thought the drug was the drug and you couldn't change it.   [information]

DOCTOR: When we give these drugs we are very concerned about the side effects. So we watch the patient's blood and his mental state—and that includes sex—very carefully. If we see anything changing, we decrease the dose and that usually takes care of things. If not, we switch to another drug. Believe me, we worry about these things and we don't want them to happen.   [genuine assertion]

PATIENT: I didn't know you did it that way. I'm really glad to hear it. Takes a load off my mind.

Sure, it does take longer to nurture. But the result is more assured. At the end of the seminar, the young doctors began to realize that there was more to prescribing than writing a few words on a piece of paper and patting the patient on the back. Many doctors take the attitude:

"I'm the doctor. I went to school for years to know what I know. The patient *should* follow my instructions. It's not my responsibility to make up for the patient's stubbornness or stupidity."

Well, many doctors are now learning that it *is* their responsibility to nurture (in our sense) their "stubborn and stupid" patients. If the doctors don't nurture, the patients don't take the medicine and all that schooling of the doctor goes for naught. Medicine not taken does no good.

Adult children with aging ill parents can sympathize with the doctor's dilemma: how to get the patient to take the medicine as prescribed and not alienate the patient. How many acrid arguments have broken out over the parent's refusal to take the medicine? If your parent is not taking prescribed medicine, you may want to play the role of nurturing physician. Let's see how it works. First, the old way:

PARENT: My knee really hurts today. I can hardly walk on it. [opening signal]

YOU-THE-CHILD: Have you taken your medicine? [question]

PARENT: It doesn't do any good. And it constipates me. [defensive]

YOU-THE-CHILD: Well, if Dr. Harris gave you the medicine he must know what he's doing. You didn't go to medical school. [attack]

PARENT: He's really not a very good doctor, you know. I know you like him, but I don't think he knows very much. [counterattack]

YOU-THE-CHILD: Well, if you think that, you'll just have to put up with your knee. [mockery]

As we put the dialogue on paper, anybody familiar with the nurturing language knows what went wrong here. Instead, the dialogue might go as follows:

PARENT: My knee really hurts today. I can hardly walk on it. [opening signal]

YOU-THE-CHILD: It does look swollen. It must hurt a lot. [nurturing listening]

PARENT: The medicine Dr. Harris gave doesn't seem to work. [more information]

YOU-THE-CHILD: You take the pills and the pain and swelling don't go away. [checking listening]

PARENT: Well, I've been skipping a few days because the medicine makes me constipated. I guess if I took the pills the swelling would go down. [more information]

YOU-THE-CHILD: But you still have the constipation. [checking listening]

PARENT: Oh, I can take care of that with doubling my bran ration in the morning. [creative solution]

YOU-THE-CHILD: That sounds like a good idea. I don't like to see you suffer. [show of pleasure]

At no time does the adult child tell the parent what to do. The adult child provides an opportunity for the parent to explore feelings and ideas so the parent can arrive at his or her own creative solution. By the way, it does no good to check up on the parent to find out if the medicine is being taken. Better to nurture and have the parent motivated from within. Then you don't have to check up. The parent will *want* to take the medicine.

Seeing a Doctor

Although older people make more doctor visits than any other age group, you may sometimes be faced with a parent who, despite clear and perhaps serious symptoms, refuses to see a doctor. Cajolery, threats, and mockery fail; or if they do succeed they open the door to dependency.

The refusal to be doctored can originate in the fear of finding out terribly bad news: "If I have cancer, it's the end and

I don't want to know it." Or because sickness stands as a symbol for aging, being sick means a loss of youth, which for some people is hard to take. Or the refusal harks back to a previous bad experience: a painful operation, an unfeeling physician, or an expense too large to bear.

Although all people over sixty-five now have extensive government medical insurance—Medicare for those who can pay, Medicaid for those who cannot—being ill means putting out scarce funds. Under Medicare, the insured person can pay out 20 percent or more of the total medical bill. Under Medicaid, although almost everything is covered, transportation and loss of work are not.

The point is: There is no way for the adult child to read the parent's mind to discover the source of the refusal. Mind reading depends on your knowing your parent's thoughts and reactions well enough to guess what he may be thinking. It almost always fails to flush out the true reason. Your parent may not consciously know his reasons for keeping away from a doctor. And if you act on the assumed reason for the parental refusal to see a doctor, the chances are you will not get your parent to budge. Instead, nurture. That way you'll find out the reason for the refusal. Your parent's unconscious may discover why. You can help your parent find the way to see the doctor.

PARENT: I can't eat that steak. It gives me heartburn.	[opening signal]
YOU-THE-CHILD: You have a pain in your stomach.	[checking listening]
PARENT: It's nothing. I've had it for a couple of months. It goes and comes.	[more information]
YOU-THE-CHILD: You have this stomach pain and it keeps coming back.	[checking listening]
PARENT: It does worry me. What should I do about it?	[question]

YOU-THE-CHILD: It must hurt a lot if you're worried about it.

[nurturing listening] (not answering the question)

PARENT: You hear so much about cancer these days. I can't help thinking about it.

[expresses real fear]

YOU-THE-CHILD: I know. Cancer is frightening. I can understand why you're scared with that pain in your stomach.

[nurturing listening]

PARENT: I know it's foolish but that's why I've been putting off going to the doctor. I'm afraid of what he'll tell me.

[coming to solution]

YOU-THE-CHILD: You really want to go to the doctor, but you can't bring yourself to go because you're scared.

[nurturing listening]

PARENT: I guess I could go. I guess I would be less anxious if you come along with me.

[solution]

YOU-THE-CHILD: You feel that if I were there, you could manage the visit more calmly.

[listening-to-speak]

PARENT: Yes. I know it's foolish.

YOU-THE-CHILD: I'd be happy to go along. It would make me feel better if I knew everything was okay.

[genuine assertion/ show of pleasure]

PARENT: How about next Thursday?

It is very important for a parent—or anybody—to express out loud the fears that hold back action. By expressing fears, parents find themselves able to act, to unblock their creative problem-solving strength. It does take longer than simply tossing out: "You ought to see a doctor." But remember: "You ought" brings on deafness. Most people with symptoms know they "ought" to see a doctor: That's not the problem. The problem is bringing themselves to do it. The nurturing language allows them the choice of doing so or not, and then coming to a thought-out solution.

(Incidentally, it may take an hour or more before a parent decides to visit a doctor. So prepare for a long siege.)

The nurturing language helps you to help your parent understand other medical problems: going to the hospital, having surgery, sticking to a special diet, doing prescribed exercise.

When the medical situation is particularly threatening— having surgery or going to a hospital—if you try to jolly your parent along or minimize the seriousness of what is happening, you will only terrify more.

Reactions to minimizing:

"There's something you're not telling me."

"If the operation is nothing to worry about why do I have to have it?"

"I've decided not to have the operation."

"The hospital is too expensive. I'll let the doctors visit me at home."

If you nurture, your parent will express the fear and then deal with it. Your parent will listen more closely to the physician, ask questions, and respond appropriately. Otherwise, the defenses come up and paralyze rational action. Recall that defensiveness means explaining one's actions or thoughts. And if your parent takes up his creative energy with explanations, he or she will not deal with the problem at hand.

As an adult child you can give a sick parent something that they may find difficult to get from others: sympathy, an understanding of what is happening to them. The nurturing language provides sympathy in abundance through listening, especially nurturing listening. In fact, sympathy literally means "having emotions in common." If you let your parent know you can feel what the parent is feeling, that is sympathy. And listening is intended to provide just that communication.

A sick parent—a sick anybody—needs sympathy, not advice. That's why many people go on endlessly about their surgery; they are trying to make you share their feelings. They would stop talking about their illness if they were assured you understood. Listening does it.

When Your Parent Has Mental Problems

Few things are sadder than to behold a once-lucid mind sink into the swamp of senility or psychosis.

As the marvels of medicine have prolonged life, we see more and more people suffering from mental problems associated with old age. The affliction may not be striking a higher proportion of old people. The same percentage of people between the ages of sixty and sixty-five, for example, may be having mental breakdowns today as did fifty years ago. It's just that so many more people are living longer. So we have more people with mental problems and we see more of it among older people than our parents did.

Even so, the frequency is not as great as it appears. Only a small percentage of older people are so mentally ill as to require hospitalization, but when it does happen it is so devastating to the victim and to the family that a wide circle of people hear of it. And that makes it seem more common than it is.

More to the point: The old person's behavior may not be mental illness at all. What you may be seeing is an unwillingness to give up habits of thought and behavior that worked tolerably well for a lifetime.

"I cannot eat anything but steak. Steak has all the vitamins I need."

"Please don't sit in my chair at the table. It makes me uncomfortable."

"I cannot take taxis. The drivers are so violent."

"I don't remember the name of your aunt's husband. I never liked him anyway."

Such statements seem to cry out for you to say: "No, that's wrong!" Maybe even: "That's crazy!"

Yet with some searching you may be able to find out what is behind the "craziness." Take the peculiar eating habits. One person we know refused to eat fish all her life. She is now seventy years old. When asked about it, she related the story that when she was ten years old—sixty years ago—she watched her uncle almost choke to death on a fishbone. The scene so frightened her of fish that she never ate it.

However, the story has a funny twist. On her seventieth birthday her friends and relatives gathered to celebrate. Included was her cousin, the daughter of the almost-choked-to-death uncle. The story was retold. But the cousin interrupted:

"But it wasn't a fishbone at all. It was a chickenbone."

For sixty years, the woman had refused fish over the wrong bone! Now she eats fish.

We are not saying that the nurturing language could reveal that mistake, but the searching could have brought out the story of the child frightened by the choking. The eschewing of fish may not seem so strange when the story is told. So with other crotchets. They are usually not indications of mental problems, but, as we said, the result of lifelong habits. You have only to discover that for yourself to realize that your parent is not having mental problems at all.

If those seemingly strange strands of thought interfere with your life, then one goes further. You make genuine assertions to reveal to your parent that you are troubled by the behavior or the thoughts that seem out of the ordinary. For example:

PARENT: I cannot take a taxi. The   [opening signal]
    drivers are so violent.

YOU-THE-CHILD: You're afraid that   [nurturing listening]
    somebody will attack you.

PARENT: It does happen.	[insistent]
YOU-THE-CHILD: Mmmm.	[wordless listening]
PARENT: Of course, if I don't like a driver's looks, I can take another cab.	[going toward solution]
YOU-THE-CHILD: You say you can manage if you had to.	[checking listening]
PARENT: Yes. Really.	[admission]
YOU-THE-CHILD: I am glad about that because I don't know how much longer I can pick you up and take you downtown every day. I've taken too much time off from work.	[genuine assertion]
PARENT: I didn't know how you were doing it. I've taken a cab before. I can take it again.	[understanding]

True senility is another and more difficult problem. The symptoms include loss of memory, inappropriate speech, confusion, and extreme "stubbornness"—the elder refuses to do anything asked of him or her. The symptoms progress in severity. The labels include senility, senile dementia, and chronic or organic brain syndrome, all deemed incurable.

Here again, caution about the diagnosis is required. Labels and medical outlook can change from one physician to another. The diagnosis can also change when the conditions of the elder are changed.

A functioning older person who is a little odd suffers an abscessed tooth with a high fever. He may lapse into confusion that looks like incurable chronic brain syndrome. A physician makes the diagnosis, and off the elder goes to an institution. All the old person needed was a dentist.

Or because older people tend to take many drugs for one condition or another, the combination of drugs may create mental confusion that looks like senility. A glance at an elder's medicine cabinet will suggest that indeed the "symptoms" may be side effects of the drugs. A doctor's reevaluation of your parent's medicines may be required. Frequently a reduction of the number and dosage of tranquilizers miraculously "clears" the mind of a parent who seems to be a "vegetable."

More often, older persons, often weak from physical ills, sink into dependency. A repertoire of behaviors and words seeks to increase the dependency or to hold on to it. Sometimes they are quite bizarre: telephone calls late at night, staying up all night, forgetting one's address, wandering the streets, crying, and complaining over trivial inconvenience or insult.

Such old people often become hypochondriacs. They believe they are suffering from every disease in the medical book. On Monday it's a brain tumor; on Tuesday it's a heart attack. The older parent no doubt suffers many aches and pains but he or she has learned to exaggerate them to gain your attention and help. Such a parent may have learned that a convenient "heart attack" can bring you running five hundred miles. Pretty soon the imagined ills become, to the parent, a reality that cannot be denied. Often, unfortunately, the parent has cried "wolf" so many times that you may ignore real illness with tragic consequences.

At this point the adult child may need professional help— a psychiatrist, a psychologist, a gerontologist—to sort out what is dependent behavior and what may be true mental disturbance. In any case, consistent application of the nurturing language cannot make matters worse; it can only help identify the dependent behavior and move the aging parent toward independence. Further, nurturing reduces the mental anguish the parent may feel and prevent the outbreak of hostility.

When a parent suffers from depression, the adult child will want to cheer up the depressed parent. That is futile. The parent needs nurturing; to feel that the terrible sadness is understood. Perhaps the parent's life circumstances are depressing: friends dying or infirm, housing poor, lack of money, loneliness. The nurturing language can discover the parent's true need, the environmental source of the depression. The adult child can then move to ease the depressing situation. Or the parent may need antidepressant drug treatment. So the nurturing language will be crucial in getting the parent —who may resist—to a doctor. Forcing won't work; nurturing will because the parent doesn't like the depressed condition. If, through nurturing, the parent comes to believe that a doctor may relieve the depression, then the parent will more readily elect to see the physician.

Some people cannot control their hostility toward the mentally disturbed because they seem so stubborn—they won't listen to reason. "She's doing it on purpose to make me feel bad," is the cry of the adult child with a parent who has severe mental problems. "He can behave in the nursing home, but he just won't because he gets all that special attention." Even professional attendants find it hard to realize that their wards cannot help themselves. That's why historically mental patients were treated so brutally in institutions. In many modern hospitals, the staffs have been deeply trained in the nurturing language. They find that their patients are calmer, less "stubborn," and less bizarre.

In nursing and old-age homes, where the staff has not been trained in one form or another of the nurturing language, it's a good guess that their clients may be the subject of verbal or even physical abuse. So if you are selecting a nursing home, listen to the way the staff talks to the old people. It is easy to detect the nurturing language or some variation of it. If you hear listening and genuine assertions, you know that you are in the right place. Both nursing and nurture comes from the same word root meaning to nourish; so those who take their nursing seriously will nurture. If you hear the clients addressed as children, or *directed* to eat their food or clean up their rooms, or admonished to be "good girls" or "good boys," or shouted down, or mocked, or they become the objects of any of the verbal weapons of the toxic language, then beware—you are in the wrong place.

When Death Looms

As the years roll on, we are more frequent witnesses to the deaths of family, friends, and beloved pets. Older people will see or have seen someone quite close to them slowly die of cancer or heart disease. These events remind them and us of the closeness of the inevitable. Recent studies suggest that while older persons fear the idea of death (as we all do), they may be more concerned with the *manner* of their death, i.e., dying alone, painfully, or among strangers, or becoming totally incapacitated while still alive (as they say, a "vegetable").

These thoughts and feelings pass daily through the minds of many persons and govern many behaviors. An aging parent, sensing the imminence of death, may, as did King Lear, begin to give away his or her belongings, even though they are few in number. Or aging parents sometimes seem to "give up." The stamp collection is no longer of interest; beloved grandchildren are regarded as nuisances; or the family home is abandoned for a tiny apartment.

Adult children will be called upon to nurture parents who face one of three situations:

The parent is gravely disabled.

The parent's close relative, friend, or pet has died or is dying.

The parent is dying.

In each case there is little one can do outside of nurturing. It does no good to force oneself on a grieving, disabled, or dying parent. That tack only produces anger or withdrawal. As with depression, being cheerful only increases the other's pain. Unasked-for cheerfulness tells the parent that the adult child does not understand. And a lack of understanding sharpens the parent's sense of being alone and without hope.

Humor can help when a parent asks for or indicates a readiness for humor. In some families, humor is a common coin of consolation. They have long experience in using it with each other and for them it is often balm for grief. They will joke at funerals to the consternation of other relatives, but it is their way of letting off anxiety and fear. For the rest of us, the adult child's stance can be one of compassionate readiness.

For three years, Frederick, seventy-five, has been confined to a wheelchair with severe arthritis. He can no longer even feed himself. Once an avid chess player, he has given up the game. It embarrasses him to have a friend move his pieces. Nancy is his forty-year-old married daughter who visits him almost daily.

FREDERICK: How's the weather outside? [opening signal/ question]

NANCY: You want to go out. [checking listening]

FREDERICK: If it's too cold my joints hurt. So I haven't been out much this winter. [information]

NANCY: It's about forty degrees out. [information]

FREDERICK: Too cold. Too cold. Winter! Winter will never end and I'll never get out of this wheelchair. [modified cry of pain]

NANCY: You're feeling depressed these days. I can understand that with your arthritis. [nurturing listening]

FREDERICK: I keep hoping things will get better but they don't. I'm a prisoner. [cry of pain]

NANCY: When I see you locked in that wheelchair, I know I'd feel the same way—not being able to do anything. [genuine assertion]

FREDERICK: Oh, I can do some things. I can watch TV. And I really would play chess if it didn't bother me so [trying to help Nancy]

much not to be able to move the
pieces myself.

NANCY: It bothers you pretty much   [nurturing listening]
not being able to handle the pieces.

FREDERICK: I know it's all in my head.   [moves to solution]
I guess it wouldn't hurt me to call
the moves and have my opponent
move them. Maybe if I tried it out
with you, I wouldn't feel so bad.

NANCY: You want to play chess with   [checking listening]
me and you would call the moves
and I'd move the pieces.

FREDERICK: We could try.

A small victory. But an important one. Nancy not only
helped Frederick start to play chess again; she has won his
confidence that she understands his predicament. The principle can be extended to a host of other situations when the
parent is seriously disabled. Note that Nancy issued her own
cry of pain, a cry that expressed her own anguish. That led
Frederick to move to help her, to ease her feelings. It gave
him something useful to do. It put his creative problem-
solving ability to work.

When Someone Dies

Grief goes through stages. At first there is *disbelief* that
the person has actually died. So strong can be the disbelief
in the death that your parent may have recurrent dreams—
day and night—that the relative, friend, or pet is merely on
vacation or is staying away because your parent did something bad. Parents under severe mental stress may find it
difficult to distinguish between those dreams and the reality.
You may find your parent "talking" to the departed, an event
that raises the specter of senility. However, with time, as
the reality of the death sinks in, the "conversations" decline.

A formal funeral tends to dispel the notion that the dead person has merely gone away, as we often foolishly tell children. In the absence of a formal service, people hold on longer to the idea that a loved one is still alive. This is especially true when the person has died far away and your parent was not present at the memorial or the burial. Adult children often try to spare their aging parents grief by keeping a death secret. That only reinforces the idea that "John isn't visiting me because I did something wrong." When aging parents learn the truth (and they frequently do from watching the faces of those around them when John's name is mentioned) they find it even harder to believe the death.

The next stage may be *anger*. Many people believe—irrationally—that the dead person died to punish them for some imagined hurt or insult. Or they are angry that God or life played a dirty trick on them by taking their daughter or son away. Old people often have the wish to die before their children do because they have deep feelings about their children and anticipate that they will suffer extreme grief at the loss. Sometimes they turn the anger against themselves. They feel they have done something to cause the death. They feel they have sinned and brought down the wrath of God. Or they did not warn the dead party about his or her health or did not feed the dead person properly. Such anger turned inward is guilt; the self-imposed "should." Guilt runs rampant when the loved one died by suicide. "I could have saved him," is the inward and (often) outward cry. This implies "I should have saved him."

Guilt can and often does lead to *depression,* a third stage. Depression itself may stem from unrelieved grief, from which it must be distinguished. Grief is normal. Your parent can be expected to be sad when someone close has died. But if grief extends beyond a few months or a year and your parent seems unable to shake it, professional help—a psychiatrist or psychologist—may be able to assist. Depression may be preventing your parent from carrying on ordinary activities of living: eating, sleeping, working, having sex. Expert help may put your parent back into life.

The last stage is *acceptance*; your parent knows that the death has occurred, that it is irreversible, that the anger, guilt, and depression have passed. Life goes on. Death is part of life. We all face it. Of course, not everyone reaches the stage of acceptance. And your parent may be one of those people who cannot accept death for themselves or others.

Nurturing, Not Forcing

Few people can be forced to step quickly through the stages of grief. The more you try to speed things up, the more your grieving parent will remain fixed at the current stage. Your parent will see your attempts as not understanding. And that will intensify disbelief, anger, guilt and depression, and delay acceptance.

We believe that a grieving parent can be made more comfortable by the nurturing language. Perhaps the intermediate stages can be shortened by nurturing and lead to more rapid acceptance.

Irene's mother, Elizabeth, has lost a favorite brother, Bill. Bill was more than a brother. He was, for fifteen years after Elizabeth's divorce, a substitute husband. He lived in the same house, shared expenses, did the chores, errands, repairs. He was a widower.

ELIZABETH: I dreamed about Bill last night. It was so real, I thought he was there. [opening signal]

IRENE: You must miss him terribly. He was so good to you. [nurturing listening]

ELIZABETH (crying): I cannot believe he's dead! That's why I dream of him so much. Day and night. [cry of pain]

IRENE: I cannot think of anything [nurturing listening]

more awful. You must be going
through hell.

ELIZABETH (crying): I find myself   [reveals feelings]
talking to him. I think I must be
going crazy.

IRENE: He must be very real to you   [nurturing listening]
now. After fifteen years, I can't
imagine how you can wipe a person
out of your mind.

ELIZABETH (a little calmer): I know   [toward acceptance]
he's gone. But I can't help myself.
Everybody tells me to carry on and
that time will heal my wounds. But
they don't understand what Bill
meant to me. Irene, you're the only
one who understands.

Irene did not try to "make things easy" for Elizabeth. She
only reflected Elizabeth's feelings back to her, adding some
interpretation each time. That allowed Elizabeth to examine
the reality of her feelings and moved her toward acceptance.
She will avoid those who try to cheer her up and seek out
Irene for understanding.

Dealing with guilt is more difficult but it follows the same
pattern. We long to say: "Don't blame yourself," when our
parent is full of self-blame, but saying that will only sharpen
the guilt. Self-blame cuts off creative problem-solving. The
victim of guilt is so concerned with easing his discomfort he
or she cannot put his attention to the problem at hand.

Benjamin, who is seventy, has been living alone since he
was widowed. His companion was Bo, a collie. The two were
inseparable. Bo accompanied Benjamin on his numerous fish-
ing and hunting trips, even though Bo was not a hunting dog.
Bo lived to the age of fifteen, a long time for a dog. Bo's death
threw Benjamin into a tailspin. He refused to accept another
collie puppy to replace Bo. Gerald, forty-five, is Benjamin's
oldest son.

BENJAMIN: It was nice of you to offer a puppy to replace Bo. But I just can't accept the responsibility of another dog.   [opening signal]

GERALD: You feel that taking care of an animal is too much for you.   [nurturing listening]

BENJAMIN: It's just the responsibility. They get sick. They get old. You have to do the right thing.   [more information]

GERALD: Hmmm.   [wordless listening]

BENJAMIN: Bo was old. But he could have lived a few years longer if I had taken care of him right.   [hidden feelings]

GERALD: You feel Bo died because you didn't take care of him.   [checking listening]

BENJAMIN: At the end when he was moping around. I knew something was not right. I should have taken him to the vet right away instead of a week later.   [guilt]

GERALD: You must feel awful. There are few things more terrible than feeling that you're responsible for a death. I can understand what you're feeling.   [nurturing listening]

BENJAMIN: Of course, Bo was very old for a dog . . . fifteen, that's like being eighty-five as a human. At that age I don't know what a vet could do for him. The vet did tell me that he was riddled with cancer . . . couldn't do much, I guess.   [backing off]

GERALD: Bo was very old. And cancer. I didn't know he had cancer.   [checking listening]

BENJAMIN: Yep. I guess I'm being a bit silly about blaming myself. I just didn't want that dog to die. I   [understands]

guess I have to calm down. After a
few months, I'll be wanting a dog
again.

Those of us who do not have pets often fail to understand
the depth of feeling others have for them. Pet owners treat
their dogs, cats, and birds like members of the family. The
departure of an animal is a psychological hurt of deep proportion. Like Benjamin, pet owners go through the stages
of grief. We have to face the fact that some of them are truly
inconsolable. Suppose Gerald had tried the usual on his
father: "Don't blame yourself." "Bo was only a dog." "You'll
forget about him when you take the new puppy." The result
would have been quite unpredictable, ranging from outright
hostility: "Bo—only a dog! He was my dearest friend, dearer
than you!" to even deeper guilt: "Don't tell me that! There
are anticancer chemicals that work like magic."

The Death of a Spouse

Husbands and wives. Few human relationships have as
many ambiguous strands as the bonds that tie husband and
wife together. There is a bond of love; love that was chosen.
A bond of partnership; the building of a life and family together. A bond of sexuality. A bond of companionship. A
bond of duty, religious or societal. The ambiguities—the
meanings of the bonds for the partners—arise because two
people come together from different families where the rules
about the bonds may differ. The more different the cultures
of the partners, the more tenuous the relationship. Where
the partners come from similar backgrounds, the bonds bind
very tightly.

In one family, the bond of partnership may be paramount;
in another the bond of love. A wife from one background and
a husband from another can "play" the marriage as if they
were two musicians reading different music. In most mar-

riages, the partners compose their differences and find ways of incorporating in the new family rules modified versions of the rules the partners bring with them.

Our society has become more heterogeneous in the selection of marriage partners—blacks and whites; northerners and southerners; Italians and Irish; Jews and Catholics; upper class and working class, and so on. When once such marriages were uncommon enough to cause scandal, today they are commonplace. In the current generation, the common bonds are weak because of the disparity of backgrounds. In the generation of our parents, these bonds can be quite strong. One has only to look at divorce rates among younger people compared to those among our elders.

Because of the strength of connection between husband and wife among our parents and their generation, the death of one can be far more powerful than an adult child of this generation realizes. The adult child may have seen his parents fighting, hating, struggling with each other. He may have observed a tyrannical father or a manipulative mother. And wonder, then, why the grief? One has only to look at the ties that bound them together rather than their differences to understand the shock of the death of a spouse.

Because the composition of a marriage relationship requires a high order of attention, the death of one partner may generate a great deal of self-blame: guilt. "I should have . . ." becomes a litany for the grieving surviving spouse. If the surviving partner has been sexually unfaithful, the remorse may be acute.

In any marriage there are long-standing disagreements. With the death of the spouse, the survivor wishes he or she had acted to alleviate the disagreement. The survivor can recall a hundred missed opportunities for speaking the words that would have made all well. "I could have done this. I could have done that."

The survivor knows that if the relationship has been a stormy one, then the children know it, too. And the bereaved has then to deal with what he or she assumes will be the children's blame for the sadnesses in the marriage and possibly for the death. It is not unknown for adult children to lay responsibility for the death of a mother or father on the shoulders of the surviving spouse.

Finally there are the losses of the bonds: the companionship, the family building, the sexuality, the duty, and the love.

PARENT: Which casket shall I buy? The wood or the bronze?	[opening signal] [question]
YOU-THE-CHILD: You seem in doubt.	[checking listening]
PARENT: I'm trying to figure out what mother would have wanted. We never discussed these things, you know.	[information]
YOU-THE-CHILD: You think she had a preference but you don't know what it is.	[checking listening]
PARENT: Well, your mother was always one for big showy things. She always worried what people would think of the house, the furniture.	[hostility]
YOU-THE-CHILD: You think she would pick the bronze but that you wouldn't like it because it's too showy.	[checking listening]
PARENT: We always fought over the things we bought because of it. She always thought I was cheap. Like I bought you the three-speed bike and she made me return it for the ten-speed. Now that didn't make any difference to you, did it?	[reveals hidden feelings]
YOU-THE-CHILD: You feel hurt that mom undercut you with me and that troubles you now.	[nurturing listening]

PARENT: I guess that's why I can't   [understanding]
make up my mind about the casket.
I keep hearing her voice criticizing
me for picking the wrong one. You
know, the wood is just as pretty as
the bronze. And in a week from now
it won't make any difference.

The adult child gave the parent an opportunity to vent
hostile and conflicting feelings and to allow the creative
problem-solving ability to come through. If the adult child
had defended the mother, that would have cut off the father's
thinking. He might have made a choice that he would regret
because the bronze casket would have depleted his small
store of retirement money.

Cornelius and Marion had been married for forty-seven
years. They had three children. The youngest, Kathleen,
thirty, lives close by. Cornelius died three months ago at the
age of seventy-two; Marion, sixty-eight, survives. Marion was
a lively person with lots of friends; Cornelius kept his nose
to business and was a rather sour but dedicated husband.

MARION: I'd just love to go to the   [opening signal]
movies. Do you think it's all right?

KATHLEEN: You think there's some-   [checking listening]
thing wrong with going to the
movies.

MARION: Well, we're still in the   [reason why]
mourning period. And some people
might say it's too soon for me to go
out.

KATHLEEN: You're worried that some   [nurturing listen-
people might say you're showing   ing]
disrespect for dad.

MARION: Exactly. He always thought   [hidden feelings]
I went out too much anyway. As if
he didn't trust me.

KATHLEEN: You have a reason for thinking he didn't trust you. [checking listening]

MARION: It's just that I always had so many friends. And I had men friends too, like James and Pat. And now James is living in Florida and Pat's dead, too. [sniffles] [information]

KATHLEEN: You must be in terrible pain with dad, Pat, and James all gone. [nurturing listening]

MARION: I know I laugh a lot [crying] but it does hurt so. Cornelius died so quickly, I didn't have a chance to make things right again. [reveals feelings]

KATHLEEN: There was something you wanted to tell dad. [checking listening]

MARION: Yes. It was Pat and me. Dad always thought the two of us did things behind his back. We never really did. Maybe, thirty years ago Pat and I were in love and we hugged and kissed a lot but we never went further than that. And then we realized it was something we shouldn't do. We just remained friends. I never told dad, but he suspected and I never let him know everything was all right [crying again]. He must have suffered so with not knowing and I should have told him. [reveals hidden thought]

KATHLEEN: What a terrible burden to carry all these years! You must feel awful about dad. [nurturing listening]

MARION: I actually feel better now that I've told you. I don't know if [acceptance]

it would have been better had I
told him. But it's all over now.

Kathleen was there for her mother. She did not judge. She
did not take sides. She allowed her mother to vent her feelings, to look at her guilt and to assuage it. Was Marion unfaithful? The point is she thought she was and that she had
hurt her husband by allowing him to suspect. When he died
she was left with the wish that she should have done something to ease his feelings. Kathleen provided a substitute
hearer. And her mother moved toward acceptance of Cornelius's death.

When Your Parent Is Dying

Helping a dying parent is the most difficult challenge of
the nurturing language. You want to do something concrete:
a miracle cure, a painkiller, something to bring your parent
back to full life. That's why so many adult children drag
their gravely ill parents from doctor to doctor and why so
many end up in the hands of quacks. The guilty need to re-
vive the dying parent is, for many adult children, overwhelming. The guilt grows out of a sense of not having done
enough for the parent over the years or in some way having
contributed to the parent's illness. Even the most sophisticated fall prey to this. A nurse we know delivered her father
to a quack cancer treatment center only to have him die
alone and in severe pain, although she knew, medically, nothing could be done for him. She just had to try.

Those who know of their impending death often go
through the same stages as the bereaved: disbelief, anger or
guilt, depression, and, finally, acceptance.

"It can't be true. I'm okay. Just feeling my years."

"I don't have to see a doctor."

"I'm not smoking too much.'"

"I'm gaining weight. How could I be sick?"

Each statement expresses the parent's disbelief in his or her death. Psychologists call this disbelief "denial." The parent denies the reality of death. Important modern psychological theories contend that the denial of death is strong in all of us. Each of us deals with death in his or her own way. We can suppress the thought by commitment to work or to another human being or to seeking pleasure. But as our parents grow older the evidence of their bodies keeps pushing the thought of mortality through the thick blanket of denial. And when death is near, the dying person can expend enormous psychic energy on denial.

The anger comes from the realization that it is happening and that it is unfair. The parent does not want to die. "Why me?" The guilt arises from the suspicion that the parent may have done something to bring on death: poor health habits, sinning against God, or in the case of cancer of the reproductive organs, sexual misconduct. There may be nothing rational here. The dying person wants to get rid of the thought that he may soon go into that "country from whose bourne no man returns."

The depression sets in when the inevitability becomes real. There is nothing more to be done and the dying person has not yet accepted the idea of death (some never do). It is at this stage that suicide can occur when the depression is a greater burden than the impending death. The dying person merely hurries things along.

The final stage of acceptance means that the dying parent realizes that death is a result of life, that regardless of how many years one has lived, one has indeed lived and has had good and bad times, and now there is peace with oneself and the world. Many dying persons cannot reach this stage: They may deny and disbelieve to the end; they may be angry or guilty to the end; or they may be depressed to the end.

Just as one cannot force the bereaved through the stages of grief, the adult child cannot force his dying parent through the stages of dying. The more one forces, the more one intensifies and prolongs the current feelings of the dying person. Again we return to nurturing; the adult child being gently available to nurture when called upon.

One of the most difficult confrontations is that of the question: "Am I going to die?" Here is how one adult child, Stephen, handled it with his mother, Helen.

HELEN: I feel so bad. My stomach hurts really bad. I don't think the medicine is helping at all. [opening signal]

STEPHEN: You're really uncomfortable. I wish I could do something to make things better for you. I don't like to see you this way. [nurturing listening] [genuine assertion]

HELEN: It comes and goes. There! I feel better. It was just a passing pain. But I do feel that the doctors didn't get it all when they operated. What do they tell you, Stephen? [information] [showing fear] [question]

STEPHEN: You're worried that the doctors didn't get all of the tumor. [nurturing listening]

HELEN: They told me they got most of it. So that must mean that some of it was left. And it's growing, isn't it? I'm going to die. Am I going to die, Stephen? [information] [question]

STEPHEN: You must be terribly scared to be asking questions like that. I can understand how all the pain and fear is upsetting you. [nurturing listening]

HELEN: I am frightened, Stephen! I have this thing growing in me. I can feel it. And nobody lives with this thing in them. I've lain here and thought about death a thousand times. I know it's coming. [expressing fear]

STEPHEN: I can see that it's on your mind a lot and that it's torturing you. [nurturing listening]

HELEN: Talking about it with you makes it seem less terrible. I know that you're here. I just don't want to be alone when the end comes. We all die sometime . . . [crying] [understanding]

STEPHEN: You'd like to have us with you when you're really feeling bad. [checking listening]

HELEN: I know you're working and you and your sister can't be here all the time. But if I knew I could telephone you anytime and just talk that would be good. And maybe if I felt real bad, one of you could come over even if it was late. [creative solution]

STEPHEN: You feel that telephone calls would be important and if Suzy or I could come over whenever you needed us that would make you feel better. [checking listening] [listening-to-speak]

HELEN: Yes. Then I don't think I'd be so scared. [genuine assertion]

STEPHEN: Of course I'll talk with you on the phone or visit you anytime, night or day. It would make me more comfortable to know that my mother was not frightened and that I could do something to ease her pain. I think Suzy would do the same. I don't know whether to ask her or leave it to you. [genuine assertion]

[giving a choice]

HELEN: I'd like you to talk to her. I find it hard to ask her for favors. You know, I do feel very good now that we've talked. [choosing]

[show of pleasure]

Stephen never answered the question: "Am I going to die?" Helen knew the answer all along. Most dying people do. In fact, he never answered any of her questions. He followed the nurturing language's rule about questions: Never ask a question; never answer one.

Helen's hidden fear was loneliness and the possibility that her loved ones would not be present to help her when the going got rough. By searching/listening Stephen discovered that hidden agenda. Notice that he did not immediately agree to telephone and visit before he listened again (listening-to-speak) to make sure that his mother was expressing her true need. Then, and only then, did he issue a genuine assertion.

At no time did Stephen try to cheer her up. To do so would mock Helen's deep feelings and fears and make her either withdraw or become more insistent that Stephen answer the question. He also avoided phrases like: "Don't worry, you'll pull through." "The pain will pass." "The drugs will kill the cancer." "Don't be silly, the doctors got it all." "Trust the doctors, they know what they're doing." "You have a long life ahead of you." "We'll be celebrating your eightieth birthday."

Such comments duck the issue Helen wants to deal with. If Stephen had tried any of these, he might never have learned Helen's true need for the calls and visits from his sister and him. And that would have made Helen's suffering greater.

You can never change the facts. Lying to dying persons usually fails. They can read your voice and face, no matter how hard you try to hide your true feelings and knowledge. There is no need to lie: You do not answer questions and you do not volunteer information until you are sure that your parent really wants what you have to say. If you do lie and they know it they lose their trust in you and with that you lose your ability to nurture them.

With a dying person, things may not go as smoothly as they did with Stephen and Helen. A dying parent can be distraught, unable to listen at all except to his or her own inner turmoil. In this situation, it is best gently and patiently to deliver as much relief through listening as possible. Much of your listening may turn out to be wordless, because you may be submerged under a torrent of thoughts, feelings, and questions.

All of which may be extremely difficult because the subject of death always raises the specter of one's own mortality, a contemplation most of us would rather avoid. But death comes, as it must, to all.

/ 13 /

Getting Along Great Even with Real Problems: II

Between parents and adult children practical problems fester that do not seem at first glance to have anything to do with nurturing. A parent needs money or does not. A parent lives in comfortable surroundings or does not. A parent works or does not. It only *seems* that these issues do not involve nurturing. Yet any adult child who has tried to advise (or respond to) his parent in these concerns knows full well that money, housing, and work often go to the heart of a parent–adult child relationship.

Money Is the Cruelest Cut

Scripture tells us that "money answereth all things"; that is, money can fulfill our wishes or desires. Indeed, studies of old people suggest that money comes first, before health and activity, in affecting morale. With money, elders can buy decent food, housing, leisure, companionship, even health. Upper-income seniors are healthier than low-income age-mates. That may stem from the upper-income person's access to medical care or from a lifetime of adequate food, safe housing, and proper health habits. The interrelationship of factors cannot easily be untangled, but it's safe to say that money plays a lead role if not *the* lead role.

As we mentioned earlier, the lives of elders have changed dramatically in the last forty years with Social Security, Medicare, Medicaid, and other special money programs for older people. They live more independently than formerly. They eat better. They get prompt and highly sophisticated medical care.

As between parents and their adult children, the money issue is: How much responsibility does a grown child have for an aging parent? Shall the parent have the same standard of living as the child? And shall the child make up the difference? These questions may also be reversed: How much responsibility does a parent have for an adult child?

The answers go to the heart of society's dilemma concerning our old people. As a society, we have agreed not to let old people starve: We give them Supplementary Security Income when Social Security or their own resources do not provide them with livable conditions. We have agreed not to allow old people to go without adequate medical care by setting up Medicare insurance for those who can afford to pay premiums and Medicaid for those who cannot. We have agreed—in some cities—to make sure that elders have safe housing. And—again, only in some places—we provide transportation, social centers, and discounts.

But as a society we scrimp on the amenities. We do not seem to want to give old people "a good time," a reward for a lifetime of work and citizenship. There are, as we have noted, millions who live just on the edge of the poverty line. Government regulations make it difficult for them to get those extra "good-time" dollars from work, friends, or family. The government deducts earnings and contributions from Supplementary Security Income and sometimes from Social Security.

For adult children, the dilemma is those "good-time" dollars. If the adult child lives in a comfortable home, what does the child owe to the parent who lives in a slum? If the adult child goes to the country for the summer, can the parent be left behind? What about clothes, movies, dining out, travel? Can there be a disparity between adult child and parent? All these questions remain between the two to be worked out through, we hope, the nurturing language. Our new language allows needs to be expressed safely without fear of recrimination. And it allows safe responses without moral judgments. The negotiation can proceed so that both parties feel comfortable.

Listen to this toxic language dialogue between Anthony, seventy-seven, and his son, Vincent, fifty-eight, a computer salesman.

ANTHONY: If you don't think you can give me the money, don't worry, I'll find a way to get by somehow. It'll be hard; I'll have to give up a little here and a little there. But *don't* worry, I'll get by.   [guilt induction by mockery]

[fake cry of pain]

VINCENT: I don't have the cash right now. Diane [wife] just had some dental work done and I have bills a mile high that aren't paid.   [defensive]

ANTHONY: I understand that Diane and your family come before your father who sacrificed vacations, good clothes and had to drive around in a ten-year-old-car so that you could have what all the other kids had.   [mockery]

I understand. Please don't worry about me. I can get by. They haven't increased my Social Security payment, but the government may   [fake cry of pain]

change its mind and give me a raise
soon. It won't be much if I get it at
all. But don't worry, I will get by.　　　[counterattack]

VINCENT: You're really a crafty old
bastard! What the hell do you want
me to do? Rob a bank?　　　　　　　　[fake listening]

ANTHONY: Now don't get upset! I'll
get by, and don't worry, I can manage.　　　　　　　　　　　　　　　　　　[capitulation]

VINCENT: Okay. You got me. I'll try to
give you the money.　　　　　　　　　[nailing it down]

ANTHONY: I don't need it. I told you
I could get by. It'll be hard though.　　[one last shot]

VINCENT: I'll have some for you by
tomorrow. Don't call me. Wait until
I call you.　　　　　　　　　　　　　　[return fire]

ANTHONY: I don't bother you. Of
course, I'll wait until you call me.

Whew! Crafty old man, indeed. Poor Vincent. There was no
way he could win against Anthony's big guns: the implied
"should" of society's rule that a father who has sacrificed deserves something in return from his children. Furthermore,
Anthony made his son choose between his father and his wife
and family. A big risk, because many adult children choose
their families. But for Anthony it worked.

By now you can see how to handle Anthony with the nurturing language.

ANTHONY: If you don't think you can　　[guilt induction by
give me the money, don't worry, I'll　　　mockery]
find a way to get by somehow. It'll　　[fake cry of pain]
be hard; I'll have to give up a little
here and a little there. But don't
worry, I'll get by.

VINCENT: You're hard up for money　　[checking listening]
now.

ANTHONY: My pension and Social Security simply don't cover my bills. And when I got sick last month, I spent an extra hundred dollars.   [information]

VINCENT: Yeah. Being sick is expensive. And you're falling short each month.   [checking listening]

ANTHONY: I keep hoping my Social Security will go up. But who knows?   [expressed wish]

VINCENT: You can't count on your Social Security.   [checking listening]

ANTHONY: Not at all. And I'm watching my savings shrink. If something goes real bad I won't have anything to fall back on. I mean, if I get very sick or if the car breaks down.   [new information]

VINCENT: So you're worried that you'll be left without any money at all in case something terrible happens. I can understand that. It's tough to see expenses go up on a fixed income.   [nurturing listening]

ANTHONY: That's why I thought we could work out something between us so that I wouldn't feel the world closing in on me.   [call for help]

VINCENT: If you could depend on some steady money you'd feel better not juggling bills all the time.   [checking listening/ listening-to-speak]

ANTHONY: That's right. I don't know how you're fixed for money now.   [checking]

VINCENT: I want to help you out as much as I can because I don't like to see you worried and scrambling all the time. I'd have to figure out how much I can put together on a regular basis. Right now I have a   [genuine assertion]

[cry of pain]

huge dental bill that I have to pay.
maybe I can pay it in installments
and put some cash together.

ANTHONY: Nobody seems to be free of   [sympathy]
bills these days. I can hold off a
little while and maybe next week
when you know where you stand
we can get together. It's very nice of   [show of pleasure]
you to do this.

In both instances, Anthony got some money from Vincent, but in the first he performed an extraction, in the second, a negotiation. In the first, father and son exchanged verbal weapons, in the second consideration for each other. With the nurturing language, Vincent brought out explicitly his father's true need, although there were clues in the first dialogue.

"Don't worry, I'll get by," Anthony had said. Although it was a ploy to generate guilt in Vincent, it also expressed the true state of affairs, i.e., Anthony could wait. That was dropped as a hint. In the second dialogue, he said out loud what he had earlier only implied. He wanted to relieve his son after the cry of pain: "I can hold off a little while." Vincent discovered new information: a savings account. That meant that his father was not in dire straits and that he, Vincent, need not feel guilty about not springing immediately to his father's aid.

Vincent also got a chance to lay his problems on the table without stirring up envy in his father. His father, then, did not force Vincent to choose between parent and family. Instead, Anthony sympathized with his son's own money hardship. Except for the opening mockery, Anthony dropped all his guilt-generating manipulations.

Suppose Anthony did not need the money at all. That often happens. Aging parents fear that they are going to be left destitute. They try to get money from their adult children to build up a nest egg, but the egg is never big enough. If that were the case with Anthony, the nurturing language would give Vincent the best chance to discover it. Usually when the true state of affairs is put into the dialogue ("Well, it's not that I need money right now; I'd just feel better if I had it"), the demand for money fades.

In Chapter 11 we pointed out that some parents often need help and cannot bring themselves to ask for it. Again, the nurturing language brings out the need and makes it safe for the parent to ask for assistance. The adult child can then offer help without fear of triggering a dependency in the needy parent. Remember this dialogue:

PARENT: Everything is so expensive these days.   [opening signal]

YOU-THE-CHILD: You're finding it hard to make ends meet.   [checking listening]

PARENT: My Social Security check seems smaller every month.   [more information]

YOU-THE-CHILD: You're finding that with inflation, you need more money.   [checking listening]

PARENT: Oh, I don't want to be a burden to anybody. You have your own family to take care of.   [feelings coming up]

YOU-THE-CHILD: You feel that if I helped you out I'd deprive my family in some way.   [nurturing listening]

PARENT: Actually, I don't need much. Probably twenty dollars a week would not make me feel so pinched. You know I don't go to the movies anymore.   [more information]

YOU-THE-CHILD: You think that twenty dollars a week would be enough for you.   [checking listening]

PARENT: Yes. But I don't want to deprive your family. [repeat]

YOU-THE-CHILD: I wouldn't find it a deprivation to help out with twenty dollars a week. In fact, it'd make me feel easier if I knew my mother was comfortable and didn't have to scrape along. [genuine assertion]

PARENT: That makes me feel very good. I'm glad you can manage it. And I do feel okay taking the money. I didn't know how I was going to ask you. [genuine assertion]

The adult child moves with care not to shred the parent's feelings. If the child rejects the parent's need, then the parent will hesitate even when a life-threatening necessity arises. The nurturing language makes the parent feel safe in turning to the child for help in small and large things.

When You Need Money

As always, roles may be reversed. The parent has the money that the child needs. Before Ned died, he set up a trust fund controlled by his wife, Edna, for the benefit of his son, Nicholas. Nicholas, now thirty-five, must ask his mother for money when he needs it.

NICHOLAS: Mom, I need money. [opening signal]

EDNA: Everybody needs money. [irony]

NICHOLAS: You have the money that dad left me and I want some. [demanding]

EDNA: Yes, he left me in control of it because I know what's best for you. [superiority]

NICHOLAS: I'm thirty-five years old. *I* [challenging]

know what's best for me. I'd like
two thousand dollars.

EDNA: What do you need it for?   [question]

NICHOLAS: That's my business. I don't   [surly]
have to tell you every time I need it.

EDNA: I won't give it unless I know.   [superiority]

NICHOLAS: This is a lousy setup! We   [name-calling]
fight every time I ask for money.
And I don't like to say it but you're
an old busybody who holds a tight
purse.

EDNA: Forget the money, Nick! No   [rejection]
dice.

Of such are sick relationships born. Nick returns again and
again to be whipped by his mother. He cannot bring himself to nurture this woman who holds such power over him.
He believes he can beat her at her own game. Of course, he
cannot. He needs some distance from her to approach her.
He simultaneously seeks her love and the money he needs.
That is a strong relationship. If he distanced himself with a
moderate relationship—seeking mutual help—he may find
it easier to nurture his mother.

NICHOLAS: Mom, I have a few extra   [opening signal]
bills this month and I need some   [mild call for help]
extra money to tide me over.

EDNA: Everybody needs money.   [irony]

NICHOLAS: You doubt that I need it.   [listening-to-speak]

EDNA: If you watched your budget   [attack]
you wouldn't be needing money all
the time.

NICHOLAS: You really do doubt that   [listening-to-speak]
I need the money this month.

EDNA: Oh, I'm sure you do.   [acknowledgment]

NICHOLAS: Mom, this month with extra   [call for help]

doctor bills and two birthdays I've
gone over my budget. I don't like
to have outstanding bills.

EDNA: You feel next month you'll be   [checking]
able to handle it.

NICHOLAS: Yes, I feel I can handle it   [genuine assertion]
once I get out of this bind.

EDNA: How much do you need?   [question]

NICHOLAS: I find it very difficult to   [cry of pain]
ask for money every time I need a
little extra. It makes me feel like a
kid.

EDNA: I have control of the money.   [superiority]

NICHOLAS: You have control of the   [checking listening]
money.

EDNA: Your dad said I should take   [superiority]
take care of the money.

NICHOLAS: I find it difficult at age   [cry of pain]
thirty-five still to have to account
to someone for how I spend my
money. I'd be more comfortable if   [call for help]
we work out a yearly budget.

EDNA: You'd like to handle this your-   [question]
self?

NICHOLAS: Yes. Within the confines of   [condition]
the will.

EDNA: I'd be relieved if you handled   [agreement]
your money! You know I don't like
being asked every bit as much as
you don't like asking.

NICHOLAS: I'm glad we won't have to   [show of pleasure]
haggle over money and get into
fights.

EDNA: That would be a relief to me!   [show of pleasure]

Nicholas did not score 100 percent on the nurturing
language. He answered a question and did not permit his

mother a choice about how to handle the money. But he came out all right because his overall performance was sufficiently nurturing. He had distanced himself emotionally from his mother. Nicholas allowed her to deal with her own moral question: how much leeway to give her son over the trust and still fulfill her dead husband's wishes.

Parent As Financial Victim

Aging parents who have put aside some money sometimes invest it badly. They keep the cash in a low-interest savings account. Or they buy tax-free bonds when their taxable income is low and there is no tax advantage. Or they hold on to stocks that have steadily declined in value and for which there is little hope of recovery. Or they buy into high-risk investments. Or worst of all, they seem to be falling into the hands of con men.

As for the last, old people are known to be primary targets of con games. The most common trick is that of the "found purse." The con artist "finds" a purse full of money in the presence of the victim and the artist's partner. There may or may not be a name and address in the purse. The con man (it may be a woman) says that the purse belongs to both him and the victim. But first they must make a good-faith effort to find the owner. If the owner is not found, they can share the contents of the purse, which appear to be several thousand dollars. The con man then asks the victim to put up "good-faith" money equal to half of what is in the purse.

Victims of this con game have been known to run to their bank to withdraw their life's savings of thousands of dollars. Of course, after the con artist takes the "good-faith" money he and his partner disappear and the victim is left with a purse containing a wad of worthless paper. Other cons include worthless stock, purchase of "off-the-truck" television sets, extortion by threats against children or grandchildren, and the gypsy's tainted money. In this last con,

the fortune teller tells the victim that a relative is dying
because the victim has tainted money and must get rid of it.
Adult children want to protect their parents against poor
investments and con games. Some simply take over their
parents' assets and dole out a weekly allowance. While such
a step protects the money, it tends to create dependency.
At the same time it demeans the parents' status; they become, with respect to money, like children. At bottom, it
is dehumanizing. (In the case of senile parents, the law
does provide children with ways to conserve assets.)

Most parents would not allow their adult children to assume responsibility for their funds. And they resist powerfully any steps in that direction. They close their ears to any
advice (for the reasons we know) and particularly resent any
interference concerning money matters. We know of one son-
in-law who is a financial consultant of high standing. The in-
laws refuse to accept his suggestions.

The nurturing language provides the avenue of approach.
The nurturing language builds trust. And as trust increases,
your parents turn to you more and more for support, i.e.,
for help, not advice, in understanding their financial situation. If faced with a con, they will more readily consult you
and not keep it secret. You can provide information if they
ask for it. For example, they may find it onerous to check
their Social Security benefits. You may find it easy to make
a phone call to get past the bureaucracy. Or they may not
know about high-interest bonds or be worried about their
safety. Sometimes you can help directly:

PARENT: I wish I had ten thousand   [opening signal]
    dollars to buy a Treasury bill. They
    pay fourteen percent interest and
    my savings account pays only five
    and a quarter.
YOU-THE-CHILD: You say you'd like to   [checking listening]
    get into Treasury bills.
PARENT: Yes. I have seven thousand   [information]

and I get three hundred and fifty dollars a year interest; I could get three times that. I could use the extra ten dollars a week.

YOU-THE-CHILD: If you had three thousand more you could buy into a Treasury bill.   [listening]

PARENT: Maybe I could borrow three thousand. It would pay. It would lower my income but it would still be more than I'm getting at the bank.   [creative solution]

YOU-THE-CHILD: Sounds reasonable.   [listening]

PARENT: Can you lend it to me?   [question]

YOU-THE-CHILD: You'd like me to lend you three thousand so that you can buy a Treasury bill.   [checking listening/ listening-to-speak]

PARENT: That's right. I think it will work.   [affirmation]

YOU-THE-CHILD: I'd feel more comfortable if we bought the Treasury bill together. That way you don't owe me anything and I collect the interest on my share from the government.   [genuine assertion]

PARENT: That would work. Yes, let's do it together!   [agreement]

Had the adult child immediately suggested lending the money or buying the Treasury bill jointly, there would have been a high risk of rejection. With the parent creating the idea, acceptance is all but guaranteed.

Let's look at a more difficult financial situation.

YOU-THE-CHILD: I see you've still got a thousand shares of Frodo Corporation.   [opening signal]

PARENT: Yes. It'll turn around.   [defensive]

You-the-Child: You feel Frodo will start paying dividends again. [checking listening]

Parent: Sure. It's a going company. They're not losing money. I've held on to it for ten years; I can hold longer. [defensive]

You-the-Child: You think that the turnaround will come soon. [checking listening]

Parent: Truthfully, I don't know. I'm disappointed. I lost a lot of money on Frodo. Cost me fifteen thousand dollars. I don't see how I'll ever get it back. I guess I'm holding on hoping. [hidden feelings]

You-the-Child: I can understand how you feel. Losing all that money can be a blow. I can see why you want to hold. [nurturing listening]

Parent: Come to think of it, I should really sell and get my money out. I could buy some bonds and at least have the interest. [creative solution]

You-the-Child: You'd have the money in your pocket. [checking listening]

Parent: Yes.

Again, had the adult child barged in with advice to sell Frodo, the parent would have reacted negatively, particularly because it was his bad judgment in the first place that lost the money. The parent's defenses would have mounted to the sky and blocked creative thinking. Frodo Corporation would have been lodged permanently in the parent's portfolio.

If Your Parent Cannot Budget

Many of your parent's money worries—as may indeed your own money worries—stem from an inability to budget or to control expenses. They spend money on trivia and then don't have enough to pay for essentials. You find them borrowing from or asking you for rent, car repairs, perhaps even food. And when you try to push your way into their lives to budget for them, they not only reject your offers of help, they accuse you wanting them to live in penury.

Here again we are dealing with habits of a lifetime. And they are very difficult to change. If your mother has been visiting the most expensive hairdresser in town, you will not be able to convince her to try someone cheaper:

"I went to the shop on Elm Street. They burned my hair. I looked like a monster for a month."

If your father has been dropping fifteen dollars a week playing poker with his friends, that cannot be easily stopped either. To leave that game would be an admission that he no longer can live a normal life. And so on. The variants are endless. In each case, the cessation of an expensive but cherished activity marks a step toward old age and death.

With the nurturing language you may be able to discover negotiable items. You may be able to help your parent transfer money from one less important activity to an important one without sense of loss. The nurturing language will aid your parent to separate the valuable from the marginal activities:

PARENT: I need thirty-five dollars to make up the rent money. I'm short this month.   [opening signal]

YOU-THE-CHILD: You've used up all the money from Social Security and what we give you.   [checking listening]

PARENT: I don't know where it goes. Everything is so expensive.   [defensive]

YOU-THE-CHILD: Hmmm.   [wordless listening]

PARENT: Do you know what hamburger costs? I watch every penny and still I don't have enough.   [question]

YOU-THE-CHILD: You're budgeting carefully and your expenses still go up. [checking listening]

PARENT: I don't have to budget. I know what I spend. I don't waste. [defensive]

YOU-THE-CHILD: You're watching your expenses on everything and that doesn't help. [checking listening]

PARENT: Oh. I can cut down on one or two things. I know I spend too much on taxis. [moving toward solution]

YOU-THE-CHILD: You feel that if you reduced some things like taxis you could do better. [checking listening]

PARENT: The taxis. The taxis. They're my downfall. I just don't like taking the bus. And I start out for appointments too late to take the bus. I guess I could make an effort on the taxis. [understanding]

YOU-THE-CHILD: You feel that if you cut back on the taxis you could make it on your own next month. [listening-to-speak]

PARENT: I really think so. [agreement]

YOU-THE-CHILD: I'm glad you've figured out what the problem is. It takes a load off my mind. I don't like to see you uncomfortable month after month. It must be very difficult for you to ask for money. [genuine assertion/ show of pleasure] [nurturing listening]

PARENT: I'd give anything not to have to do it. [reveals feelings]

You will find it hard going if there is a striking gap between your standard of living and that of your parents. And that will bring you to the philosophical questions: Can I let my parents live at a much lower income level than I? What do I owe them? Your answers can be negotiated with your parents.

What, No Will?

Families who do have some money face severe disruption over the aging parent's last will and testament. Mishandling of the will can foster lifelong enmity among brothers and sisters. Even when there is not a good deal of money involved, relatives jockey for favor to get a bigger piece of the pie. The parent is buffeted first this way and then that.

"Momma promised me the pearl necklace."

"I should get the Tiffany lamp. It was in my room."

"I know dad has General Motors stock that I told him to buy. In a sense I should get the profit he made."

"I don't think father should leave his money equally to the grandchildren. You have three kids and I only have one and that's unfair."

On the other side, parents use the will to control their adult children, promising one child one thing and another child something else (sometimes the same thing). To bring a child to heel, a parent may threaten to eliminate that child from sharing in an estate. Needless to say, a relationship based on such a severe imbalance of power—with the parent holding the power—cannot be anything but sick in the sense we have described: Both parties are punished and rewarded by their mutually hostile behavior. At least one of the parties needs to recognize the sick character of the ties that bind. Only then can repairs begin.

Sometimes the parent has refused to make a will, leaving his or her estate open to high taxes and excessive legal entanglements. Elders often wish to escape from family pressures surrounding wills, so they do not make one. The making of a will also speaks to mortality, and that is a subject that elderly people would often rather avoid. So they suppress the idea of a last will and testament.

Alas, the emotions, the conflicting objectives, the greed and the fears associated with wills sometimes make peace and fairness almost unattainable. Occasionally it even becomes impossible to get a will written. In this situation, the person with the nurturing language skills has the best chance of playing the mediating role. The nurturing person need not submerge his or her own needs and feelings, but more than others the nurturer will be heard (and will hear others) without generating hostility. The nurturer will, in part, infect others with the nurturing style and calm the storms of conflict.

Where Will Mother or Father Live?

Even though so many parents do live by themselves, many more families struggle with the problem of where to put grandpa or grandma. There are many more old people today than there were a century ago. Life expectancy is at an all-time high. Today one person in twelve is over sixty-five; a hundred years ago the figure was one in twenty-five. In addition, housing standards were lower then: A bathroom or bathtub was not required. An extra person meant only an extra bed. We now expect these and other amenities as necessities. But small urban apartments cannot provide them easily for three-generation families.

Mostly parents will be living alone. The death of a spouse, particularly for women, raises the issue sharply. Because women live longer than men, there are far more widows than widowers. Most older men live with a wife (or a woman not a wife). Perhaps a quarter of older women live without a husband or male companion. The widow alone is becoming a major social issue.

Here are the questions faced by more and more families today:

"Shall we let mom live in that big old house alone?"

"The neighborhood has turned bad. Let's get dad out of there."

"I can't put mother up here. Mildred can't manage that. Why don't you take her?"

"I can't live with my parents anymore. It's driving me crazy."

"Pop wants to sell the house and move to Florida."

"With that broken hip—even when it gets better—mother cannot live alone."

"Daddy really can't take care of himself at all— mentally."

"Mother is eighty-two. Wouldn't she be better off in an old-age home?"

"We've got to get mom out of the state mental hospital."

You are hearing the voices of the adult children. They are taking on the problem of parental housing as their own. In most cases, parents make up their own minds where to live. With adequate financial backing, they do have choices, although among the poor the choices—as for everything— dwindle down to few; sometimes none.

To place mother in an old-age home; to move father out of the family house; to get mother out of the mental hospital—each implies that the decision involves the parent only minimally. That leads to conflict and resistance on the part of the parent to accede to the decision. If the parent has been given no choice, he or she is made to seem a ward of his or her own children.

Living with Grandma and Grandpa

Here are some common conflicts and how they might be handled by the nurturing language. First, the parent living with the adult child's family.

Mother or father at home intensifies the normal stress of living together. The adult child and spouse have worked out a set of rules for coexistence that covers the children, meals, bathrooms, gardens, leisure, sanitation, sharing of chores. The parent suddenly finds himself or herself thrust into a little social group whose rules the parent did not establish or negotiate. As an independent adult and former head of household, the parent expects to be able to change the uncomfortable rules and to set a few. To the adult child, the spoken or unspoken guiding principle is: "This is my house and I expect to have my rules followed."

Unless some compromise is negotiated, both sides will mount verbal weapons and manipulations. Without mutual agreement, either the parent gives in—grudgingly—and becomes a docile childlike member of the household, or the parent eventually moves out in a climate of hostility. The problem mimics the tension between spouses. When the rules of living together cannot be modified to suit both parties, there are three possible consequences. One: somebody—usually the parent—moves out; two: somebody capitulates; three: the relationship becomes sick—all the parties receive punishments and rewards from the hostility.

With the nurturing language, you have a chance to change the rules to suit everyone in the household. You can get the cooperation of your live-in parent and your spouse. And win the benefits of a loving helpful parent living with you.

After her husband died in their retirement home in Arizona three months ago, Nell, sixty-eight, has moved in with her son, John, and his wife, Alberta. John had bought the old family home from his parents so Nell is really living in her original home.

NELL: Dear, don't you think that the chair would look better over there? [opening signal/ question]

ALBERTA: I like it where it is. [answers]

NELL: Dear, let's put it over there just to see how it looks. [tries again]

ALBERTA: It looks just fine. [rejection]

NELL: It would fit nicely there by the small table. [once more]

ALBERTA: It's staying where it is and I don't want to move it! [final]

NELL: My, you certainly are an opinionated person! [name-calling]

We all know where that leads. Nell wants to change things to suit her needs. Alberta thinks: "This is my house." Nell has no recourse but to bring out the weapons. Let's try it with the nurturing language.

NELL: Dear, don't you think the chair would look better over there? [opening signal/ question]

ALBERTA: You think it would look better over there. [checking listening]

NELL: Yes. It would balance off the room. [reason]

ALBERTA: You feel the room needs to be balanced. [checking listening]

NELL: Yes. Good decorating says the room should be balanced. [superiority]

ALBERTA: I feel that my way of arranging doesn't please you. [genuine assertion]

NELL: Oh, dear, it's nice! I just want to move the chair. [backing down]

ALBERTA: You feel the room won't be right until that chair is moved. [checking listening]

NELL: It's a nice room. Perhaps it isn't the chair that needs moving. Maybe it's the small chest. [backing down again]

ALBERTA: You think the small chest needs moving. [checking listening]

NELL: Yes. I guess I have that feeling. [confused]

ALBERTA: You feel something has to be moved but you're not quite sure what. [checking listening]

NELL: Why, yes, I have that feeling. [agreement]

ALBERTA: You feel uncomfortable in this room. [nurturing listening]

NELL: Yes.

ALBERTA: You have a reason for feeling uncomfortable. [nurturing listening]

NELL: I guess it's that that chair be- [reveals hidden feel-
longed to my mother and she always ings]
kept it by the window.

ALBERTA: You'd like me to put the [nurturing]
chair by the window because it
would feel right to you because of
your mother.

NELL: Yes, Alberta that would be nice. [show of pleasure]

It may occur to many: Why put up with all that nonsense? It's Alberta's house now. Nell simply has to do what Alberta wants. Nell is just an interfering mother-in-law.

One has to assume that because Nell has moved in with her adult children they want her there and they want her to be comfortable. And everybody wants the daily give-and-take to go smoothly. In the first dialogue, Alberta aggressively asserted her power over her mother-in-law. To keep her dignity, Nell fought back. And that will lead to more and more confrontation. John will be brought in and he will face the impossible task of choosing between his mother and his wife. Marriages have foundered when a parent moves in with the adult child.

By speaking the nurturing language, Alberta acknowledged that her mother-in-law is an adult, entitled to express her feelings and to be involved with the establishment of rules of the house. The nurturing language revealed to Alberta that the placement of the chair had deep emotional meaning for Nell, something completely hidden in the first dialogue. Alberta could then weigh her need to keep the chair the way it is against Nell's need to satisfy that longing. Even though the chair event seemed trivial, Alberta laid a foundation for the negotiation of matters more important to her.

Indeed, there were more critical issues:

ALBERTA: We have such a jam-up at [opening signal]
the bathroom every morning with

John getting to work and the kids to school. Everybody leaves here in a rush. [call for help]

NELL: Once Nancy [grandchild] is in there you can't get her out. [shifting blame]

ALBERTA: You feel Nancy takes too long in the bathroom. [checking listening]

NELL: Just yesterday she was in there combing her hair for ten minutes. [shifting blame]

ALBERTA: You think ten minutes is too long for combing hair. [checking listening]

NELL: At least she can do it in her room. She did it this morning. [solution]

ALBERTA: You're saying that if Nancy combed her hair in her room we wouldn't have the rush for the bathroom. [checking listening/ listening-to-speak]

NELL: It would help.

ALBERTA: We still had the jam this morning even though Nancy combed her hair in her room. John barely had time for breakfast. We've set up a time when each person can use the bathroom and when the schedule is not kept, we run into this trouble. It's getting on all our nerves. [genuine assertion]

NELL: Well, I can't help it if I go in before my time. I just have to. I can't wait. [defensive]

ALBERTA: You're saying that your time is too late and that it's too hard for you to wait. [checking listening]

NELL: Yes. Maybe if I went real early before John and then again much later I won't hold anybody up. [creative solution]

ALBERTA: That would certainly help   [show of pleasure]
everybody. I'm glad we worked it
out. I just couldn't take another
morning like today.

Alberta discovered that Nell had a physical problem that
prevented her from keeping to the bathroom schedule. Again,
the nurturing language takes longer but the results are more
permanent and the feelings warmer. It's a good idea to work
out the rules as soon possible after your parent moves in.
That way there are no hidden rules to cause friction.

When You Live in Your Parents' Home

Although you may be well past your teens and you live in
your parents' home, your parents may continue to treat you
as if you were a small child. They want you to keep to their
schedule, their rules, and their moral standards as if nothing
had changed since you were in diapers. And if for economic
or other reasons you cannot move out, you are stuck unless
you decide to do full battle with them or you rely on the
nurturing language. Hostilities end with pain or promote a
sick relationship. The nurturing language will give you peace
and parents.

DAUGHTER (arrives home at 8:45 P.M.)
MOTHER: (screams): Where have you   [question]
been all day?
DAUGHTER: Excuse me.   [wordless listening]
MOTHER: Where have you been all   [question]
day? I've had dinner waiting on the [hidden informa-
table and now it's cold.   tion]
DAUGHTER: You were worried about   [checking listening]
me because you didn't know where   [listening-to-speak]
I was all day.
MOTHER: Yes. You know how that up-   [superiority]

sets me. I had dinner waiting and   [nearly a cry of
you didn't come home. After all the   pain]
work I did!

DAUGHTER: If it irritates you that din-   [genuine assertion]
ner gets cold, you don't really have
to fix it for me anymore. I really
don't mind because I'll be coming
home late a lot during this semester.

MOTHER: You really don't mind? [re-   [question]
lieved]

DAUGHTER: You sound relieved.   [nurturing listening]

MOTHER: I am.

Here's a tougher and equally common problem:

FATHER: You can't stay out late to-   [superiority]
night.

DAUGHTER: Bobby is in trouble with   [defensive]
the cops and you let him stay out all
night. But I have to be in by mid-
night. It's not fair.

FATHER: Your brother is different. He's   [superiority]
a boy. Besides, we don't want to
make the same mistake with you.

DAUGHTER (storms out of room)   [retreat]

Very hard to handle. Why not try this:

FATHER: You can't stay out late to-   [superiority]
night.

DAUGHTER: I only want to stay out un-   [genuine assertion]
til one A.M. with Tommy because
we're going out with some friends.

FATHER: One o'clock is too late. I want   [superiority]
you home by twelve. Young girls
should not be out in bars at that   ["should"]
time of night.

DAUGHTER: You're saying that it's okay for young men to stay out late but not young women.	[checking listening]
FATHER: Yes. It's dangerous out there at that time. A girl can't be too careful.	[superiority]
DAUGHTER: I can understand that you're worried about me. You feel Tommy and my friends won't protect me.	[nurturing listening]
FATHER: I wouldn't say that. Maybe if you gave me a call around midnight I wouldn't be so worried.	[creative solution]
DAUGHTER: I can stay out until one o'clock if I give you a call earlier . . . around twelve.	[checking listening]
FATHER: Yes. That would be good.	
DAUGHTER: I'll be glad to telephone. I don't want to worry you unnecessarily.	[show of pleasure]

This daughter had to be ready to compromise. Some adult children would balk at the telephone call as demeaning unless they realize that the call is intended to ease the father's worry, not as a requirement for a child. The daughter avoided defending herself, avoided the usual "I am not a child." "I am not a girl; I am a woman." Etc.

The father may have a hidden agenda. He may be concerned about his daughter's sexual activities and feel that an early curfew would reduce the chances of her engaging in "forbidden" behavior. We'll deal with sexual issues in Chapter 14.

When Your Parent Has to Go to an Institution

Putting an aging parent in a nursing or old-age home or a mental hospital can rip a family apart. Lifelong feelings of guilt wash over adult children in great waves. Many adult children refuse—as they say—to abandon their parents. And when they examine available facilities, they find a few of high quality. The rest often lie on the edge of being prisons or poorhouses. Even though Medicare pays (in part) for nursing home care after an elder has been hospitalized, the payments are limited and the burden then falls back on the old person or on his adult children. When all resources are exhausted, the elder becomes the ward of welfare—Medicaid—to be placed in a nursing or old-age home of uncertain quality.

More and more adult children and their parents face the dilemma of the institution. All of us would like to see our parents in a lovely garden apartment near their friends with nearby social and medical facilities. But illness and poverty intervene to narrow the choices. Often it is a matter of economics—what the family can afford. Most often, creative solutions have been overlooked because the parent has been eliminated from the deliberations on where he or she is to live. The nurturing language plays a double role: allowing the parent a choice so that creative skills can come into play and giving the parent a voice in selecting the kind of living arrangement best for the parent.

As for the latter—picking the place—we have already alluded to the function of the nurturing language in assessing the quality of the staff. If you hear the nurturing language spoken between staff and patients, then despite poor physical appearance the institution probably has high service standards. They care. Your parent will preserve dignity and vitality. Listen for this:

ATTENDANT: Good morning, Mrs. Oliver. I hope you're feeling well today.　　　　　　　　　　　　[opening signal]

MRS. OLIVER: Okay, I guess.　　　　　　　　　　[hint]

ATTENDANT: Something's troubling you.　　　　　　　[checking listening]

MRS. OLIVER: I have a slight burning when I go to the bathroom.   [reveals problem]

ATTENDANT: You have a burning sensation when you urinate.   [checking listening]

MRS. OLIVER: No. It's when I do the other.   [corrects attendant]

ATTENDANT: You have a burning near the rectum.   [checking listening]

MRS. OLIVER: That's right. I'm very constipated. I haven't taken my Metamucil* regularly.   [reveals more]

ATTENDANT: You think your constipation is causing the burning. Well, you must be very uncomfortable.   [checking listening]
[nurturing listening]

MRS. OLIVER: It's really my own fault. I should take the Metamucil regularly. I'll let you know in a couple of days how it's going.   [creative solution]

ATTENDANT: I'm glad to hear that. I don't like to see you suffer. If it doesn't get better we'll have somebody take a look.   [show of pleasure]

If you hear such dialogues, you know you're in a good place. On the other hand:

ATTENDANT: Well, Mrs. Oliver, what's bothering you this morning?   [question]

MRS. OLIVER: Nothing.   [answers]

ATTENDANT: How's your constipation?   [question]

MRS. OLIVER: It's all right.   [answers]

ATTENDANT: Been taking your Metamucil every day?   [question]

---

* Metamucil: a bulk laxative.

MRS. OLIVER: Oh, yes.   [answers]
ATTENDANT: That's a good girl.   [condescending]

If you hear such conversations in your presence, you may be assured that in your absence the language gets rougher and more demeaning. The attendants, nurses, and doctors in such a place treat their patients as children.

"Now be a good boy and take your medicine!"

"I told you to sit in that chair!"

"The rules are: no smoking. And we mean no smoking!"

"If you keep on complaining, we'll have to give you another shot!"

"Now clean up your bed! It looks like a baby's crib."

"Get over to that side and stay there or you'll regret it!"

No matter how pretty the scenery or tasty the food, such behavior by staff will make your parent miserable. There is another version of this directiveness: It's called wheedling—using flattery and honeyed words to get a person to do your bidding.

"Don't we look pretty with our face washed!"

"What a clever person you are! You've finished your carrots."

"Look, look! Mr. Harris has taken three more steps today! Isn't that wonderful!"

"I just love your frock! It fits you very well. I hope you'll keep it clean."

Wheedling demeans an older person's status just as effectively as directiveness. The wheedler assumes that his target is too stupid to see through the flattery or that the elder is as a little child and must be spoken to accordingly. If you hear wheedling, your parent may be very unhappy. Elders visiting such places are very quick to pick up directiveness and wheedling. They will say: "I don't like this place." And then not be able to explain why. You may point out the lovely grounds, the beautiful rooms, the good food, all to no avail. They hear the demeaning sounds of the toxic language.

Letting Your Parent Decide

If you keep your parent from full partnership in choosing living arrangements, your parent will never be satisfied. Parents tend to find fault when they have not been consulted. It is their way of establishing their status and regaining or attempting to regain control over their lives. If you are moving toward an institutional arrangement, the nurturing language will give your parent the best chance at deep participation in his or her fate.

YOU-THE-CHILD: When you leave the hospital we need to arrange where you'll live. [opening signal]

PARENT: You're not sending me to an old folks home! I'd rather die! [defensive]

YOU-THE-CHILD: You're afraid of an old-age home. [nurturing listening]

PARENT: They're terrible places! I know. Chuck Sealey is in one. He's miserable. Why can't I live at home? [defensive] [showing fear] [question]

YOU-THE-CHILD: You think you'll try to manage at home. [checking listening]

PARENT: We can get a nurse or a housekeeper until I can take care of myself. Maybe Jill [a niece] can sleep over at night. I don't care what it costs. [creative solution]

YOU-THE-CHILD: You feel a nurse can give you the medicine, feed you, and put you through the rehabilitation exercises. [checking listening]

PARENT: I've started rehabilitation here. But I won't have the machines. Do you suppose I could rent them? [information] [question]

You-the-Child: If you could rent them you could do the rehabilitation at home.   [checking listening]

Parent: They must be expensive, huh? And the nurse, too. What do nurses get these days? I don't suppose they cook either. I'll need a housekeeper. Hmmm.   [backing down]

You-the-Child: The costs seem to be mounting up. Maybe Medicare will pay.   [checking listening]

Parent: No. They only pay for nursing home care. I could get rehabilitation in a nursing home. They're not bad. And they're only temporary. Maybe, I could go there first and then home.   [information]   [another solution]

You-the-Child: You're saying that with a month or so in a nursing home you'd be ready to live at home.   [checking listening]

Parent: I don't know but it's worth a try.   [likes idea]

You-the-Child: It does sound that way.

Dialogues of this kind may last an hour or more as you go over each detail with your parent several times. Your parent may perseverate, i.e., repeat the same sentence over and over. "I don't want to go to an old folks home." "Chuck Sealey is miserable." The repetitions express uncontrolled fear, fear that can be made easier to bear by consistent nurturing.

You rarely achieve a resolution as quickly as in the above version. You will itch to give advice: "Why don't you . . .?" Or: "How about this idea . . . ?" If you scratch the itch, your parent will hear the implied "should" and back off. He will think you are trying to get him to do something he does not want to do. You may have to delay your own genuine assertions until the perseveration ceases. Only then will your parent hear you.

The prospect of institutionalization may trigger extreme hostility in your parent, who may heap blame on you for the present predicament. You may expect all the verbal weapons of the past to come into active play. It will be hard to stick with the nurturing language as you long to get back at your parent. It is helpful at such times to distance yourself emotionally from your parent by temporarily moving a step or two down the ladder of relationship.

Let's see what such a confrontation sounds like:

YOU-THE-CHILD: I worry about you alone in that apartment, especially after you fell last week. I'm glad nothing was broken, but I think about the possibility of your being helpless there.　[genuine assertion]

PARENT: You're leading up to something. What is it?　[question]

YOU-THE-CHILD: You think I have something in mind.　[checking listening]

PARENT: Yes. What is it? What are you leading up to?　[question]

YOU-THE-CHILD: I'm worried about you alone in that apartment, especially after you fell last week.　[genuine assertion]

PARENT: You're hinting that I should move out, aren't you? What are you leading up to?　[question]

YOU-THE-CHILD: You've thought about moving.　[checking listening]

PARENT: I'd like to move in with you and Jane.　[expresses wish]

You-the-Child: You think that's the best thing.   [checking listening]

Parent: Oh, I know how you feel. You don't want me anywhere near you. And Jane would be happy if she never saw me again.   [attack]

You-the-Child: How unhappy you must be to feel that Jane and I don't want you or want to see you!   [nurturing listening]

Parent: It's not pleasant being old and rejected by your family.   [expresses feelings]

You-the-Child: I can understand how you feel. It seems to you that because we can't have you live with us that we don't love you or want to help you. I didn't realize how deep your feelings are.   [nurturing listening]

Parent (crying): Now you know why I don't want to move.   [expresses feelings]

And so on. For several hours perhaps. Until the parent gets it all out for you to hear. It takes will not be defensive: "But Jane and I want to see you! Why not come for dinner Thursday?" Defensiveness will only make your parent close his or her mind to what you have to say. Constant nurturing will eventually open his or her hearing so that a solution may be negotiated.

/ 14 /

Getting Along Great Even
with Real Problems: III

Sex. A little word. A large issue. In American life, we have
made it unseemly for older people to think, to talk, or to
behave sexually. We have invented the idea of "the dirty
old man," a man past the half-century mark who advances
sexually toward women younger than himself. We mock the
woman who at forty or fifty acts coquettish, although in
women of twenty or thirty we call the same playfulness
"cute." We assume that sexual ability declines sharply with
age and disappears by age sixty-five or thereabouts. We cannot imagine that older people have any interest (except
salacious) in sex.

In the real world of older people, sex figures heavily in
their lives. Many, the exact number is unknown, have almost
undiminished sexual activity well into their eighties. Old-age
homes have set up "private rooms" so that elders may enjoy
sexual companionship. Women do not lose their physical
capacity for orgasm nor men their ability for erection and
ejaculation. Their sex behavior differs from that of younger

people. Older men may take longer to reach an erection and it may be less firm than in their younger days. And it takes them longer to achieve ejaculation and then be ready again for intercourse. Better than younger men, they can engage in long love-making before ejaculation, a skill often appreciated by their partners.

Older women suffer from dryness of the vagina and loss of tone of the vaginal walls and both may lead to uncomfortable or painful intercourse. Both conditions may be treated successfully with hormones or lubrication.

Older people are less interested in the frequency of sexual acts—how many orgasms—than they are in the quality—how comforting, how pleasant, how romantic. Cuddling and hugging may be more important to them than genital contact. And most of all, they need and treasure the intimacy that sex promotes.

Recent studies suggest that older people are far more liberal in their attitudes than younger persons believe. For example, the Social Security laws financially punish older people who marry. A woman may be getting a widow's benefit that she loses on marriage. Many older people, loath to lose the money, just move in together without benefit of clergy and keep the benefit of money. Age differences are growing between sex partners, although by and large elders prefer sex mates close to their own ages.

Because sex may have been a taboo subject between parent and child growing up, it continues to be between parent and adult child. Because parents attempt to control their young children's sexual behavior, they may continue to do so as the children become adults. And as roles reverse, i.e., as the adult child assumes parental authority over the parent, the child seeks control over the parent's sex life. What the parent experiences may appear unseemly, immoral, or dangerous to the adult child.

Edgar, fifty-four, was widowed a year ago. Gene, twenty-seven, is his son.

GENE: Dad, people are talking because you're seeing Sue Anne.

EDGAR: Yes. Don't we look well together?

GENE: Dad, everyone doesn't think so.

EDGAR: Why not? She's a pretty little thing, and a senior in college, too.

GENE: Everyone knows she's a senior in college.

EDGAR: Isn't that great? I plan to go to her graduation in June.

GENE: Dad, that's just the point!

EDGAR: What do you mean? I went to your graduation, too. Didn't I?

GENE: Yes. But, dad, she's too young for you.

EDGAR: No. I think we hit it off very well.

GENE: She is six years younger than I am! Young enough to be your daughter.

EDGAR: Well, she isn't young enough to be your daughter. So keep your nose out of my life! No more advice, sonny!

The father had warned his son five times in this dialogue about making a judgment. Each time the son persisted. Finally, Edgar fired off his salvo. He was expressing an opinion held by many parents, namely, "Don't meddle in my sex life."

Gene might say: "But don't I have a responsibility for preventing my father from doing something foolish, something that will make him the laughing stock of his friends?"

Is Gene really concerned about his father's reputation or is he more concerned that his, Gene's, friends will make rude remarks about his father whom he might have to defend? Is he more fearful for his own reputation as being the son of a "dirty old man"? If so, perhaps Gene may want to take the burden and express it to his father as follows:

GENE: Dad, people are talking be-   [opening signal]
cause you're seeing Sue Anne.

EDGAR: Yes. Don't we look well to-
gether?   [show of pleasure]

GENE: You like being seen with Sue   [checking listening]
Anne.

EDGAR: Oh, yes. She's such a pretty   [reveals feelings]
little thing. And a senior in college,
too.

GENE: You seem very pleased with   [nurturing listen-
yourself about the conquest you've   ing]
made.

EDGAR: Not bad for a guy my age, eh?   [question]

GENE: I can understand you feel   [nurturing listen-
younger going out with Sue Anne.   ing/listening-to-
                                           speak]

EDGAR: I know not everyone likes the   [understanding]
idea of a man my age dating a
young girl. But I'm enjoying it.

GENE: People do talk to me about it   [cry of pain]
and I have a hard time with it be-
cause Sue Anne is six years younger
than I. I find myself getting angry
with what people are saying.

EDGAR: I'm sorry I'm making things   [sympathy]
tough for you. But I'm having a
very good time. I know it won't last.
She's very young, and she knows it,
too. I'll try not to take her to places [creative solution]
where you know the people.

GENE: That'll help. Maybe people will [show of pleasure]
cool down if they don't see you so
much with her.

In this dialogue, Gene recognizes that gossip won't force
his father to give up Sue Anne. Gene also understands that
the problem is his; it is he who cannot stand the gossip. And
by listening to his son's feelings, Edgar came up with a

partial solution. In this case, Gene cannot hope to have his father solve the problem completely. The nurturing language retained the bond between father and son and improved the son's position; the old toxic language estranged the two and brought no improvement.

More commonly the parent disapproves of the adult child's sex activity, particularly when the child still lives with the parents. Jan is twenty-one, a senior in a local college and living at home with her father, Raymond, and mother, Helen. The following conversation was reported by Jan after a role-playing session in a special class in the nurturing language conducted for adult children at Adelphi University.

JAN: Daddy, I've something I want to tell you. I've decided to go to Florida for my vacation. I'm going with Tommy. [opening signal] [incomplete genuine assertion]

RAYMOND: Who else is going? [question]

JAN: No one, just me and Tommy. [answers]

RAYMOND: What do you mean just you and Tommy! Over my dead body! I won't permit it! [superiority]

JAN: But, daddy . . . [argues]

RAYMOND: No. No. No! [superiority]

JAN: Daddy, I want to talk to you about this. I want to discuss it calmly. I can't talk to you now. I feel nervous when you scream. I'll discuss it with you when you calm down. [walks out of room] [call for help]

Later that evening:

JAN: I really want to talk to you about my vacation with Tommy. Can we talk now? [incomplete assertion] [question]

RAYMOND: Yes. Why Tommy? Why can't you go with one of your girl-friends?   [questions]

JAN: I could have, but I wanted to go with Tommy.   [answers]

RAYMOND: It's all Tommy's idea. I know he just wants to . . .   [judgment]

JAN: Dad. It wasn't Tommy's idea. It was my idea. I want to go with Tommy.   [contradicts] [assertion]

RAYMOND: In my day . . .   [superiority]

JAN: Daddy, this is *my* day. I could have lied to you or covered it up, but I wanted to be honest with you.   [contradicts] [defensive]

I know it's hard for you, but I'm not your little girl anymore.   [seminurturing]

RAYMOND: I know that, Jan, but I don't see why you can't bring some-one else with you.   [trying for solution]

JAN: I already said I could but I don't want to.   [not listening]

RAYMOND: I won't allow it.   [authority]

JAN: I'm not asking for your permis-sion. It would have been easy for me to get it by lying. But I don't want to lie to you. I've made up my mind. It's my decision and I'm ask-ing you to accept it, not to like it.   [aggressive]

RAYMOND: I don't like it and I don't accept it, but I'll try to get used to it.   [part agreement]

Jan learned some things from the nurturing language, enough to be able to stand up to her father, enough to pro-vide some nurturing so that Raymond would not feel com-pletely rejected. Our analysis of this dialogue is that Jan had been dominated by her father for many years. The nurturing language gave her a few tools to fend off her father's dominance. Her newfound freedom, however, diverted her attention from fully nurturing her father. She seemed intoxicated with being able to control her father. And that is a danger when you apply the nurturing language incompletely. For a while, it can give you the upper hand . . . power. And power can corrupt.

Jan's intermediate result came from her call for help ("I want to talk to you about this . . . etc.") and the seminurturing ("I know this is hard for you . . ."). Her call for help opened the possibility of later discussion. And the seminurturing allowed her father to search for a solution ("I don't see why you can't bring someone else with you").

The dialogue does show the strength of the nurturing language. Jan applied only a part of it and still gained something from her father, however grudgingly he delivered it. Had Jan fully used the nurturing language, we suspect that her father might have come around to a more friendly, helpful and understanding position.

It may be worthwhile to look at some alternate responses. The toxic language response is indicated by bold face; the nurturing language in italics.

RAYMOND: Who else is going? [question]
JAN: No one, just me and Tommy. [answers]
JAN: *You are concerned that I'm going alone with Tommy.* [checking listening]

RAYMOND: Why Tommy? Why can't you go with one of your girlfriends? [questions]
JAN: I could have but I wanted to go with Tommy. [answers]
JAN: *You feel it would be safer if I went with one of my women friends.* [checking listening]

RAYMOND: In my day . . . [superiority]
JAN: Daddy, this is *my* day. I could [contradicts]

have lied to you or covered it up   [defensive]
but I wanted to be honest with you.
I know it's hard for you but I'm not   [seminurturing]
your little girl anymore.

JAN: *I know that it is hard for you to*   [nurturing listen-
accept what I am doing. It must   ing]
seem to you that I am about to do
something terribly immoral and
dangerous.

RAYMOND: I won't allow it.   [authority]

JAN: I'm not asking your permission.   [aggressive]
It would have been easy for me to
get it by lying. It's my decision and
I'm asking you to accept it, not to
like it.

JAN: *This is something I really want to*   [genuine assertion]
do. When I'm told that I'm not al-
lowed to do it, I feel as though I
were a little girl and not permitted
to be an adult and make adult de-
cisions.

These were four critical points in the dialogue. Had Jan responded fully with the nurturing language, her father would have had a chance to understand his objections. He would have seen her point of view and perhaps reached toward her to help her. He might have come up with a creative solution that would have assuaged his feelings of danger. Jan and her father could have discussed the sexual issues more frankly. Raymond tried to open up the subject ("I know he just wants to . . . "), albeit crudely, but Jan rejected the opportunity. Our new language permits safe explorations of sexual problems.

Cecil is sixty, living alone after a divorce many years ago. His son, Douglas, is thirty-four, married with two children. They meet for dinner from time to time.

CECIL: How are things at home? [question]

DOUGLAS: Fine. [answers]

CECIL: I mean between you and Linda. [question]

DOUGLAS: You have a reason for asking. [checking listening]

CECIL: Oh, nothing really. I just know how it can be with married couples. [reveals part feelings]

DOUGLAS: You think Linda and I could have the same problem that you and mom did. [checking listening]

CECIL: It's not out of the question. [comment]

DOUGLAS: Hmmm. [wordless listening]

CECIL: I mean your mother and I never did have a good sex life. [reveals hidden material]

DOUGLAS: That must have been hell for both of you. [nurturing listening]

CECIL: Especially for me. It was always very important to me. You know since the divorce, I haven't been alone for more than a few weeks at a time. I have a new woman now. I'd like you to meet her. [more material]

DOUGLAS: You're anxious to get together soon. [checking listening]

CECIL: Harriet's really very sexy. She's about forty years old. I must say she's something to keep up with. [more material]

DOUGLAS: You sound as if you're having a good but strenuous affair. [nurturing listening]

CECIL: Actually, I'm not my old self with Harriet. I really don't know what's wrong. And it worries me. [more revelations]

DOUGLAS: You sound very unhappy with the sex part; as if you lost it. [nurturing listening]

That must be very difficult for you
because sex is so important for you.

CECIL: I've been losing my erection. I   [profound material]
don't know what's causing it.

DOUGLAS: Oh, that's terrible. You must   [nurturing listen-
be beside yourself. And you don't   ing]
have any clue. That's worse.

CECIL: Actually, I do have a clue. My   [moving toward so-
prostate is getting bigger and when   lution]
I was to the doctor last he asked me
was I having trouble with my potency. I told him, "No." But I was
having trouble. Maybe I should go
back and have him check again.

DOUGLAS: It sounds like a good idea.   [show of pleasure]
I'd be relieved to know that you're
getting at the reason for all this.

CECIL: I think I should go next week.   [agreement]

Note that Cecil had some very personal business on his
mind, but his inhibition would not allow him to go directly
to it. Instead, he first made a foray at Douglas's private life.
Psychologists call this projection: We attribute to someone
else the trouble or the characteristics that we have. If Cecil
is having sex problems, he suggests that Douglas may be
having them, too.

The new language gently made it safe for Cecil to reveal
his difficulty and to open his creative problem-solving skills.
On the first visit to the doctor, Cecil did not answer the physician's question about potency for reasons we now understand. But Cecil understood the implication of the question.
His son made it possible for him to bring the information to
bear on his current embarrassment.

In some families, sex is never discussed. There is just too
much taboo surrounding it, even with parents and adult
children who have been close and supportive all their lives.

At most they will deal with the technical and medical problems—i.e., infections, having babies—but never with the intimacy and feelings of sexual interaction. Many adult children, therefore, have no opportunity to get help or information from their parents. The loss may be critical for young adults.

Jean, twenty-seven, has a good job as a copy writer in an advertising agency. She has her own apartment on Chicago's Near Northside. Her mother, Rose, fifty-two, lives in the suburbs where Jean grew up. They talk almost every day either in person or on the phone. Theirs is a close mother-daughter bond. Up to now sex talk has been outlawed by mutual silent consent. But Jean has learned the new language and she wants to share something intimate with her mother.

She has been having a love affair with Phil, thirty-four. They do not live together.

JEAN: I have a problem I want to share because it will help me think it through.	[opening signal/ genuine assertion/ call for help]
ROSE: Not something terrible, I hope! Tell me.	[sympathetic]
JEAN: It's about Phil and me.	[information]
ROSE: You haven't broken up?	[question]
JEAN: You're worried about that.	[checking listening]
ROSE: No. No. I think you're a lovely couple.	[corrects]
JEAN: I do like him a lot. That's what makes it so difficult. Sometimes when we make love he makes demands on me that I can't meet.	[genuine assertion]
ROSE (embarrassed): You mean you're sleeping with him?	[question]
JEAN: You thought I wasn't.	[checking listening]
ROSE: I guess I knew it but I didn't want to admit it to myself. After all, you're my little girl.	[admission] [irony]

JEAN: And you feel your daughter shouldn't be going to bed unmarried.   [checking listening]

ROSE: I'd rather you were married. But I guess you're old enough to know what to do with your life. I just don't want to see you hurt. Although Phil is a nice guy and wouldn't hurt you.   [reveals feelings]

JEAN: I still do have a problem that I'd like to get off my mind.   [repeat assertion]

ROSE: You were saying he makes demands you cannot meet.   [reaching out]

JEAN: Yes. He wants oral sex and I cannot bring myself to do it. I don't think it's immoral.   [cry of pain]

ROSE (very embarrassed): I can understand how you feel. It's something that some men seem to want very much. I had the same problem.   [nurturing listening]

JEAN: You had the same problem.   [checking listening]

ROSE: It's hard for me to talk about it with you.   [cry of pain]

JEAN: Yes. We've never talked about sex, I know. I can understand if you want to stop.   [nurturing listening]

ROSE: No. No. This is okay. I want to help you with this.   [reaching out]

JEAN: You have some idea in mind.   [checking listening]

ROSE: Well, I made up my mind that I loved your father very much and I simply had to get over whatever it was that stopped me from doing it.   [reveals material]

JEAN: So you overcame it.   [checking listening]

ROSE: Not without work. [laughs] I told your father how I felt about it.   [information] [suggests solution]

I tried to get him to help me and he was not so insistent while I worked things out. After a time because he helped I was able to do it. And we also found other things we both enjoyed. So it didn't become the main thing for us.

JEAN: I'll have to think about this. [show of pleasure] This has been so helpful. I thought there was something wrong with me. I'll figure out some way to deal with it now.

There was no way that Jean could have learned what she did without nurturing. Jean proceeded cautiously, opening up the subject step by step and nurturing her mother all the way. If she had burst in on her mother with the oral sex problem immediately, it is likely that Rose would have not contributed anything to the dialogue except a few embarrassed coughs. Rose gave Jean valuable insight into her dilemma: that one solution is to approach Phil (with the nurturing language) for help.

Suppose Rose had responded with: "I would never do that. I don't care who he is. It's disgusting!" Jean would at least have support for her own initial attitude; namely, that she was not alone in her feelings. Jean would then have to work something out with Phil.

A third possibility:

Rose: Oh, it's nothing at all. I rather enjoy it. And if Phil wants it you ought to give it to him.

Jean would first have to deal with the "ought" but if her mother does it, then that gives Jean "permission" to do it also. In sex, permission from a person significant in your life may be critical to your participating in sexual behavior that you believe may be forbidden.

In any sexual problem, the nurturing language opens up the

possibility of dialogue, and a dialogue means shared concern. By sharing your burdens with your parent, you may learn how to carry them better. By encouraging your parent to share, you may provide a chance for the parent to put creative effort to work.

Grandchildren As Conflict Pawns

To parents, grandchildren symbolize life's continuity. It is a way of warding off old age and death because the grandchildren carry the biology and tradition of the family. The grandparent can say: "I made it to here." So grandchildren have deep symbolic importance for your parents.

Grandparents also invest in their grandchildren many of their disappointments with the way they brought up their own children. They try to correct what they have done by offering advice, or more, demands about the way in which the grandchildren should be reared. They try to compensate for those errors by showering their grandchildren with love, attention, presents, and their presence. They seek to extract from the grandchildren the love they may have lost from their own children.

Parents also try to extend control of their adult children through the grandchildren. It may be as simple as withholding baby-sitting services or as complex as dividing the estate to manipulate the adult child. In response, adult children control their parents through the grandchildren, denying their parents access to the grandchildren or holding them hostage to some requirement. Some adult children who refuse to have children frustrate their parents' need for the continuity they seek.

"I have to make an appointment to see my own grandchildren!"

"My daughter-in-law is ruining the children! She spoils them rotten!"

"My son says he's not having any children. Too much trouble. What a waste!"

"My grandchildren live a thousand miles away. I wish they were closer."

"I try to tell my daughter what she's doing wrong with the kids. But she doesn't listen."

Problems over grandchildren can be resolved—if at all— with our new language. Nurturing allows you-the-child to make clear to your parents where you stand. At the same time, you help them to deal with the realities of family life; that is, your family is separate from them and they do not call the turns.

Here's a sampling from many conversations between Norma, a new mother, and Bertha, her mother.

BERTHA: Jeff doesn't look well.
NORMA: Do you think he is sick?
BERTHA: I'd take his temperature.
NORMA: Okay.
BERTHA: Let me do it. It must be done carefully.
NORMA: I know how.
BERTHA: I have more experience. This is only your first baby.

BERTHA: Don't you wash his dishes separately?
NORMA: No.
BERTHA: Do you think they are clean enough?
NORMA: Sure.
BERTHA: I used to sterilize your dishes.
NORMA: When I sterilize his mouth, I'll sterilize his dishes.

BERTHA: The window is open in the baby's room.
NORMA: I like to have fresh air.
BERTHA: There is a draft on him.
NORMA: He has his sleepers on.
BERTHA: When he has a cold you'll remember to close the window.

The dialogues clearly reveal Bertha's concern for her grandchild and Norma's resentment at her mother's interference. Bertha still believes that she knows and can do better than her daughter in child-rearing and she takes every opportunity to show it. If Bertha continues down that path, Norma will make it more and more difficult for her mother to visit. Bertha will "lose" her grandson and her grandson will "lose" his grandma.

Norma could deal with any of the three examples above by simple checking listening. In time, Bertha probably would back down and offer fewer and fewer suggestions. A cry of pain could speed things up and bring Norma's discomfort to her mother's conscious attention. As you read the dialogue below, keep in mind that Bertha could just as well be a mother-in-law:

BERTHA: Don't you wash his dishes separately?	[question]
NORMA: You think Jeff's dishes need to be extra clean.	[checking listening]
BERTHA: Babies do get infections. I used to sterilize your dishes.	[authority]
NORMA: You felt sterilizing my dishes made me have less infections.	[checking listening]
BERTHA: Oh, yes. You were never sick.	[superiority]
NORMA: I was never sick.	[checking listening/ listening-to-speak]
BERTHA: Well, you did have some of the usual childhood things but less than other children.	[backing off]
NORMA: Mom, I have a new baby in the house and it's difficult enough without having my every move questioned or pointed out as wrong. It gets on my nerves and makes me feel like a baby myself.	[genuine assertion]

BERTHA: I only wanted to help.	[defense]
NORMA: You think you're being helpful.	[checking listening]
BERTHA: I'm so nervous myself about little Jeff that I want nothing to go wrong.	[reveals feelings]
NORMA: I can understand you love him and want him to be well cared for.	[nurturing listening]
BERTHA: I know you can do it. It's just . . . that . . .	[backed off]
NORMA: Hmmm.	[wordless listening]
BERTHA: I'll try not to interfere too much.	[reaching out]
NORMA: That'd make me feel very much better . . . to be able to do things by myself and not worry about doing them wrong.	[show of pleasure]

We emphasize again that the show of pleasure is important in rewarding your parent and sealing the bargain. It also helps you recognize that your parent has made a move in your direction and offered a compromise. Some people simply continue to bombard their parents with cries of pain, long after their parents have agreed to quit the noxious behavior. Such adult children cannot take "yes" for an answer. They risk losing the cooperation of the nurtured parent.

"When Can I See My Grandchild?"

In the reversal of power that often occurs between adult children and their parents, keeping the grandchildren hostage must rank high as an odious manipulation. It plays against all the fears of the aging parent: the desire for continuity, the indication of aging, the loss of the adult children, loss of love, of presence. Rather than nurture their parents, many adult children resort to hostaging to keep their parents from interfering (as with Bertha and Norma). Others find the grandparents' demands for time with the children too onerous. And because grandparents do tend to spoil children, the adult children often find their children returned to them with a notable lack of discipline.

The problems can be erased by nurturing. It takes patience, but is more effective in the long run. And in that way your child doesn't lose the grandparent, the grandparent doesn't lose the grandchild, and you don't lose your parent.

Here's what can happen:

MOTHER: I'd like to see the children tomorrow if you're not busy.

DAUGHTER: I'm busy and they're so busy. I really don't know when would be a good time. Why don't you call early next week and we can make a definite appointment for sometime early next month.

MOTHER: I am your mother! I'm *entitled* to see the children!

DAUGHTER: Yes, you are. But at my convenience. I'm a busy person and all *you* have to do is come over and leave when you feel like it.

MOTHER: I get the feeling that my coming over is trouble for you.

DAUGHTER: Oh, mother, you know I want to see you, but you must learn to come only when you're welcome and I can have time for you.

MOTHER: Well, I don't feel you have to entertain me! But if that's the way you feel . . . please check to see if you're too busy five weeks from today!

This mother needed to nurture her daughter. Something in the history of their relationship led the daughter to hostage her children against her mother. We obtained the dialogue in an interview with a sixty-five-year-old woman in a senior citizens club. Others chimed in over their severe problems at getting to see their grandchildren. Here's another from a seventy-two-year-old woman.

MOTHER: I'm thinking of coming to see you on Tuesday.
DAUGHTER: Tuesday I'll be busy with the painters.
MOTHER: I think then I could come over on Wednesday.
DAUGHTER: I'll be going to a meeting.
MOTHER: Friday you're usually home. I could come then.
DAUGHTER: Oh, this week, I'll be meeting a friend for lunch.
MOTHER: I really could come over and just visit with the children if you're not home.
DAUGHTER: Oh, mom, don't you want to see me?

There is a lot of history behind that dialogue. A lot of fights. A lot of hostaging. If you want to prevent isolating your parent, the new language offers, as it did with Bertha and Norma, a way of bringing your parent close without interfering or spoiling your children. We have an example from the Adelphi University program. Alex, fifty-eight, lives with his wife in the country fifty miles from his daughter, Felicia, who has two boys, seven and five. Alex is visiting.

ALEX: I have a good idea. Why not have the children visit us for a week? [opening signal]

FELICIA: That's worth thinking about. They have a vacation in a few weeks. [comment]

ALEX: You think they'll fight with each other? I hope they'll get along. [question]
It'd be terrible if they fought all the time the way they do here. [assertion]

FELICIA: They don't fight any more than other boys of their age. [defensive]

ALEX: Oh, yes they do! I never see [judgment]

Edna's children fight like that.
They have excellent manners; seem
to really like each other.

FELICIA: That's because you're never around them for more than five minutes.	[attack]
ALEX: The other day Bobby tore Chris's shirt for no reason at all.	[judgment]
FELICIA: If that's the way you feel about it, don't take them!	[counterattack]

After instruction, Felicia was able to role-play in a nurturing way:

ALEX: Do you think they'll fight with each other?	[question]
FELICIA: You're worried about not being able to control them.	[nurturing listening]
ALEX: Yes, they won't listen to me. If you were there, they'd listen.	[creative solution]
FELICIA: I can't go down with them. Dennis and I planned to be away for a few days. That would spoil our trip.	[genuine assertion]
ALEX: I'd like to have them down, but I don't want trouble.	[genuine assertion]
FELICIA: Don't take them unless you feel comfortable.	[advice]
If you want, they could stay a couple of days instead of an entire week.	[choice]
ALEX: We'll talk it over and let you know.	[toward a solution]

Not perfect, but enough to ward off the hostaging and to give grandpa a chance to reflect on whether he really wants to have the two active boys without their mother around.

Now let's deal with a big issue: visiting grandchildren. How much is enough? How can you, the adult child, come to some reasonable agreement with your parent about visits and your parent's behavior toward your children? How can you avoid spoiling, lack of discipline, etc.? Here is an extended dialogue that can take place over several days because there are many issues covered.

PARENT: When can I come and see the children?	[question]
YOU-THE-CHILD: You want to visit soon.	[checking listening]
PARENT: Today if possible.	[reveals desire]
YOU-THE-CHILD: I have a problem with that because I have to take Ellie for her piano lesson and Bill has his Little League. I couldn't pick you up.	[call for help]
PARENT: But you always pick me up! Why can't you do it today?	[question]
YOU-THE-CHILD: You have some way I can do that and still get Ellie and Bill where they have to go?	[checking listening]
PARENT: I guess not. Tomorrow?	[question]
YOU-THE-CHILD: You have time to visit tomorrow.	[checking listening/ listening-to- speak]
PARENT: Yes. Tomorrow is a good day.	[information]
YOU-THE-CHILD: It's awful hard for me to arrange visits on short notice because the children and I have so much scheduled.	[genuine assertion]
PARENT: They have no time for their grandmother?	[question]
YOU-THE-CHILD: You feel we're avoiding you.	[nurturing listen- ing/listening-to- speak]

PARENT: I don't know. You and the children always seem too busy for me.

[reveals feelings]

YOU-THE-CHILD: It's just awful hard for me to arrange visits on short notice because we have so much scheduled.

[repeats genuine] assertion]

PARENT: You mean if I gave you more notice it would be easier for us to get together.

[creative solution]

YOU-THE-CHILD: That would be very helpful because that would take the pressure off me to try to fit you in.

[show of pleasure]

PARENT: If I knew what the schedule was I could organize myself better.

[call for help]

YOU-THE-CHILD: I can write it out for you.

[answers call]

They work out schedule:

YOU-THE-CHILD: Mom, I have a problem with the boys each time they visit with you. It's getting harder and harder for me to deal with.

[call for help]

PARENT: What is it? I don't have any problem with them. We get along fine.

[question]
[superiority]

YOU-THE-CHILD: You don't have any problems with them.

[checking listening/ listening-to- speak]

PARENT: Not at all.

[genuine assertion]

YOU-THE-CHILD: Well, my problem is that during the visit they have eaten a lot of candy when they know that they're not supposed to to eat any candy at all. It's bad for

[call for help]

their teeth and I have a hard enough time controlling their candy without their getting it somewhere else.

PARENT: I never give them any candy. I wouldn't do that. [hearing the implied "you"]

YOU-THE-CHILD: You're saying they never get any candy from you. [checking listening]

PARENT: Never. [affirmation]

YOU-THE-CHILD: I wish I knew where they were getting it. I worry so about their teeth. [genuine assertion] [call for help]

PARENT: Maybe they're buying it by themselves. I've seen them buy it. [creative solution]

YOU-THE-CHILD: You've seen them buying candy by themselves. [checking listening]

PARENT: Yes.

YOU-THE-CHILD: I didn't realize that. I don't give them any money for anything when I'm not there to supervise what they buy. I know they'll spend it on candy. [genuine assertion]

PARENT: They're probably using the money I give them. And they run off so fast I can't stop them. Maybe I shouldn't give them the money unless I'm right there with them. [admission]

[creative solution]

YOU-THE-CHILD: That would be enormously helpful and I would know they weren't sneaking candy when I'm not there. [show of pleasure]

In the same way, you can make deals with your parent about discipline, excessive gifts, interfering with your management, criticizing the children, or any number of behaviors that grandparents fall into. The sequence is the same: listen, listen-to-speak, genuine assertion, listen, show pleasure. Your parent will want to help you and you will not fall back on hostaging to get your way.

"I'm Too Busy"

Sometimes the shoe is on the other foot. Your parents show little interest in your children. They never visit. They never call. They never send gifts. When you do visit they shout at the children and keep them out of the way. It's hard to say what brings parents to such a pass. It may be buried in the history of the family or in the relationship between you and your parents. Some people have taken the psychological position that they do not like children and attempt to live up to their words. In any case, you may find the analysis too difficult; or having done it, you are still faced with what to do.

You may want closer contact between your children and your parents because you feel that all children should experience their grandparents. Or you view the distance between your parents and your children as another expression of the distance between you and your parents. Or you need help with the children—babysitting, money, medical care. A proper call for help gives you the best chance of achieving the result you want.

YOU-THE-CHILD: We're having a cookout next Sunday. We'd like to have you come. It'll be fun with the children.	[opening signal]
PARENT: Mother and I are going to a concert that evening and it'll be too much for us.	[refusal]
YOU-THE-CHILD: You're saying that having some food with us will tire you out for the concert.	[checking listening]

PARENT: It's not the food. But the kids are so wild that they knock us out. [reveals problem]

YOU-THE-CHILD: Oh, you must be pretty upset with the children to pass up a cookout. [nurturing listening]

PARENT: They're children and we're getting old. If they wouldn't climb all over us, we'd be all right. [reveals feelings] [creative solution]

YOU-THE-CHILD: You feel that if we found a way to keep the children off you, you'd come visit us. [checking listening]

PARENT: Oh, yes! But you can't do that. They're just too wild. [authority]

YOU-THE-CHILD: You think it's impossible to keep the children under control. [checking listening]

PARENT: I couldn't do it. [admission]

YOU-THE-CHILD: I always thought you and mom enjoyed having kids on your laps. Now that I know what you feel, I can certainly get Allen and Virginia to keep off you because I really want you to come visit us more often. I like having you and so do the children. [genuine assertion]

PARENT: Well, we can try it. [agreement]

YOU-THE-CHILD: I'm so happy! I'm sure we're all going to have a good time. [show of pleasure]

If you defend your children against the criticisms of your parents you are—as we explained in discussing defensiveness—attacking your parents, just as your parents attack you by being defensive. By nurturing you get to the root of the problem and then, with your parent's help, solve it. Your parents may dislike many things about your children. Some parents let you know; others hide their feelings and avoid contact with the children. Sometimes their objections are minor and get blown out of proportion because they see nothing being done about them; and nothing is being done because you don't know.

Let's look at a complex issue: Your parents have no interest in your children and you want them to be interested.

YOU-THE-CHILD: I was very disappointed that you didn't show up at Cary's birthday party. I would have liked to have his grandma there to celebrate with us.	[cry of pain]
PARENT: I had my regular Saturday afternoon bridge game. You know I can't give that up. Besides, it was a children's party, not for adults.	[defensive]
YOU-THE-CHILD: I do suppose that the bridge game is very important to you after all these years. I know you enjoy it so much.	[nurturing listening/listening-to-speak]
PARENT: I didn't mean to hurt Cary's feelings. I'm sure he didn't even know I wasn't there.	[defensive]
YOU-THE-CHILD: You feel that Cary doesn't take notice of you when you are around.	[checking listening]
PARENT: He's only a child.	[defensive/shifting blame]
YOU-THE-CHILD: He is only a child.	[checking listening]
PARENT: I wish I could be more interested in him. It's just that children that young bore me.	[reveals feelings]
YOU-THE-CHILD: You're saying that because he's so young you find it hard to be interested in him.	[checking listening]

PARENT: Oh, he's cute and all that. [defensive]
And I do love him. I am his
grandma, after all.

YOU-THE-CHILD: I'd be very happy if [call for help]
Cary could have the experience of
a grandma more often than he
does. I remember your mother, and
she and I spent a lot of happy times
together. I'd like that for Cary.

PARENT: You don't think I do enough [question]
for him?
Didn't I get him that nice sweater?

YOU-THE-CHILD: You feel you've done [checking listening]
enough and you're upset that I
might think you haven't. [nurturing listening]

PARENT: I did think I heard an accu- [defensive]
sation.

I suppose I could do more than I [reaching out to
do now. Maybe I could take him on help]
a special birthday trip to the park.
I could make it just Cary and
grandma. Maybe I'll get us some
funny hats, too.

YOU-THE-CHILD: You really sound ex- [nurturing listening]
cited by your plans.

PARENT: I guess I could make it not [creative solution]
so boring by planning my time with
him.

YOU-THE-CHILD: I'm so pleased you're [show of pleasure]
making the effort. I did so want
you two to get together.

It is extremely difficult not to be sarcastic under these
circumstances; difficult *not* to say: "A bridge game is more
important to you than your grandson!" Nor do we think such
a grandmother can be turned around as quickly as the
dialogue suggests in its condensed form. You will get your

parent to come closer to what you want in one session, but you may need several to get most of what you want.

Society is on your side: Grandmas are supposed to take an interest in their grandchildren. So if you nurture consistently, your parent will yield to the societal pressure and to your call for help in giving your child a grandmotherly experience. We have illustrated our point with a grandmother, but the same might be said of cold and uninterested grandfathers.

Some Other Practical Problems

The nurturing language works in less pressured situations:

Leisure

Many old people do not like to socialize because they fear leaving their homes. Although more than ever we have senior citizen clubs with many activities, your parents may keep away from them. They may feel "only old people go there," meaning that they do not like to be reminded of their own advancing age. Or they feel that the social class of the club is beneath them (or, too far above them). By nurturing, you may help them work through their doubts just as nurturing helps them work through their medical problems.

Older people sometimes resist almost any leisure activity: going to the movies, out to dinner, on vacation, or engaging in the sports that once held their interest. They prefer to stay home and watch television or amble to the local bar, which has become their club. As such people get older their activity level winds down until they do very little with anybody else. Such aloneness increases mental disturbance and can aggravate senility.

Your nurturing will help them to get out with other people and to be involved as they once were. Nagging always fails. But if you can work out a genuine call for help, they may reach out to help you by helping themselves.

Work

A majority of parents of adult children still work for a living. But as they get older the specter of being fired looms larger. They know that each decade past forty cuts by half the chances of getting another job equal to the one they have. They may or may not have a good retirement plan or put away enough money to live comfortably.

For many, work also provides a reason for living. To be working is to be a useful human being; not working is to be useless, perhaps not human. Work also gives daily opportunity for meeting with other people. It's like belonging to a club, which is why many people will work for less money in a place they like.

So when your parents have work problems, they are deep problems indeed. Advice comes last. Nurturing comes first. With nurturing, your parents can separate the practical from the emotional in their job difficulty. With nurturing, your parents can feel useful when they have lost a job: They will know somebody cares even though they are out of work. It's no use saying: "Cheer up! You'll get another job." Those words will have the same effect as saying to a new widow: "Cheer up! You'll find another husband."

Better to recognize the pain your parent is feeling at the loss and reflect it back (nurturing): "You must feel awful that Zilch Watch Company laid you off after twenty-five years. That seems very unfair. I'd be terribly angry!" Now your parent's feelings seem real. The nurturing gives permission to feel angry so the anger won't be turned inward. You liberate the creative problem-solving skill and your parent will get down more quickly to finding another job or making other useful plans.

Religion

It is not uncommon for older people to return to the religion of their youth. They often do so in a fundamentalist way; i.e., they have very simple ideas of God, sin, right, wrong, the Scriptures. Sometimes they get involved with a sect that is out of the mainstream and may appear to you to be more a cult than a sect. In America, we have been so concerned with young people's being taken into cults that we have missed the obvious: Cults have for a long time seduced older people.

You will find it hopeless to argue with your newly religious parent. If you nurture, you have the best chance of keeping the bond between you so your parent will not be afraid to turn to you for help in case it is needed. Suppose your parent converts to a cult that demands all your parent's money. If you are estranged, your parent will not call on you for guidance.

If you nurture, you may help your parent modify the fanaticism that often attaches to conversion or reconversion. You may be able to ward off without hostility your parent's attempts to convert you. If you provide a respectful audience through listening, you avoid pushing your parent into taking a position from which he or she feels ashamed to retreat. With the experience of your listening to his ideas, your parent need not defend himself. His creative skills will be unblocked.

You may not get everything you want but you may be able to prevent your parent from doing serious harm to himself and his pocketbook.

/ 15 /

Why It Works

"I know my father. No matter what you do he will talk the same way and do the same things."

"Hear me? My mother is so wrapped up in herself she wouldn't hear a bomb going off next to her ear."

"She's my mother and I love her but there is no way she can solve her own problems. She hasn't in forty years. I've had to do everything. I've been the parent."

'The old man is senile! What's the use trying to talk to him?"

"My mother-in-law has manipulated her son and me for twenty years. If I change the way I talk that won't change her manipulations."

At first glance, it does seem unlikely that your change of language alone will change the behavior of others. You have seen people behave in a fixed manner for years and frustrate all your efforts to talk them out of it or to counter their aggressions and manipulations. Why then do we believe that the nurturing language will achieve what other methods have failed to accomplish?

Here's a summary of the modern scientific evidence that supports the effectiveness of the nurturing language. We cannot hope to be exhaustive because this, after all, is a helping book, not a psychological text. We merely outline the main ideas and findings so you can have some confidence that what you are about to do will succeed.

Nurturing Is Better Than Attacking

Though aggression may be exciting and interesting in literature, it destroys human relations. It creates an unequal power situation: One individual dominates another. In the dominated individual it produces a learned helplessness and dependency. And like an infected person, the aggressed individual aggresses against others. Unfortunately, aggressors in our society often reap huge rewards in money, sex, power, and status. So aggression seems like a good thing. Companies often advertise for "aggressive young men." Such firms are proud of their "aggressive sales campaign" or "aggressive competition."

A parent–adult child relationship based on aggression—in either direction—cannot be happy for at least one of the parties and probably both. A helpless adult child or a helpless aging parent demeans human dignity. In an ironic way, a helpless parent (or adult child) puts a greater burden on the aggressor because the aggressor now is faced with solving problems that might have been solved by the helpless one. And finally, aggression—attack—inflicts pain on the victim. That's why it works. To avoid pain, the victim is willing to do the aggressor's bidding.

Nurturing—as in listening and reflecting back the other's feelings, thoughts, and needs—builds human bonds. It equalizes power. It fosters independence. It unblocks problem-solving skills. In our democratic society with authority no longer holding its once-vaunted power, nurturing more and more wins the rewards formerly achieved by aggression. Companies now look for young men and women with "human relations skills." Modern business management now seeks to create an atmosphere free of aggression. In an aggressionless environment, people work better with higher morale. If salespeople have been nurtured, they make more sales than in aggressive campaigns.

A parent–adult child relationship based on nurturing—in either direction—can be happy for at least one and probably both parties. Nurturing supports human dignity. Because nurturing counters helpless behavior, the nurturer shoulders a lighter burden. The nurtured person tends to solve problems unaided. And, finally, nurturing inflicts no pain.

Even if there were no proof that the nurturing language can change a person's behavior, one could choose nurturing over aggression purely on the fact that nurturing is more humane than aggression, that nurturing causes no wounds, and that it is less disruptive than aggression. Now let's look at some of the evidence that supports nurturing.

We Have Seen It Work

The most dramatic evidence comes from our own experience. We have seen nurturing change people's behavior. Dr. Flax observed it in her many years as a therapist; Mr. Ubell as a journalist and former manager of a large news organization. In both cases, the effort was not easy.

Dr. Flax, as a co-therapist in treating a married couple with sexual problems, was verbally attacked by a hostile husband who said that Dr. Flax did not fit his image of a therapist:

PATIENT: You don't look like a thera- [judgment]
pist.
DR. FLAX: You feel that therapists [checking listening]
look a certain way.
PATIENT: I thought you'd look a little [reveals thoughts]
different than you do.

DR. FLAX: You feel I don't look like someone you had in mind. [checking listening]

PATIENT: I expected someone who'd look a little older and more experienced. [reveals thoughts]

DR. FLAX: You're concerned that I may not be experienced enough to help you. [nurturing listening]

PATIENT: Yes. Yes. That's exactly what I mean. [reveals thoughts]

DR. FLAX: As we go along in the therapy I hope the process will become more comfortable. I'll make every effort to make it so. [genuine assertion]

PATIENT: Okay. Let's see how it goes. [agreement]

DR. FLAX: I'm pleased that you've agreed to give it a try. It'll make things much easier. [show of pleasure]

The patient entered into the therapy. Although at several points the patient blocked the road to sexual effectiveness, he tended to cooperate and soon lost his reservations about Dr. Flax as a therapist. All psychotherapists speak one form or another of the nurturing language. They know it helps the patient bring hidden material to the surface of consciousness.

As a journalist, Mr. Ubell was trained to ask questions. Questions, as we have shown, generate hostility. When he acquired the nurturing language, Mr. Ubell reduced the number of questions he asked. He found that he elicited more information than when he asked questions. A typical interview might go like this:

UBELL: I'm interested in knowing about your work on fiber in the diet for a news report. [genuine assertion]

SCIENTIST: I've found that with a high- [information]

fiber diet there'll be fewer cases of cancer of the colon and other diseases of the intestine.

UBELL: You're saying that if you eat more bran the risk of cancer goes down. [checking listening]

SCIENTIST: Yes. When we looked at the diets of native African peoples we found that they were very high in fiber and low in fat. At the same time, those peoples had practically no cases of colon cancer. We in the West eat a diet low in fiber and high in fat and colon cancer is one of our leading killers. [more information]

UBELL: I really don't understand how a high-fiber low-fat diet prevents cancer. [call for help]

SCIENTIST: Well, we cannot prove it yet. Our evidence is circumstantial so far. But we believe that the bacteria in the gut convert some fat into cancer-causing chemicals. With less fat, you have fewer of those dangerous substances. The high-fiber food moves the cancer chemicals through the gut faster so that they don't remain in longtime contact with the lining of the intestines. [reveals hidden information]

The interview continued in this vein for a half hour. No questions were asked. By the end the scientist had provided all the information plus his doubts about his ideas. His attitude toward the reporter was one of eager respect. The reporter had listened.

We could cite many examples of how nurturing can be

employed in everyday life to elicit help and to help others. But such evidence is only anecdotal, not scientific.

How It All Began

The story of nurturing begins with Sigmund Freud, the Viennese father of psychoanalysis. Although his ideas circulated among mentalists of his time, Freud brought them together and enlarged them. Freud theorized that we all have memories from early childhood that deeply affect our current behavior. Some of the remembered events stand brightly in our memory and we know they govern what we do. Recall the woman who watched her uncle choke on a bone. She refused to eat fish for sixty years.

Other events cannot easily be brought to the forefront of consciousness; we have "forgotten" them. But, Freud suggested, those "forgotten" memories are still in our minds, in what Freud called our unconscious, and they still govern our behavior. For some people those "forgotten"—Freud would say "repressed"—memories force us into bizarre or malfunctioning behavior.

It was part of Freud's theory of treatment that if those repressed events could be brought to the foreground of our thoughts, we could relive them and detoxify them so they would no longer lead us into strange behaviors. Dealing with those memories requires a complex series of therapeutic maneuvers, which are irrelevant here. The main point is that Freud found a way of bringing up those lost memories. Initially, in 1893 while he studied with Jean Martin Charcot in Paris, he tried hypnosis, which worked with some patients but not with others. In the same year, he discovered the basic tool of psychoanalysis: free association. He asked his patients to report all daydreams, fantasies, nightmares, dreams, and random thoughts, without *censoring* them. Freud realized that society abhors many of those thoughts: memories of incest, fantasies of murder, thoughts of unlimited power and lust. So we keep them secret and sometimes censor them from ourselves.

As Freud progressed with the method of free association, he realized that the more he interrupted the stream of words the less material his patients brought up. Also, if he made judgments of their dreams—good or bad—the flow of association would halt or slow down. He also understood—and this we put simplistically—that if he explained too much about the meaning of the oncoming thoughts, the patient would withdraw from the free association.

Here is the kernel of what we call nurturing: the skill of listening without interruption and without judgment. Freud created an environment in which the patient felt safe to dredge up the repressed feelings, thoughts, and needs. The conscious mind threw away its censor.

Let the Client Solve His Problem

Since Freud, thousands of psychiatrists and psychologists have refined and elaborated that single Freudian idea (of course he had many others). Of all therapists, Carl Rogers stands out as the one who first deeply subjected nurturing to scientific test. He wanted to know: (a) does nurturing lead to an increase of communication; (b) does it lead to personality change; and (c) does it bring about behavior change? On all three counts, Rogers and his associates produced evidence in the affirmative.

Rogers undertook the scientific test because he believed that clinical and anecdotal stories were not enough. He said it beautifully:

Science is a way of preventing me from deceiving myself in regard to my creatively formed subjective hunches which have developed out of the relationship between me and my material. It is in this context, and perhaps only in this context, that the vast structure of operationism, logical positivism, research design, tests of significance, etc., have their place. They exist, not for themselves, but as servants, in the attempt to check the subjective feeling or hunch or hypothesis of a person with the objective fact.

Rogers believes that individuals have the power within themselves to become mature personalities and to change their behavior. The role of a therapist is to facilitate that process. That's why Rogers calls his treatment "client-centered therapy." Originally, he spoke of "nondirective therapy" to describe the fact that the therapists did not direct their clients.

To help the client mature, Rogers reflects back to the client the expressed thoughts, feelings, and needs. In our sense, the therapist responds with wordless listening, checking listening, or nurturing listening. Through listening, the therapist tries to understand and to feel the client's inner emotional world. Rogers ranks high an ability to climb into the client's emotional shoes. Without that capacity for empathy (which Freud also required), the therapist is merely following a formula, which the patient quickly discovers.

Rogers and his associates recorded and made transcripts of many therapy sessions. In one study, his scientific group analyzed the therapist's responses into categories: nurturing, interrupting, or psychological interpretation. They then examined the client's response to the therapist's response. Only nurturing encouraged the client to go on, to dig deeper into his memory bank and to bring up more material. Only nurturing allowed the client the creativity of solving his own problems. Any other therapist response—interruption, explanations, judgments, or advice—stopped or slowed the flow.

Such experiments suggest that even in the nontherapy situation nurturing does bring out the hidden material of the nurtured person because that person feels "safe."

Rogers has many examples in which clients subject therapists to severe verbal attacks using the weapons we have outlined earlier. If the therapist responds with nurturing, the attack dies down and the patient examines even more deeply his or her own motivations for the attack. Which is exactly what one wants to happen in a parent–adult child dialogue.

As for personality and behavior change, Rogers and his group proved that at the very least their clients' language changed from aggressive to assertive. They demonstrated that the client's self-concept changed; i.e., the client self-concept more closely approached the client's ideal concept of himself. And there was strong evidence for changes in the client's behavior.

Essentially, Rogers laid the groundwork for the rapid spread of the nurturing language (although he did not call it that). He made it accessible to psychologists and to ordinary people because he stripped it of the convoluted theory that Freud attached to it. While Freud's theory of personality and behavior fills many books, Rogers's is contained in a few pages in one of his many books. For Rogers the theory is simple: Client, heal thyself.

We Can Learn from Pigeons

Additional support for the nurturing language comes from B. F. Skinner, the man who developed to its highest form the psychology of reward and punishment. Skinner and Rogers disagree on some fundamental theoretical grounds, but they agree in their humane approach to human psychology. Skinner developed the idea that if you reward an animal following a behavior by that animal the behavior is likely to be repeated; if you punish, the behavior is not likely to be repeated.

If, for example, you reward a pigeon with a kernel of corn every time the pigeon turns to the right, you can, in short order, make the pigeon turn in a circle. You can quickly stop the turning if you punish the bird with a mild electric shock at each spin.

Skinner and many who followed him developed the idea in a thousand different ways. In practical applications, behavioral psychologists have trained animals to incredible feats. Skinner himself taught pigeons to guide bombs to their targets during World War II. Others have trained severely mentally retarded human beings to feed and to toilet themselves where other training methods had failed. Juvenile delinquents have been kept on the straight and narrow. Mental patients have given up their bizarre behavior. Normal children have been taught to do chores and have improved their performance in school.

Skinnerian techniques become very difficult to apply to more complex interpersonal behaviors. First there is the nature of the rewards. With animals and retarded humans one usually uses food or water. Because both are under the control of institutions, juvenile delinquents and mental patients can be offered an elaborate schedule of rewards: free time, ice cream, games. Some mental institutions have established a system to pay inmates in tokens for desired behavior. The inmates exchange the tokens for food, cigarettes, clothing, free time. Children in school also fall under the control of the school, so there too one can provide the necessary rewards.

Skinnerian methods succeeded within families whose members made contracts to reward each other for the desired behavior. Usually, the behaviors are quite specific: cleaning up one's room, working in the garden, coming home on time, etc. When the behavior is more general—not losing one's temper, being polite, not shouting—compliance is harder, but not impossible with the usual rewards.

A problem arises over the rewards: What may be rewarding for one person may be neutral or punishing for another. In one experiment in a school, a number of children elected, as reward for doing homework, the cleaning of guinea pig cages. After cleaning the cages twice, the children discovered that the reward felt more like a punishment. Unless you elicit the cooperation of the other in setting the rewards, you are likely to misjudge the power of the reward for the other.

In a Skinnerian scheme, rewards, to be most effective, must be given immediately following the desired behavior. The longer you wait the less likely will you get a repeat of the act you want repeated. The longer you wait after a child completes the homework, the less likely will the child complete the homework the next day. Further, to make the behavior occur consistently—that the child does the homework day after day—the rewards must be frequent.

To get around the barrier of immediate and frequent rewarding, Skinnerian psychologists organize schemes of self-reward. For example, if the child marks an X on a card when the homework is completed, the X becomes the immediate reward if the X can later be exchanged for free time, games, or whatever. The child can give himself or herself as many X's as needed as quickly as required.

In interpersonal relationships—parent to adult child—you would find it difficult to arrange any effective scheme of rewards that could be applied immediately and consistently. Imagine asking your parent to select a menu of rewards to be used whenever your parent does what you want or need! Or even if you could surmise a reward that is rewarding, there are few that can be applied with frequency and immediacy. Could you give your parent a token or ask your parent to mark an X on a card?

Nurturing As a Reward

Although Carl Rogers might deny it, nurturing fits within the Skinnerian scheme. You can look upon nurturing as a reward. Rogers's and other evidence suggest strongly that nurturing causes the repetition of behavior that is nurtured. Most people, even the most severely disturbed, respond to

nurturing in this way. Nurturing may be the universal reward.
Let's take a simple example:

PARENT: I'm so upset with my new   [opening signal]
apartment. It's so small.

YOU-THE-CHILD: After being in that   [nurturing listening]
big house for so many years you
must be pretty cramped for space.
I can understand why you're so unhappy.

PARENT: Oh, I have it pretty well or-   [reveals thoughts]
ganized. It's not as though I'm in
a cage.

YOU-THE-CHILD: So you think you can   [nurturing listening]
live there comfortably even though
it's small.

PARENT (weeps): It's really the house   [reveals hidden feel-
and your father and all the children   ings]
that I miss. Moving out ended a
part of my life. But I'll get on.

The behavior here was the parent's revelation about her
feelings. After the first nurturing (reward) the behavior
was repeated with a second exposure of her truer feelings.
A second nurturing revealed her deepest feelings. (We have
seen how the nurturing/reward allows your parent to hear
what you have to say in your genuine assertions.)

Of the three genuine assertions, only the show of pleasure
can be classed as a reward. By telling your parent how
pleased you are and why following an agreement, you are
rewarding your parent's problem-solving behavior. You are
insuring that such behavior will be repeated.

A cry of pain comes close to being a punishment for unwanted behavior. Although a cry of pain does not directly
attack the parent, it displays to the parent another human
being being hurt. Experiments show that given a free choice

most people do not like to see others continue in pain. It is painful for them. Such pain is like a mild shock given to a pigeon; it tends to shut off behavior. Similarly, a cry of pain by you will tend to shut off your parent's pain-generating behavior.

Punishment, however, has a side effect. It evokes hostility in the punished party. That is why a cry of pain by you may often be followed by an attack by your parent. Your parent not only hears the implied "you," he or she also feels the pain of your cry of pain. That is one reason why it is so important to follow a cry of pain with nurturing. The rewarding nature of nurturing applies balm to the hostility.

A call for help is neither reward nor punishment. It is an invitation. It offers a choice to your parent to help or not to help; it permits your parent to choose the manner of help. If you demand help, you are punishing. If you specify the way in which you get the help, you are punishing. And punishment stops behavior—the move toward help—and engenders hostility.

What We Do Unto Others

More evidence supporting the nurturing language comes from the theory and research on social learning. In this, Albert Bandura, of Stanford University, is the leader. In brief, social learning theory holds that we learn complex behavior by mimicking others. In particular, we emulate those we see being rewarded for their behavior. We also follow the lead of role models, people whom we have adopted as someone we want to be. We may want to behave like our parents, teachers, friends, somebody on television or in the movies.

If we see someone rewarded for aggression, we tend to be aggressive. Children appear to be particularly sensitive to picking up aggression in this way from their parents and they continue their aggressive behavior well into their teens. Boys lean more toward aggression than girls, who are more nurturing. Aggression, says social learning theory, breeds more aggression; nurturing more nurturing.

If we nurture someone we can expect, in time, to be nurtured in return. If we attack—bring out our verbal weapons and manipulations—we will be attacked in turn. Social learning theory and its evidence, therefore, give us confidence that the nurturing language will bring about the change in behavior that we seek, a turn away from dominance, hostility, and helplessness and toward equality, nurturing, and independence.

Nurturing for Everyone

In the welter of how-to books in popular psychology, Thomas Gordon's *Parent Effectiveness Training,* more than any other, gave the nurturing ideas to the widest public for practical application. Gordon, a colleague of Carl Rogers's, simplified all the previous material on nurturing for parents with growing children. Since the first P.E.T. book, Gordon and his team produced three more for teachers, managers, and women. All follow the P.E.T. outline. Millions have read and applied the P.E.T. ideas.

Gordon's formulation of the nurturing language is leagues ahead of all the others in the field. Many other available books on child-rearing written for the public have grievous faults. Some are written in such complex psychological jargon that it is almost impossible for an ordinary mother or father to understand them. Others treat case by case with brilliance, but you are left with no skills to deal with your case, which may be different from the cases treated in the book. You are left with the thought: "Gosh, I wish I could think of such things with my children." Others give such general instructions as to leave the parent in a fog or worse. Instructions to love, or to be warm, or nurturing without being specific as to how to perform those operations simply confuse or create guilt in a parent.

Gordon provides descriptions (as we do) of the essential

skills of the nurturing language. He composes Rogers's ideas of reflection of emotions, thoughts, and needs into active and passive listening. We have divided the category into wordless checking and nurturing listening. Our genuine assertions derive from Gordon's "I-Messages." We feel it is easier to understand a call for help, a cry of pain, and a show of pleasure. Also, adult children will find these concepts more adaptable to their problems with their parents. Gordon also helps parents decide whether a problem is theirs or the child's.

Gordon established a nationwide network of P.E.T. workshops at which parents can study and practice the P.E.T. principles. In addition he sponsored a number of research projects. One shows that people can easily learn the language. Another proves that parents undergoing P.E.T. training gain in empathy; they are able to share in and feel the emotional experiences of others, a prime skill if one is to speak the nurturing language.

We owe a debt to Gordon, who led the way in showing that deep psychological ideas can belong to a wider public than a few professionals.

Some Recent Evidence

Since Rogers's first work, psychologists have been very busy proving various aspects of the nurturing language. Many of them have approached the problem from their particular theoretical viewpoint, as did Bandura with social learning theory. Recently, a good deal of work has focused on learned helplessness. The experiments suggest that when people fail at a task they are in danger of becoming helpless in the face of the next task. Science supports the old adage about getting back on the horse immediately after you fall off. If the person who fails does not immediately attempt the same task he or she tends to be helpless the next time.

Studies in nursing homes show that attendants teach their

clients to be helpless by taking over many of their self-grooming activities and by not speaking the nurturing language. In general, any dependent relationship breeds learned helplessness. Incidentally, controversial data exist to suggest that learned helplessness leads to depression.

Whenever nurses, counselors, or institutional workers have been taught some aspect of the nurturing language, they have been able to learn it and to apply it. In many studies now, the objects of the nurturing language change their behavior in the desired direction. It does not produce a 100 percent change; but it improves conditions significantly.

Finally, there is the work of Lorna Smith Benjamin, of the University of Wisconsin. She has identified seventy-two different kinds of interpersonal communications between the self and another person.

Each communication can be located on a diagram that reveals how much attack, support, freedom, or control it contains. The diagram looks like this:

Allowing Freedom

Empathetic Understanding

Annihilating Attack   Tender Sexuality

Blame

Total Control

For example, *blame* sits between *annihilating attack* and *total control*, meaning that it has elements of each. *Empathetic understanding* contains parts of *allowing freedom* and *tender sexuality*.

When a parent accuses or blames a child, those words contain elements of attack and control. When a parent ignores a child, the communication attacks and allows freedom. A nurturing response, in our sense, contains the allowance of freedom and tender sexuality.

Benjamin's structure of communications is too complex to be completely described here. But Benjamin's investigations of the interpersonal responses of normal and mentally ill people clearly show that the nurturing language elicits the responses we say it does. Not all her classes of communication are like those in the nurturing language, but they come close. Benjamin's category of *empathetic understanding* is like our nurturing listening. And like nurturing, empathetic understanding evokes a clear expression of feelings from the other.

Friendly exploration (checking listening) results in revelations of thoughts and feelings. *Confirmation* of the other's behavior (a show of pleasure) brings about an enthusiastic sharing of things and ideas. To *ask trustingly* (a call for help) brings a helpful response.

We do not find a cry of pain explicitly in Benjamin's work. It is similar to her *desperate protest,* although not as strong. A desperate protest brings on an attack, just as a cry of pain often does. That is why a cry of pain needs to be followed by nurturing. A cry of pain is useful in stopping hurtful behavior even though it brings on an attack.

Benjamin also shows clearly that advice, overhelpfulness, and control produce all the signs of dependency: clinging, deference, overconformity, submergence of the self, and complete yielding. According to Benjamin, the weapons and manipulations of the toxic language create in the victim all the responses we know. Blame induces defensiveness; superiority brings on sulkiness; punishment produces appeasement; and manipulation makes people agree with you but they do not understand why.

Benjamin has taken the communication idea one large step further. She has explored what each type of communication does to the inner feelings and thoughts. She shows that, for example, *blame* evokes *sulkiness* as a behavior (external) and *guilt* as an emotion (internal). Which is what we said the weapon of blame or judgment does.

Empathetic understanding (nurturing listening) encourages *clear expression* of feelings and thoughts outside and induces *self-examination* inside. Again, this is exactly what we want our nurturing language to accomplish. When we nurture by nurturing listening we want our parents to examine themselves, their thoughts, their needs, their feelings. If they are attacking us, self-examination will expose the attack to themselves. If they have a need, they will more carefully weigh that need against our ability to fulfill that need or they will come to some creative solution on their own.

In summary, except for a few details, the whole of the nurturing language in principle and practice appears to be confirmed by Benjamin's investigations.

Finale

We feel that the nurturing language holds great power to reconcile parents and adult children, just as it has shown power to create helping and emotionally supportive relationships between parents and young children, therapists and their clients, teachers and students, and managers and the people who work with them. Nevertheless, reconciliation takes time. The nurturing language has no magic and won't work unless applied consistently, genuinely, and sincerely, i.e., that you adopt the language as your normal way of speech with its full range of emotion, not only with your parents but with everyone.

Perhaps we should all remember what Oscar Wilde said about children and parents:

Children begin by loving their parents; as they grow older they judge them; sometimes they forgive them.